2009

THE BEST 10-MINUTE PLAYS
FOR TWO OR MORE ACTORS

Smith and Kraus's
Short Plays and 10-Minute Play Collections

For more information about upcoming Smith and Kraus titles, to sign up for our
eNewsletter with special promotions and private sales, or to order books, visit
smithandkraus.com. Or call toll-free (888) 282-2881.

2009

THE BEST 10-MINUTE PLAYS
FOR TWO OR MORE ACTORS

Edited by Lawrence Harbison

CONTEMPORARY PLAYWRIGHT SERIES

A Smith and Kraus Book
Hanover, New Hampshire

Published by Smith and Kraus, Inc.
177 Lyme Road, Hanover, NH 03755
www.SmithandKraus.com
(888) 282-2881

First Edition: October 2009
10 9 8 7 6 5 4 3 2 1

Manufactured in the United States of America
Cover design by Dan Mehling, dmehling@gmail.com
Text design by Julia Hill Gignoux, Freedom Hill Design

ISBN-13: 978-1-57525-759-4 // ISBN-10: 1-57525-759-9
ISSN 1550-6754
Library of Congress Control Number: 2009936732

Contents

PLAYS FOR THREE OR FOUR ACTORS

Foreword

This year, Smith and Kraus has combined its two annual ten-minute play books into this one volume, divided into three sections: Plays for Two Actors, Plays for Three or Four Actors, and Plays for Five or Six Actors. Now, you can get the best ten-minute plays produced during the 2008–2009 theatrical season all in one book!

In years past, playwrights who were just starting out wrote one-act plays of thirty to forty minutes duration. One thinks of writers such as A. R. Gurney, Lanford Wilson, John Guare, and several others. Now, new writers tend to work in the ten-minute play form, largely because there are so many production opportunities. Fifteen years ago, there were none. Actors Theatre of Louisville used to commission playwrights to write ten-minute plays for their apprentice company. When I was senior editor at Samuel French, it occurred to me that there might be a market for these very short plays, so I compiled and edited an anthology of ten-minute plays from Actors Theatre, which did so well that Samuel French has now published six such anthologies. For the first time, ten-minute plays were now widely available, and they started getting produced. There are now a multitude of ten-minute play festivals, not only in the United States but all over the world.

In this volume you will find fifty-one ten-minute plays, culled from the hundreds I read last year. All have been produced successfully. Some have even won awards. These plays are written in a wide variety of styles. Some are realistic, some are not. Some are comic (laughs); some are dramatic (no laughs). I think this form lends itself well to experimentation in style and subject matter. A playwright can have fun with a device that couldn't be sustained as well in a longer form. Many of these plays employ such devices.

What makes a good ten-minute play? Well, first and foremost I have to like it. Isn't that what we mean when we call a play, a film, a novel "good"? We mean it effectively portrays the world as I see it. Aside from this obvious fact, a good ten-minute play has to have the same things any good play has — conflict, interesting characters, and compelling subject matter. It also has to have a clear beginning, middle, and end. Many of the plays I read for this book were scenes, not complete plays—well-written scenes, but scenes nonetheless. They left me wanting more. I chose plays that were complete in and of themselves. I also chose plays that I knew would interest those of you who produce ten-minute plays, because if a play isn't produced it's the sound of a tree falling in the forest, far away. In the back of this book you will find information on whom to contact when you decide which plays you want to produce.

There are a few plays in this book by playwrights who are pretty well established (Don Nigro, Jacquelyn Reingold, and Eduardo Machado are three examples); but most are by terrific new writers you never heard of, playwrights destined without a doubt to become far better known when their full-length work gets produced by major theaters. And you read their work first here!

Lawrence Harbison
Brooklyn, New York

PLAYS FOR
TWO ACTORS

PLAYS FOR
ONE MAN AND
ONE WOMAN

All Good Cretins
Go to Heaven

KATHLEEN WARNOCK

All Good Cretins Go to Heaven was originally produced by
Metropolitan Playhouse, New York City, June 5–22, 2008,
as part of The East Village Chronicles, Volume V.
Directed by Michael Hardart. Cast: Lulu — Amy Fulgham;
Joey Ramone — Will Cefalo.

CHARACTERS

    LULU: Early forties, kind of a solid citizen now, still a punk at heart. Maybe a tattoo or two, not someone you'd ever see in a business suit. In jeans (work-worn, not expensive ones) and work shoes or boots. Has had a lot of fun in her life, not a lot of which she regrets.

    JOEY RAMONE: Punk icon (May 19, 1951–April 15, 2001).

SETTING

    The Bowery, New York City. Joey Ramone Place. It's not too cold out, one of the recent New York winters where it's strangely warm at the wrong time.

TIME

    Late at night, early morning. Winter: late 2006, early 2007.

• • •

The Bowery, 3 or 4 A.M. Even in 2006, not the safest place in New York City. Lulu is coming down the street, projecting a "don't fuck with me" attitude. She's coming from a party, but she's not (too) drunk. Sound of something metal and loud; maybe a trash can being thrown, or a grate clanking down. It makes Lulu start and look around.

LULU: Who's there? *(She looks around, up, spies a street sign.)* "Joey Ramone Place." *(Turns and looks at a boarded-up storefront.)* CBGB? Is that you? *(She goes up to it and lays her hand on where the door used to be.)* Damn. Fuckin' old dive. New York fuckin' City. Joey Ramone, give me strength. *(She turns to go. Maybe there's a change of light. Joey Ramone is there. Yeah, that's Joey Ramone. He's not of this world anymore, and it shows; like maybe, there's an unearthly sheen or glow to his leather jacket. You could even give him a set of wings. Otherwise, he looks exactly like Joey Ramone. He's drinking a beer.)*

JOEY: 'ey. Whattaya want?

LULU: *(She takes it in.)* Joey? For real?

JOEY: *(He shrugs.)* I guess.

LULU: But you're, like . . .

JOEY: . . . Not living in the same neighborhood. No.

LULU: I don't live around here anymore, either. But, I'm just over in Astoria. If I can ask . . . where you hangin' out these days, Joey?

JOEY: Around. Haven't been down this way in a while. But like, if you believe in forever . . .

LULU: . . . then life is just a one night stand. IS there a rock-and-roll heaven?

JOEY: *(He looks at the boarded-up door.)* You know we have a helluva band.

LULU: I would guess. So, does that make you like, an angel, or something?

JOEY: I guess. A Jewish angel.

LULU: From Queens. 4-5-6-7 . . .

JOEY: . . . all good cretins go to heaven.

LULU: So Deedee's an angel now, too? A rapping junkie angel? He made it to heaven?

JOEY: They have kinda different standards for rock-and-roll heaven.

LULU : And Johnny? Did you and Johnny ever make up?

JOEY: You know, when I was sick, people kept telling Johnny, "You don't have forever to make your peace with Joey." But now he does. And it's probably gonna take that long.

LULU: You still play?

JOEY: All the time. Anytime we want. And the sound system never sucks, and you never lose your voice. I was walkin' down the street the other day.

LULU: In heaven.

JOEY: Yeah, in heaven. I was walkin' down the street in heaven, and suddenly it was the Bowery, and I saw CBGB, and I walked in the door, and it was just like it was. Nearly broke my ankle on a fuckin' hole in the floor. And I was like, dude?

LULU: What about the bathrooms? Were they still shitholes?

JOEY: You don't have to piss in heaven.

LULU: A nice touch. But you shoulda seen the blowouts they had here, Joey. The last few months. All the people who came together to try and save it. Little Steven Van Zandt . . .

JOEY: I like Little Steven. He's cool.

LULU: Lotta people came and did last shows. I saw Joan Jett in June.

JOEY: I like Joan. She's cool.

LULU: But they still shut it down. I can't say I was completely bummed. Its time really had come . . . and gone.

JOEY: Like mine . . .

LULU: No way, man. You left way too early. You were young.

JOEY: Lotta younger guys than me in heaven. Hey, lemme ask you a question . . .

LULU: Sure. Anything.

JOEY: Johnny Hef . . .

LULU: The Bullies. Yeah. I knew him.

JOEY: I like him. He's cool. He turned up . . . didn't want to talk about how he got there. Most I could get out of him was a building fell on him. He was a fireman, you know that?

LULU: Yeah.

JOEY: So, like, what happened? Do you know?

LULU: OK. *(She turns toward the spot that is "downtown" from where she's standing.)* Look downtown.

JOEY: *(He does.)* What?

LULU: Look at the skyline, Joey.

JOEY: *(It takes him a minute.)* Hey . . . I don't see the . . . you know . . . the two . . . the twin . . . the World . . .

LULU: This happened after you left town, Joey. You died in the spring. I remember how I heard about it. I was comin' home from Easter with my family. And on the radio. 1010 WINS. "The entertainment world mourns the loss of Joey Ramone." That was April. 2001. I worked to your party that year. "Life's a Gas." Your bro and your mom, they threw you a birthday party at the Hammerstein. Cheap Trick, Debbie Harry, Howie Pyro. Those guys.

JOEY: Cheap Trick. I like them. They're cool.

LULU: They played "Surrender." Good song.

JOEY: That was May. What about — *(He indicates downtown.)*

LULU: You know, I was down there right before. I was running sound for Ladyfest East, at the Knitting Factory. Lotta girl bands. Karyn Kuhl, Lourds. Sarah Jones.

JOEY: Karyn Kuhl from Sexpod? I like her. She's . . .

LULU: Cool. I walked outta there about . . . this time of night, September 10. 2001. And I thought, "Damn we still got a scene. Downtown still has its moments."

JOEY: There'll always be a downtown.

LULU: But different. Next day . . . a building. Those buildings. Both of 'em. Fell on Johnny Hef and 342 of his brothers. And about three thousand other people.

JOEY: You're shittin' me.

LULU: Wish I was, man.

JOEY: No way! What the fuck happened?

LULU: I don't like to talk about it, Joey. You got the people like me, and you got the ones who are obsessed with it. It still fuckin' kills me, so I don't discuss it. OK?

JOEY: Yeah. Wow. Things have really changed around here, right?

LULU: Dude, you do not even know!

JOEY: All the buildings going up. Where's the bums? Where's the kids puking and trying to talk their way in with a fake ID?

LULU: Doin' it somewhere else, Joey. Just not here anymore. High-rises. Restaurants.

JOEY: Whoa.

LULU: Yeah. Sometimes I wonder . . . is it still New York City?

JOEY: Greatest fuckin' city in the world.

LULU: It's different. I mean, things have always changed, but you wonder now if something's . . . gone. Forever. I wonder if I'm over it. Or it's over me.

JOEY: *(Sees the street sign.)* Joey Ramone Place? They named this corner after me?

LULU: They did. Some fans got a petition together, went to the city. I guess the mayor thought it was a good idea. Bloomberg.

JOEY: That's cool. Who's Bloomberg?

LULU: The Mayor. Rich guy. Lotta rich guys around now. Everywhere. Even around here. I used to come downtown before the Tompkins Square riots, visit friends in squats that are million-dollar condos now.

JOEY: Squats, man. And shooting galleries. Remember those?

LULU: The only galleries around here now sell art.

JOEY: But you're still here. Whatta you do?

LULU: Little bit of everything: run sound, lights for bands. Book some rooms. Sometimes I go on tour as a guitar or drum tech.

JOEY: You still make the music happen. You're still here.

LULU: Well, in Astoria.

JOEY: I like Greek food. You're still here.

LULU: I'm still here.

JOEY: If I need more vocals in the monitor, I look at you, and you do it.

LULU: Turn it up to eleven.

JOEY: Spinal Tap. I like those guys. They're cool.

LULU: They're, you know . . .

JOEY: . . . fictional? Yeah. I'm dead, not stupid. You're not stupid, either. So the Bowery isn't the Bowery anymore. So what? You'll just move along somewhere else. Right? There's other places, right? The music never really goes away, right?

LULU: Even if this old joint is gone, there's still basements and storefronts and shitty holes-in-the-wall where kids with guitars think they invented punk. And some of 'em keep the faith and still manage to grow up to be . . . semirespectable citizens. Like myself.

JOEY: Don't get too, you know, GOOD. Or boring.

LULU: Don't worry about it, man. I am usually not like this. I am not going to bitch about how nothin's like the old days. After all, I'm one lucky joker who got to see you and your brothers play many times, and a lot of other bands, some really good and some that totally sucked, in that boarded-up craphole over there. I guess . . . it just hit home . . . really. Tonight. That's why I called you, man.

JOEY: OK. Well, you know, don't.

LULU: Don't what?

JOEY: Don't think it's all in there, man. Just, you know, look for what's there now, in this city. It's a wonderful world.

LULU: Dude . . . you sing the hell out of that song.

JOEY: Thank you. It's good 'cause it's true. Right?

LULU: Right. So, I guess . . . I'm going to keep on having a good time, and see my friends, and remember the ones who've gone on, and kick ass till it's my time. I mean, I gotta, there's no choice, but I guess there is the choice to fuckin' like it. Like you did.

JOEY: I like you. You're cool.

LULU: I know. *(Pause.)* Hey. Can I ask you one more question?

JOEY: Sure. You want some of my beer?

LULU: Heavenly Rolling Rock? What's it taste like?

(He offers it to her. She takes a sip.)

LULU: Heavenly backwash is more like it. Jeez, Joey. Angel spit still tastes like spit.

JOEY: Sorry, man.

LULU: OK, so here's the question. It's more of a favor. Would you and your brothers sing for me, Joey? One more time?

JOEY: Wish I could do it inside.

LULU: Me too.

JOEY: I used to get up on that stage, and I'd look out, and you'd think you couldn't see anything because of the lights, but you know, you got used to 'em.

LULU: I'm sure the shades helped.

JOEY: They did. And I'd look down that long, long room, and I'd see people packed in and standing up on the sides, and climbing on the speakers, and the bartenders slamming drinks on the bar, and the waitresses squeezing through, and some guys squeezing them, and at the end of it all, I could see the door, and if I looked harder, you know what I saw?

LULU: What did you see, Joey?

JOEY: It was like the back wall was blasted away, and I was lookin' out in the universe. I could see all these fucking stars and galaxies. And comets and shit flying across the universe, and it was like I was beaming out the song to the whole fuckin' universe. That's what I saw.

LULU: In heaven?

JOEY: No, at CBs.

LULU: I saw it too, Joey. I'd like to see it one more time.

JOEY: I can do that. Yeah.

(Suddenly, there is a mic stand [it doesn't have to have an actual microphone in it]. Joey assumes his classic singing position, splay-legged, head down. He begins the superfast Ramones count-off.)

JOEY: 1234!

(Black out.)

END OF PLAY

The Can Can

KELLY YOUNGER

The Can Can was originally produced by Craig Sabin and B.K. Willerford at Avery Schreiber Theatre, Los Angeles, February to March 2004, as part of Can Festival III, Can-nections. Directed by Julie Fischer. Cast: Candie — Cyanne McClairian; Duncan — Brian Catalano.

CANDIE: Twenties to thirties, moody.
DUNCAN: Twenties to thirties, stubborn.

SETTING
Bare stage.

TIME
The present.

• • •

Candie and Duncan stand apart onstage. They each hold an aluminum can connected by a long piece of string stretched taut between them. It's a childhood toy string-phone. As Duncan speaks, he holds his can to his mouth and Candie holds her can to her ear, and vice versa. They do not make eye contact nor acknowledge each other's presence. During the first part of the play, however, they will walk back and forth across the stage, eventually becoming entangled in the string connecting their cans.

The dialogue should play as if the couple is arguing on the phone. The tone of the argument should follow this basic model: fast-paced, heated, sarcastic, comical, and increasing in volume until it finally ends in a tender realization that the argument is pointless and cliché. Lights up.

CANDIE: If you expect to soar with the eagles during the day, you can't hoot with the owls at night.

DUNCAN: You can't legislate morality.

CANDIE: If you can't do the time, don't do the crime.

DUNCAN: Don't open that can of worms.

CANDIE: You can run, but you can't hide.

DUNCAN: You can say that again.

CANDIE: What can that mean?

DUNCAN: You can't please your honey without money.

CANDIE: Money can't buy happiness.

DUNCAN: You can't squeeze blood out of a turnip.

CANDIE: Money can't buy you love.

DUNCAN: You can't make a silk purse out of a sow's ear.

CANDIE: You can bet your bottom dollar.

DUNCAN: You can bet your boots.

CANDIE: You can't get there from here.

DUNCAN: If you can't stand the heat, get out of the kitchen.

CANDIE: If you can't stand the kitchen, get a real job.

DUNCAN: You can dress her up but you still can't take her to town.

CANDIE: You can dress up a pig, but he'll still be a pig!

DUNCAN: Appearances can be deceptive.

CANDIE: You can't be counted on in the clutch.

DUNCAN: You can't hit the broad side of a barn.

CANDIE: You can't see beyond the end of your nose.

DUNCAN: You can't find your way out of a paper bag.

CANDIE: You can't see the forest for the trees.

DUNCAN: You can't teach an old dog new tricks.

CANDIE: If you can't run with the big dogs, stay on the porch.

DUNCAN: Why buy the cow when you can get the milk for free?

CANDIE: You can't fit a square peg in a round hole!

DUNCAN: Your mouth is writing checks your body can't cash.

CANDIE: I can't stomach this.

DUNCAN: She who cannot dance blames the DJ.

CANDIE: You can put glitter on a turd, but it still stinks.

DUNCAN: You just bit off more than you can chew.

CANDIE: You can screw up a two-car funeral.

DUNCAN: Beggars can't be choosers.

CANDIE: Better light a candle than curse the darkness.

DUNCAN: Women: can't live with 'em, can't live without 'em.

CANDIE: You can never go home again.

DUNCAN: Never put off tomorrow what you can do today.

CANDIE: You can't take knickers off a bare arse.

DUNCAN: You must crawl before you can walk.

CANDIE: You can't learn to swim without getting in the water.

DUNCAN: Brother, can you spare a dime?

CANDIE: Well, he can eat cookies in my bed.

DUNCAN: You can't have your cake and eat it too.

CANDIE: You can't hold a candle to him.

DUNCAN: He can talk the leg off a chair.

CANDIE: The empty can rattles most.

DUNCAN: You can't judge a book by its cover.

CANDIE: As far as the eye can see.

DUNCAN: I'm gonna open a can of whoop ass.

CANDIE: You can't win 'em all.

DUNCAN: Enough ants can eat an elephant.

CANDIE: You can't swing a dead cat without hitting one.

DUNCAN: How many ways can you skin a cat?

CANDIE: You can't fool a fool.

DUNCAN: Try as hard as you can.

CANDIE: Can you top this? You can fool some of the people all of the time, and you can fool all of the people some of the time, but you can't fool all of the people all of the time.

(Beat. By this time they are both entangled tightly in the string, back to back. They both sigh.)

DUNCAN: Can't a cat look at a queen?

CANDIE: I don't know how much more of this I can take.

DUNCAN: This can't be easy for you.

CANDIE: You can't call your soul your own.

DUNCAN: Any old stocking can find an old shoe.

CANDIE: You can't make orange juice out of lemons.

DUNCAN: Can't you take a joke?

CANDIE: Nothing can be done.

DUNCAN: You can hardly blame me.

CANDIE: You can't be too sure.

DUNCAN: Can you forgive me?

CANDIE: You can't put the toothpaste back in the tube.

DUNCAN: Can you forgive me?

CANDIE: You can lead a horse to water, but . . .

DUNCAN: Can I buy you a drink?

CANDIE: You can catch more flies with honey than with vinegar.

DUNCAN: We can work it out.

CANDIE: You can't win for the sake of losing.

DUNCAN: You can decide your own life.

CANDIE: Catch as catch can.

DUNCAN: You're so close I can taste it.

CANDIE: Ask not what your country can do for you . . .

DUNCAN: . . . but what you can do for your country.

(Beat. They put their cans down, turn, and look at each other for the first time.)

DUNCAN: Can you hear me now?

CANDIE: I think I can. I think I can.

DUNCAN: Candie.

CANDIE: Duncan.

(Tangled tightly, they embrace. Lights out.)

END OF PLAY

Déjà Vu All Over Again

ROBIN RICE LICHTIG

Déjù All Over Again was produced by New Jersery Repertory
Company, May 2008, as part of their Theatre Brut series.
Directed by John FitzGibbon. Cast: Yogi Berra — Stephen
Innocenzi; Yolanda — Michele Tauber. *Déjù All Over Again*
received a reading at the Arthur Seelen Theatre, New York
City, February 2008. Directed by John FitzGibbon. Cast:
Yogi Berra — Bob Marcus; Yolanda — Robin Rothstein.

Extra thanks to Bernard L. Jones for his expertise and Yankee shirt.

CHARACTERS
> YOGI BERRA: Thirty-one, the real man, feeling old.
> YOLANDA: Ageless, loves to laugh, very positive, ethereal in a quirky way.

SETTING
> Yankees locker room.

TIME
> April 1957.

• • •

"Take Me Out to the Ball Game" fades as lights rise on a locker room. A few wet towels scattered around. Yogi, a towel around his waist, waves to the exiting team.

YOGI: *(Forced cheerfulness.)* Go. Yeah. Tip top. See ya tomorrow. We'll pulverize 'em tomorrow! *(He sinks on a bench beside a Yankee gym bag and a bat, depressed, wet towel around his neck like an albatross.)* Didn't used to make so many wrong mistakes.
> *(He takes a carton of Twinkies from his bag, squints to try to read the ingredients on the label. Yolanda enters. He is unaware of her.)*
YOLANDA: Oh fairies and fancies A great man is down; Bring light to his aura Renew his renown!
YOGI: *(To himself.)* Stupid small print. Nobody could read this. Oughtta be a law. *(More depressed. He eats a Twinkie.)*
YOLANDA: Oh spirits, it's me I'm not kidding now; This man needs my help You must show me how!
YOGI: Holy schmoli!
YOLANDA: Greetings.
YOGI: You can't be in here.
YOLANDA: But I am.
YOGI: It's a men's locker room.
YOLANDA: Excellent specimens. Except for tubbies who should cut back on Twinkies.
YOGI: *(Depressed again.)* Thanks a heap.
YOLANDA: Is that a gray hair?

YOGI: Pull it out! Pull it out!

(She pulls out the hair.)

YOGI: Please don't tell nobody.

YOLANDA: Buck up, Yogi. So you weren't hitting today —

YOGI: It was Kansas City for cripesake.

YOLANDA: You've had slumps before.

YOGI: This time it ain't déjà vu all over again. It feels different. Like SLUMP in the curve of life. Up, up, up; then down, down, down. Then you die. No. First people laugh and boo. Then you die. *(He stuffs gum in his mouth.)*

YOLANDA: It's April. The season is young.

YOGI: *(Wistfully:)* Young.

YOLANDA: What's your average?

YOGI: .230.

YOLANDA: Some are lower.

YOGI: Who?

YOLANDA: Well not this year yet, but —

YOGI: Juicy Fruit?

YOLANDA: Maybe later.

YOGI: Later I'll be dead.

YOLANDA: There's always tomorrow.

YOGI: Tomorrow I'll be another day more decrepit. Can I please be alone?

YOLANDA: How old are you?

YOGI: Twenty-nine.

YOLANDA: Try again.

YOGI: Thirty. All right. Thirty-one.

YOLANDA: Yup. One foot in the grave.

(He moans, buries his face in his hands.)

YOLANDA: Where's the goofs and chuckles, Yogi?

YOGI: I really didn't say everything I said.

YOLANDA: *(Chortles.)* Like that. And like when you said about a restaurant in your old neighborhood in St. Louis, you said: "Nobody goes there anymore. It's too crowded." *(Laughs harder.)* Or when you said: "A nickel ain't worth a dime no more."

YOGI: *(Not laughing.)* Yeah. I'm hysterical.

YOLANDA: *(Laughs.)* When you said: "We were overwhelming underdogs."

YOGI: *(Not laughing.)* We were.

YOLANDA: "The other teams could make trouble for us if they win."

YOGI: I'm splitting a gut.

YOLANDA: "Ninety percent of the game is half mental."

YOGI: Mr. Barrel-of-Monkeys has given his name to a bear.

YOLANDA: All this because of one game?

YOGI: The future ain't what it used to be.

YOLANDA: That's funny!

YOGI: My hair's receding. My knees pinch. My ears sag. I'm half deaf. My eyebrows are bushes. I fart all the time. Send for a bib. Send for diapers. Send for a body bag! Send for something they oughtta invent so a man can satisfy Carmen when his hormones fail him.

YOLANDA: So that's it.

YOGI: Last night.

YOLANDA: It happens.

YOGI: It's a symptom of decrepitude!

YOLANDA: I'm sure Carmen understands.

YOGI: Who are you anyway?

YOLANDA: Yolanda, the Oracle of the Yankees.

YOGI: Oracle?

YOLANDA: You know. Ancient. Long stringy white hair . . .

YOGI: I thought that was a whatchamacallit.

YOLANDA: Seer, soothsayer, oracle — same ballpark.

YOGI: Like in Shakespeare?

YOLANDA: You like Shakespeare?

YOGI: Ooooh yeah! Smart man.

YOLANDA: He can't help you. I can.
    (Yogi shakes his head.)

YOLANDA: 'Cause I'm a woman?
    (Yogi shakes his head.)

YOLANDA: 'Cause I'm old?

YOGI: That word — like a dagger in my heart.

YOLANDA: OK. Skip it. I only deal with Yankees and you won't be one for long the way you're going. *(To herself.)* No, Yolanda. Help the Yankees is what you do. It's your raison d'etre. *(To Yogi.)* Lawrence Peter Berra, I'm going to help you whether you cooperate or not. Lie down.
    (He stretches out on the bench. She gives him a vigorous rubdown as they continue.)

YOGI: Who have you helped in the past?

YOLANDA: Over half your team.

YOGI: I never heard of you.

YOLANDA: Have you been listening?

YOGI: I've been depending on myself.

YOLANDA: Aye, there's the rub.

YOGI: See. Shakespeare again. Man, if he was here —

YOLANDA: They don't even call it baseball where he's from.

YOGI: Name some guys you helped.

YOLANDA: Privileged information.

YOGI: Thought so.

YOLANDA: Whitey, Hank, Billy, Mickey —

YOGI: Mantle?

YOLANDA: Not "Mouse."

YOGI: How?

YOLANDA: That spree at the Copacabana. That's all I'm going to say.

YOGI: How much do you charge?

YOLANDA: Nothing.

YOGI: Don't pull my leg.

(Above said as she is stretching his leg.)

YOLANDA: I'm a fan.

YOGI: That's it?

YOLANDA: That's everything.

YOGI: *(Depressed.)* It was. *(He puts on his pants.)*

YOLANDA: In the future, if you run into another oracle, you should know: Oracles never charge a fee. We do, however, accept gifts of appreciation. Gratuities. I actually am in great need of a small gift of appreciation. It actually has been three days since I ate, but I haven't been focused on my stomach growling. I was focused on helping you. I was committed to trying everything in my power —

YOGI: Like what?

YOLANDA: Whatever works.

YOGI: For instance?

YOLANDA: Come here.

(He reluctantly stands in front of her. She puts her hands on his head, suddenly shoves him backward, almost knocking him over.)

YOLANDA: Get thee gone, Specter of Old Age! *(To Yogi.)* Better?

YOGI: I dunno.

YOLANDA: Wiggle your shoulders.

YOGI: Gave me a cramp.

YOLANDA: Come here.

YOGI: *(Backing away.)* Never mind. I'll ice it later. *(He puts on his socks.)* It ain't specters. It ain't the pitches. It ain't the bats. It ain't nerves. It ain't the crowd. I love the crowd. It ain't the pressure. It ain't pebbles in my shoes or lack of concentration.

YOLANDA: Have you tried prayer?

YOGI: No dice.

YOLANDA: *(Praying.)* Dear God —

YOGI: I'm doomed I tell ya. The 57 season is doomed. The 58 season is —

YOLANDA: *(Continuing, louder.)* Your humble servant Yogi Berra needs a divine hand. With each game his average sinks lower and lower. He strikes out and strikes out and —

(Yogi starts to interrupt. She puts a hand over his mouth.)

YOLANDA: His youthful, positive attitude has been swept away in a flood of self-doubt. He needs a sign pointing to the end of this dark, dark vortex. A sign would be greatly appreciated. Amen.

(They wait for a sign. Nothing.)

YOLANDA: Gum.

(He gives her a stick. She chews. He chews. They look heavenward. Nothing. He offers her twenty dollars.)

YOGI: You did your best.

YOLANDA: *(Shaking her head:)* No solution, no gratuity.

(He puts on his shoes. She feels something in her pocket. Perhaps she forgot it was there.)

YOLANDA: Well I'll be a Harvey Wallbanger!

YOGI: Huh?

YOLANDA: In my pocket all this time. Shame on me.

YOGI: What?

(She pulls out a pair of . . .)

YOLANDA: Eyeglasses!

YOGI: Yours?

YOLANDA: Yours!

YOGI: Oooh no.

YOLANDA: Put them on.

YOGI: *(Fierce explosion.)* I don't need glasses! Nothing's wrong with my eyes! Glasses are like a billboard with flashing lights: Old! Older! Oldest! They'll hear the crowd in fifty states: "Take a hike, Four Eyes! Get a cane, Granpa!"

(She turns away as if he had struck her.)

YOLANDA: Every game the Yankees lose will be my fault. I'm an oracle failure. Nobody will have confidence in me. Nobody will come to me for help. I'll be useless. Hungry too. Really, really hungry.

(He tries to give her money. She slaps it away.)

YOGI: Tomorrow —

YOLANDA: You'll strike out again. I see it clear as day. If you don't stop moaning and groaning about how old you look and put on the damn glasses, the Yankees will never win again.

(Yogi puts on Yankee uniform shirt number 8.)

YOGI: I can see a speck of tobacco on a pitcher's lip. I can see the twitch in his eye. When the ball's coming at me, it floats in slow motion. I can count the stitches on the cowhide. Every one — 108 stitches. I have the eyes of a newborn eagle! *(He flings the towel that's been around his neck to the ground.)*

YOLANDA: So how come you're throwing in the towel, Eagle Eye?

(Yogi picks up his gym bag.)

YOGI: See you in a retirement villa.

YOLANDA: It ain't over 'til it's over.

(He was exiting. This stops him in his tracks.)

YOGI: Says who?

YOLANDA: Shakespeare.

YOGI: Damn. You sure?

YOLANDA: The Bard himself.

(Yogi ponders this a moment, then squares his shoulders, makes a momentous decision.)

YOGI: When you come to a fork in the road, I guess you just gotta gosh darn take it.

(She holds out the glasses. He puts them on. Lights shift. He picks up a bat, touches "home base" with it a few times, holds it ready to slam an incoming pitch. [Note: Yogi is a leftie.] Sound: roar of a crowd.)

YOGI: "It ain't over 'til it's over." Speaks to me. Like in person.

(He swings. Sound: crack of ball meeting bat. Her eyes follow the ball over the crowd, out of the stadium. Yogi breaks into a huge grin. Yolanda holds out a hand for the twenty dollars. Black out.)

END OF PLAY

Feeding Time at the Human House

DAVID WIENER

Feeding Time at the Human House was originally produced at
Compass Theatre, San Diego, April/May 2008, as part of
6th @ Penn Challenge III Festival. Directed by Jessica Seaman.
Cast: Fran — Michelle de Francesco; Bernie — Ivan Harrison.

CHARACTERS

FRAN: A mature, omnivorous, intelligent, adaptable, ground-dwelling female baboon.

BERNIE: A nondominant, omnivorous, intelligent, adaptable, ground-dwelling male baboon.

SETTING

A zoo in a large city.

TIME

The present.

NOTE: There are no sets or scenery; the actors wear street clothes and mime all the props.

• • •

An empty stage: Bernie and Fran are on opposite sides of the stage. Bernie is happily munching a big handful of grass as Fran eyes him, annoyed.

FRAN: *(Beat.)* Must you make that noise when you eat?

BERNIE: *(Looking up, interrupted.)* What noise?

FRAN: *(Mimicking him.)* Chomp, chomp, crunch, gulp!

BERNIE: Well, pardon me. *(Stuffs the handful of grass under an imaginary rock or bush.)* I'll finish it after you go to sleep. All right?
(Fran just sighs, sits, and drags a finger through the dirt. Bernie glares at her for a moment; trots downstage and picks up a big handful of something. He looks out at the audience and beyond, making a quick survey. He finds a likely looking target, winds up, throws, and gleefully runs around in a little circle.)

BERNIE: Didja see that? Whaddya think of that, huh?

FRAN: *(Shrugs, barely glancing up.)* Yeah, it was all right.

BERNIE: All right? Fran — I nailed her right between the shoulder blades! Bam! Made her drop her popcorn and everything! BAM! Weren't you even looking? *(Runs downstage and gleefully shouts after his unseen victim.)* Forget it, lady! No dry cleaner on earth is gonna get that out!

FRAN: I really —
(Pause.)

BERNIE: *(Looks at Fran, confused.)* What? Really what?

FRAN: Bernie — I really — I just wish you'd stop throwing poop.

BERNIE: *(Like she's nuts.)* What're you talking about?

FRAN: *(Pause.)* Do you have to throw poop at people?

BERNIE: — I'm a baboon, yeah, it's, like, part of our job description? *(Beat.)* Besides, it relaxes me.

(Fran sighs.)

BERNIE: What?

FRAN: . . . nothing . . .

BERNIE: *(Fed up.)* Oh, for God's sake . . . *(Beat.)* You know, you've been really impossible lately, you know that?

FRAN: Well, maybe it's because I wind up having to do everything around this enclosure!

BERNIE: Oh, please.

FRAN: No, I'm serious. Like, for instance, maybe you could groom yourself a little more often.

BERNIE: OK, OK . . .

FRAN: Why does it always have to be my job? It's not as if I don't have anything else to do.

BERNIE: You said you liked eating lice!

FRAN: For a snack, yes, but not as a constant diet! *(Gestures out toward the audience.)* You're always going on about what a bunch of slobs they are, maybe you could make a little more of an effort with your own appearance occasionally.

BERNIE: *(Checking his skin.)* Are you going to start in with this again? I'm not that lousy, for crying out loud . . .

FRAN: Fine, have it your way, I'm wrong.

BERNIE: No — I — no, look —

FRAN: It's fine, I'm always wrong. You're always right.

BERNIE: *(Sits, his head in his hands.)* Ohh-h-h-h-h . . .

FRAN: Never mind. *(Pause.)*

BERNIE: Boy, you sure mated down when you mated with me, right? That's what this is all about, isn't it? You might as well say it. It's what everybody thinks, anyway.

FRAN: Oh, who cares what everybody thinks.

BERNIE: Oh — well, thank you very much!

FRAN: That is not what I meant.

BERNIE: Oh, of course it is! *(And now here's Bernie's chance to make fun of Fran.)* My great-great-great grandmother's troop was studied by the Leakeys — the Olduvai Gorge Leakeys. Oh, yes, and my grandmother's troop was written up by Jane Goodall. Goodall studied us for several seasons. And my mother's troop was personally acquainted with Dian Fossey — *(A refined eye-roll, complete with a hand-upon-bosom gesture.)* that poor woman. We tried to warn her the natives were getting restless, but, well, you know how very stubborn these humans can be . . .

FRAN: *(Stung.)* I never said we knew Dian Fossey.

(Bernie snorts.)

FRAN: . . . but we were studied by Leakey and Goodall.

BERNIE: Oh, well, whoopee for you . . .

FRAN: Oh, who cares! Just — go watch the people and leave me alone for a while . . .

BERNIE: OK, fine. *(Crosses, looks out over the audience, watching the zoo visitors.)* You know, with that special treat they put out this morning, I thought you'd be in a better mood.

FRAN: Yes, it was very nice.

BERNIE: There are plenty of zoos where they don't do a damn thing for birthdays, you know. Nice, big basket of green grass with chunks of fresh fruit all in it. Delicious.

FRAN: I'm not ungrateful.

BERNIE: I mean, we could just as easily have wound up somewhere they consider us a delicacy.

FRAN: Not at my age . . .

(Beat.)

BERNIE: Is that it? You're depressed because it's your birthday?

(Beat.)

FRAN: My rear end doesn't swell up like it used to. And I'm really starting to spread, I can see it. *(Sighs.)* I'm fifteen years old, I guess it's inevitable . . .

BERNIE: Your rear end swells just fine. I still like the way your rear end swells.

FRAN: *(Looks out at the unseen zoo visitors.)* It's funny. Their rear ends don't swell up at all.

BERNIE: *(Joining her.)* Well, some of them do — like that one over there.

FRAN: Oh — yeah, well, hers is huge, you're right.

BERNIE: Did you know their females are always in heat?

FRAN: Don't be disgusting.

BERNIE: It's a medical fact! Their mating habits are really shocking. You see, they don't have a certain time when they're receptive; their females don't come into heat — they're constantly in heat, perpetually in season. The result is — and I know you're gonna laugh — they copulate at will.

FRAN: That's just stupid.

BERNIE: I'm telling you, it's the truth!

FRAN: You're just making stuff up. You're always doing that.

BERNIE: Not only that, but they eat even when they're not hungry.

FRAN: I'm hungry all the time. I could eat a tree.

BERNIE: You do eat trees.

FRAN: You know what I mean.

BERNIE: You eat trees, you eat bushes, you eat grass —

FRAN: Oh, shut up.

(Bernie picks up another handful.)

BERNIE: *(Trying to cheer her up.)* C'mon. Come on over here. Go ahead and chuck this at the tall guy over there. Nice, big target, he'll never know what hit him — he's too busy screwing around with his Blackberry.

FRAN: *(Sighing.)* . . . if only throwing poop was all it took . . .

BERNIE: *(Facing Fran, his back to the zoo visitors.)* Come on, baby. Go on, let him have it right in his double-breasted cashmere coat. You know you wanna.

FRAN: He saw you. He's moving away.

BERNIE: *(Disappointed, drops the handful and grunts.)* Hmph.

FRAN: Amazing how fast they learn.

BERNIE: Don't kid yourself. They're idiots.

FRAN: Is that why they're out there and we're in here?

BERNIE: I'm telling you, they're morons. They still don't have the slightest idea what the dolphins are up to.

FRAN: *(Feels a headache coming on.)* Oh, God, Bernie, please, I'm in no mood to listen to more of your conspiracy theories.

BERNIE: I heard it myself!

FRAN: *(Weary.)* Yes, I know, you told me. Before the remodeling.

BERNIE: Yes. That's right. Before they moved us into the new enclosure, back when we were in the old pens, next to the aquatic mammals.

FRAN: Bernie, please.

BERNIE: Everyone's terrified of killer whales and sharks and giant squid — but I think they're just doing the dirty work for the dolphins! If people had any idea what they were really up to, they'd turn 'em all into cat food.

FRAN: Bernie, I — yes, I remember, you told me all about it.

BERNIE: They even tried to get me involved; did I ever tell you that?

FRAN: *(Sighs.)* Bernie, right now, all I want to do is watch the people and try to relax a little, OK? *(She moves away from Bernie to do just that.)*

BERNIE: "We need friends," one of 'em told me. "Friends who can climb over fences — friends with hands, who can pick things up, and do little jobs for us. And once we take over, we'll make it all worth your while." Said he'd been in the Navy and learned how to use explosives. I'm telling you, those dolphins mean business.

FRAN: *(Rubbing her temples.)* Well, then, it's a good thing we don't live next to them anymore.

BERNIE: *(Gesturing at the zoo visitors.)* Even if you told them, they wouldn't believe it! "Oh, Flipper wouldn't hurt a fly!" That goofball grin, all those cute, little noises. Boy, are they in for a shock. They don't know anything.

FRAN: Well, Bernie, they must know something. After all, they went to the moon.

BERNIE: *(Beat.)* You believe that?

(Something in the crowd catches Fran's attention. She takes a step or two downstage.)

FRAN: *(Watching intently.)* Hmn.

BERNIE: — What?

FRAN: See that female over there?

BERNIE: What female over where?

FRAN: In the Roberto Cavalli chiffon silk blouse.

BERNIE: Uh — yeah. Must have bucks.

FRAN: Do you notice anything else about her?

BERNIE: *(Is this a trick question?)* Uh — ahm . . . she — ah — looks great for her age?

FRAN: Bernie. No. She was part of a mated pair. Remember? Every time she came in here, it was with the same male.

BERNIE: Oh! Yeah! The fat, old guy with the hair plugs and the chunk-gold jewelry, sure.

FRAN: Well, he's not with her anymore. She's been showing up all alone for weeks.

BERNIE: Oh.

FRAN: I think — I think he died, Bernie.

BERNIE: Or she dumped him. They do that, you know. Their females have this highly formalized ritual that drives the male away and leaves them in full possession of the enclosure and everything in it. It's a fascinating behavior; I believe it's unique to humans.

FRAN: No. The male died, Bernie. I can tell.

BERNIE: If you say so.

FRAN: I always liked seeing them. They were so affectionate and bonded, you know? Even at their age. Just look at her — she must be nearly twenty in baboon years.

BERNIE: Twenty-five, if she's a day. I think she had that face-stretching procedure that's supposed to be some sort of visual aphrodisiac or somatic pheromone or something.

FRAN: That's not the point, Bernie! She used to be together, bonded, with someone and now — she's alone. She's just — alone.

BERNIE: Oh. Yeah, I guess so.

(Pause, as Bernie occupies himself hefting and trying out new handfuls.)

FRAN: Bernie — do you ever think — do you ever think about what would happen to me if something should happen to you?

BERNIE: *(Distracted.)* What's gonna happen to me in here?

FRAN: I'm not talking about being shot by poachers or eaten by a leopard.

BERNIE: Well, all right then.

FRAN: I mean — over the normal course of events. In the fullness of time. If you go before I do — what's going to happen to me?

BERNIE: *(Shrugs.)* I dunno. You'd probably get passed around until one of the guys decides to take you on permanently. S'what usually happens.

FRAN: *(Tearing up.)* But I don't wanna get passed around! I wanna be with you.

BERNIE: *(Puts an arm around her.)* It's OK, it's OK — you're staying with me, I'm not going anywhere! Take it easy, Fran; everything's fine.

(Pause.)

FRAN: *(Sniffling a little.)* And — and — if I went first — what would you do?

BERNIE: *(Uh-oh.)* Why do you have to bring this stuff up?

FRAN: I'm serious, Bernie. These are important issues. Not to males, I know, but females think about these things.

BERNIE: How should I know what I would do?

FRAN: *(Mad.)* Well, you'd do something, wouldn't you?

BERNIE: *(Scrambling for an answer.)* Well, I — I wouldn't mate again.

FRAN: — You wouldn't?

BERNIE: No.

FRAN: — Never?

BERNIE: Not ever. I'd get old throwing poop at people, and then one day, I'd just keel over.

FRAN: — Promise?

BERNIE: I promise.

FRAN: *(Walks up to the edge of their enclosure.)* Bernie? What do you think they see when they look at us?

BERNIE: How should I know?

FRAN: *(Looking out at the audience.)* I'm serious, Bernie. What do you think they see?

BERNIE: I dunno — buncha monkeys, I guess.

FRAN: Sometimes, I see them looking up at the sky — or at the stars. Even the juveniles.

BERNIE: So?

FRAN: I think — things must look really different to them.

BERNIE: Well, sure — they're there and we're in here. Like you said.

FRAN: No, not just that. They can see stuff. Different stuff, you know? More stuff.

BERNIE: Yeah. So what?

(Pause.)

FRAN: I'd like to see more.

BERNIE: Not me. That's probably what makes 'em crazy. Who wants to see what they see?

FRAN: I would. I really would. Sometimes, when they look at each other — the mated pairs? It's like they see so much more than just each other. It's like they see — whole oceans. We never see anything like that, do we, Bernie?

BERNIE: *(Shrugs.)* Like I said — idiots.

FRAN: *(Annoyed.)* Well, they may be idiots but at least they don't throw poop.

BERNIE: They throw a lot worse than poop.

FRAN: Yeah . . . but they also built this zoo. It's not like we could trade places with them.

BERNIE: The dolphins think they can.

FRAN: Well, Bernie, I think the dolphins are gonna be disappointed.

(Bernie notices something in the crowd and takes a couple of quick steps downstage.)

BERNIE: Hey — hey, look — the guy in the cashmere? There he is again — and he's got his back to us! (Dashes over to scoop up a handful and dashes right back.) OK, now watch this time, OK?

(Just as he starts his wind-up, Fran interrupts him.)

FRAN: Bernie?

BERNIE: *(Freezes in midthrow.)* Now what is it?

FRAN: — Nobody can sling it like you do, Bernie.

BERNIE: *(Smiles.)* I love you, Fran.

FRAN: *(Smiles.)* I love you, too, Bernie.

(Bernie pitches a line drive.)

BERNIE: *(Raising both arms in triumph.)* BAM!

(Black out.)

END OF PLAY

Life Coming Up

SHARYN ROTHSTEIN

Life Coming Up was originally produced as part of New York
University's Tisch School of the Arts New Works Festival,
March 2007. Directed by Matthew Arbour.
Cast: Abby — Kelly Van Zile; Chris — Kaolin Bass.

CHARACTERS
ABBY: Mid- to late twenties.
CHRIS: Late twenties to early thirties.

SETTING
A trendy bar in an East Coast city not too far from Maryland.

TIME
The present.

• • •

A dark, trendy city bar. Abby, in a button-down shirt too tight for her and a pair of khakis far too big for her, downs her beer. Chris, in a well-fitting suit, watches her, sipping a Mojito. Abby puts down the beer and lets out a big belch. Chris is slightly taken aback, but he smiles.

ABBY: So how long have you worked at Slimeballs Sleazeballs and Sons?
CHRIS: 420 years. This spring.
ABBY: So that's what I have to look forward to.
CHRIS: That and the Christmas party. They give you nonalcoholic eggnog instead of a bonus.
ABBY: Ha. Excuse me, I've gotta burp again — *(Abby stops herself from burping.)* Wait. Is this a date?
CHRIS: I thought so.
ABBY: Oh. Then I won't burp. Unless you want me to. Unless that does something for you — ?
CHRIS: No, not usually. But if it does something for you —
ABBY: So this is a date.
CHRIS: Well I asked you —
ABBY: I'm glad. I'm glad it's a — Actually. I'm in a bad place right now.
CHRIS: OK. Should we move — ?
ABBY: No. I mean I can't date you. I'm having an emotional breakdown.
CHRIS: Right now?
ABBY: Yes.
CHRIS: Because of me?
ABBY: I don't think so.
CHRIS: You can burp if you want to —
ABBY: No — thanks, that's very nice — but, look: you don't want to date me.
CHRIS: I do want to date you.

(Beat. Chris regrets laying his cards on the table.)

CHRIS: At least, I think I want to date you?

ABBY: You don't. You can't. It's like, psychologically impossible.

CHRIS: Um, OK, can I at least finish this drink with you?

ABBY: No. I have depression.

CHRIS: *(Lighting up.)* Me too!

ABBY: Medicated or nonmedicated?

CHRIS: Depends on the day.

ABBY: Good. So you understand.

CHRIS: Depression? Yes. Unending feelings of despair and hopelessness. Sinking. Drowning. In a vat of dirt or —

ABBY: Sludge.

CHRIS: Yes!

ABBY: Something viscous.

CHRIS: Oh viscous, good word.

ABBY: Looking out a window and seeing —

CHRIS: Death.

ABBY: Well, that's a bit extreme —

CHRIS: Sorry —

ABBY: No. No, don't apologize. Just for me, it's more like . . . acid reflux.

CHRIS: Yes!

ABBY: Like perpetual acid reflux. Like your life coming up on you.

CHRIS: Exactly!

(Beat.)

ABBY: Wow. We have a lot in common. *(Beat.)* I don't think this will work.

CHRIS: I think it's working.

ABBY: The last guy I had a lot in common with turned out to have a rare fungal infection. I was on antibiotics for a year.

CHRIS: None of my fungal infections are rare; you'll be off meds within a month. *(She smiles.)* Do you want another drink?

ABBY: That's not fair. I'm an alcoholic. I always want another drink.

CHRIS: I'm addicted to online gambling.

ABBY: I've always wanted to try that.

CHRIS: Come over. I'll show you how.

ABBY: Great. I'll bring the wine.

CHRIS: Nice. *(Slight beat.)* You were saying? Emotional breakdown?

ABBY: Oh yes. My mother.

CHRIS: Mine too! A monster!

ABBY: A vampire.

CHRIS: With a moustache.

ABBY: No.

CHRIS: It glows in the dark. Just like her undead soul.

ABBY: Mine's not so bad. Only she's terrible. She demands things I can't provide.

CHRIS: Like what?

ABBY: Love and respect.

CHRIS: Who has the time?

ABBY: That's what I said! I work, I take classes, I recycle, I barely have time to breathe. And also: people are dying.

CHRIS: Yes!

ABBY: All the time. Like everywhere.

CHRIS: Yes, yes! Like: Africa.

ABBY: And she doesn't even notice.

CHRIS: Notice. Care —

ABBY: Because she's so fucking —

CHRIS AND ABBY: Depressed!

CHRIS: And my father —

ABBY: An anxious mess —

CHRIS: The weather. The laundry. Dental hygiene.

ABBY: Everything.

CHRIS: Totally spineless.

ABBY: That's why he loves her. She tells him what to do. Who to be.

CHRIS: He needs her. He's addicted to gambling. Craps, principally.

ABBY: Booze. Jack, principally. Principally now. *(Beat.)* She's been sick. My mother.

CHRIS: *(Sincere.)* I'm sorry.

ABBY: Chronic death type stuff.

CHRIS: That bad?

ABBY: All the time sick. Constant care. Like running a marathon for years, hoping you never get to the finish line, but kind of hoping you do. Running and running. And there's nobody giving you water on the sides.

CHRIS: I could. Give you water.

ABBY: No.

CHRIS: Why not?

ABBY: You're already depressed.

CHRIS: There's nothing a depressed person likes more than another reason to be depressed. We could share meds.

ABBY: And shrinks.

CHRIS: And pain.

ABBY: I've got enough.

CHRIS: We all have enough. That's why we share it.

ABBY: Why did you ask me? On a date? It's not normal. For me.

CHRIS: *(He laughs.)* Me neither. I saw you talking to the water cooler. The other women they talk at the water cooler. You were talking to it.

ABBY: Yeah.

CHRIS: What did you say?

ABBY: I made a wish.

CHRIS: For your mom.

ABBY: For my boss. That her hair would fall out and she'd grow a pair of tits on her chin. She makes me staple everything twice.

CHRIS: Did it happen? The wish?

ABBY: I'm still waiting.

CHRIS: Saw you talking to the water cooler. Forgot my depression. For, like, a split second.

ABBY: Then it came back.

CHRIS: It always does. But for a split second —

ABBY: Are you a coward?

CHRIS: Only when it counts. Do you get mean?

ABBY: I did once. But I never got nice again.

CHRIS: Are your parents still married?

ABBY: Yes. Yours?

CHRIS: Thirty-five years. Do you ever wonder how?

ABBY: No. Never.

CHRIS: Me neither.

ABBY: They've got —

CHRIS AND ABBY: Chemistry.

CHRIS: Come over tonight. I can teach you how to ruin your credit.

ABBY: I have work tomorrow.

CHRIS: So do I.

ABBY: I left my anxiety pills at home.

CHRIS: You can take mine.

ABBY: And my birth control.

CHRIS: I'll be a gentleman.

ABBY: I hate gentlemen.

CHRIS: I meant the kind of gentleman who ties you up.

ABBY: I have a scar.

CHRIS: I have three. Self-inflicted.

ABBY: Wow.

CHRIS: I thought I'd bleed to death. But instead I just got kind of nauseous. I think I'm better now. I think. How's that for honesty?

ABBY: I see why you don't date a lot. *(Beat.)* My mom's having surgery tomorrow. I was supposed to go home. But I'm not.

CHRIS: Where's home?

ABBY: Maryland. Not even that far. My father said I was heartless. *(Slight beat.)* My father said I was heartless. *(Beat.)* Do you still want me to come over? *(Beat.)* I told you this wouldn't work out. *(Abby gets her coat. She starts to leave.)*

CHRIS: Wait. Do you want me to go with you? Home?

ABBY: Why would you do that?

CHRIS: I told you: there's nothing a depressed person likes more —

ABBY: You want a wife.

CHRIS: I want to feel like a grown-up. I want to be responsible for somebody else so I don't have to be responsible for myself. *(Pause.)* What do you want?

ABBY: I want to be absolved.

CHRIS: I can do that.

ABBY: How?

(Chris takes her hands.)

CHRIS: Tonight, we'll gamble. Tomorrow, we'll go to Maryland.

(Abby takes a deep breath.)

ABBY: You're intriguing. For a tax attorney.

CHRIS: If by intriguing you mean tormented.

ABBY: I do.

(Abby sits down again. Chris lets out a burp. They smile at each other.)

END OF PLAY

Novices

MONICA RAYMOND

Novices was originally produced by CentAstage at
Arts Black Box Theatre, Boston Center for the Arts,
February/March 2008, as part of Plays on Tap. Directed by
Joe Antoun. Cast: Kate — Lisa Tucker; Pete — Steve Triebes.
Novices was also performed at the Stanford Calderwood
Pavilion, Boston Center for the Arts, May 11, 2008,
as part of the Boston Theater Marathon. Directed by
Doug Lockwood. Cast: Kate — Molly Schreiber; Pete —
Antonio Ocampo-Guzman.

    KATE: Twenties, sparky, bright, thin.
    PETE: Thirties, large, smart, very badly dressed.

    Au Bon Pain.

    The present.

• • •

PETE: I'm looking for the young woman who wants to be tamed.
    (Pete walks over to Kate, who continues reading her book. Pete pulls out a letter and reads to her from it.)
PETE: "I am a wild animal. Ravish me! Tame me! Torture me!" That wouldn't be you, would it?
KATE: Shut up! I DO NOT know you.
PETE: No? Hmm. *(Reads.)* "I am five feet three inches tall and I'll be in my 'office drag,' a white silk shirt under a red-lined black jacket, but you'll know me by my 'fuck-me' shoes." Those wouldn't be your fuck-me shoes, would they?
    (Pete bends down under the table to examine them. Kate kicks him.)
PETE: I'll ignore that, my precious, because — we haven't started yet.
KATE: *(Bitter whisper.)* Oh, haven't we?
PETE: *(Reading.)* "And I will be reading a copy of *(He mispronounces the title horribly.)* Lay Lie-a-Song Dang Geroos.
    (Kate tries furiously to obscure her book, but it soon becomes evident to both Pete and the audience that this is indeed the very title she's reading.)
KATE: Forget it. Just forget it. After the way you pronounced it, forget it —
PETE: And how should I have said it?
KATE: *(Pretty good French pronunciation.)* Les Liasons Dangereuses.
PETE: *(Repeating after her, impeccable French pronunciation.)* Les Liasons Dangereuses.
KATE: That's it, exactly. And now, I'm going —
    (Pete blocks her way.)
KATE: Let me pass, please.
PETE: "I will be wearing my fuck-me shoes and reading *Les Liasons Dangereuses*. Your humble slave, awaiting the first of your many commands."

KATE: I did not write that.

PETE: Then who? Justine, your alter ego?

KATE: All right, I wrote it. But it was a terrible, terrible mistake.

PETE: Those aren't your fuck-me shoes. Your fuck-me shoes are at the cobbler's.

KATE: You suck!

PETE: You wish! Maybe if you're very, very good —

KATE: Oh, forget that! You could not turn me on if this were the Garden of Eden. Before the fig leaves!

PETE: That's pretty strong.

KATE: If this were the Garden of Eden, I would rather make it with the snake!

PETE: Really? Hmm . . .

KATE: At least he had some backbone!

(A beat. Pete looks at her. He laughs. Kate is too angry to look, but eventually she does. She laughs, too.)

PETE: Kate, please.

KATE: Don't call me that.

PETE: I thought you said that was your name.

KATE: It is.

PETE: That's a very bad idea. You should never give some creep on the Internet your real name.

KATE: Tell me about it.

PETE: He might just thrust your name, Kate, into the conversation constantly, Kate, like somebody at a convention, Kate, whom you've unwittingly allowed to corner you, and Kate, he can read your name tag pinned to your lapel, Kate, and he clings to you, Kate, like some infuriating used-car salesman, Kate, who thinks that if he acts like he already knows you, Kate, you will finally buy something just to get away from him, Kate, and his constant Kate, Kate, Kate, and that is why, Kate, you should never give your real name, Kate, to a stranger on the Internet. *(Pause.)* Kate, what am I doing wrong?

KATE: That jacket. Ugh. Hideous.

PETE: So?

KATE: You knew it was hideous? And you wore it anyway?

PETE: I was afraid it wasn't hideous enough, actually.

KATE: You're not taking this seriously at all. You have totally the wrong attitude. This is like surgery. The least you can do is give it the same attention you'd give to a job interview. You should be wearing a really well-tailored suit. Spotless. Commanding.

PETE: I'm not applying for a job as an investment banker.

KATE: You should look as if you are.

PETE: Oh. *(Pause.)* You've done this before, then?

KATE: Never. I'm a novice.

PETE: Why, me, too. You don't seem like a novice. You seem — so sure — about how it should go.

KATE: That's how I can be. Sure.

PETE: Um, I don't follow.

KATE: Have you ever noticed how, after you do something, you're less and less sure about how it should go?

PETE: Well, no. I don't think I have noticed that.

KATE: Don't contradict me! Like with a recipe, after you make it, you might want to keep it in the oven a little longer. Or add more butter or something. But before you make it —

PETE: You know how to make it. Or think you do, anyhow. So — you know how it should go?

KATE: Completely and precisely.

PETE: What a relief!

KATE: I mean, not between us! There's no way you can redeem yourself. That jacket. That salesman pitch. It's excruciating.

PETE: I thought it was supposed to be excruciating.

KATE: It should be like being riven to the heart by an ecstatic sword. Not like stubbing your toe.

PETE: I want you to eat salt.

KATE: What?

PETE: Would you — if I asked you, if I commanded you — would you eat salt?

KATE: What an odd request. (This isn't the way it's supposed to go, by the way.) Why?

PETE: I thought about it. You see, there ought to be a lot of ways to torture someone at a place called Au Bon Pain. But that was the only thing I could think of.

KATE: You could fling me over the counter and put on those plastic gloves and fill my orifices with chicken salad!

PETE: That hadn't occurred to me. I am woefully limited.

KATE: You ARE!

(Pete tears open a salt packet and spills salt on the table.)

PETE: Go ahead! I COMMAND you to eat that! Every grain!

(Kate sucks her finger and applies it to some grains of salt on the table. She licks her finger.)

PETE: Ooh, you look so cute!

KATE: You shouldn't say that!

PETE: Why not, if it's true? Aren't I the one who's supposed to be giving orders, by the way?

KATE: Because you should find something wrong with the way I'm doing it. You have to be very exacting.

PETE: *(Sternly.)* Very well, then. You will just quietly eat your salt, and, if I tell you something pleasant, like that you are adorable, you will just patiently endure it. *(In his own voice.)* How was that? Any better?

KATE: *(Grudging.)* A bit.

(Kate eats salt. Pete watches her.)

PETE: You are so —

KATE: We need a safe word!

PETE: A what?

KATE: A safe word. Something I can say when it all gets too much for me.

PETE: Isn't that the point?

KATE: Yes, well, you are supposed to push my boundaries, but not to the point where they snap.

PETE: I see. For a novice, you are certainly quite experienced.

KATE: I've read all the books. Shouldn't you be telling me to take my underwear off by this point?

PETE: Just eat your salt.

KATE: I don't want to. It's not sexy and it's boring.

PETE: Do I get a safe word when I have had enough?

(Kate is silent.)

PETE: Look, this is a task! You are my slave — at least you said you wanted to be.

KATE: That was of passion!

PETE: *(Fiercely.)* Just eat your goddamn salt, while I think of something else!

KATE: Penis!

PETE: What?

KATE: That's my safe word. Penis.

PETE: Shouldn't it be something like elevator?

KATE: Too many syllables. Like if I'm tied up and it starts to pinch —

PETE: Well, what about a color, then? How about BLUE?

KATE: It can't be blue! Blue is like blue movies, and black and blue. Blue is not the least bit safe!

PETE: And penis is? Just tell me, what is so safe about a penis? It is rearing, it is fierce, it has a total mind of its own, it is completely uncontrollable —

KATE: PENIS!

PETE: What — what's the matter?

KATE: I just needed — a breather.

(Pete puts his arm around Kate to comfort her.)

KATE: PENIS! PENIS! PENIS! PENIS! PENIS!

PETE: *(Removing his arm.)* What —

KATE: You are pushing my boundaries.

PETE: But all I did was —

(Pete puts his arm around Kate again.)

KATE: PENIS! We hardly know each other.

PETE: It was just an affectionate —

KATE: Affection has to come last. After you've tied me to the mast, blindfolded me, seared me with the cat o' nine tails, when I am a whimpering pulp of submission, then, just then, a tinge of affection may be possible. Not before.

PETE: Oh.

KATE: I thought you wanted this, too. I thought you wanted what I wanted.

PETE: I thought I did, too.

KATE: Tell me I'm fat.

PETE: But you're not, I think —

KATE: Go on, tell me.

PETE: — you're perfect.

KATE: You're not even trying.

PETE: What should I say?

KATE: Tell me I'm a blimp, that my body's disgusting.

PETE: Oh, Kate —

KATE: Please —

PETE: You're a blimp. Your body's disgusting. You need to go on a diet of — water and watercress — and pepper — hot pepper — and from now on that's all I will let you eat. And I insist on your going to the gym and doing the exercycle for — FIVE HOURS! *(Getting into it.)* You are horribly fat, you're obese, with your pudgy little butt and your — flabby thighs and your mushy little cheeks — I don't even want to see you without clothes until you've committed yourself to a tremendous regime.

KATE: *(Swooning.)* Oh . . .

PETE: What is it?

KATE: I just feel — that finally I've met a man who sees me the same way I see myself . . .

PETE: But you know, I don't see you —

KATE: Penis! Penis! Penis!

PETE: Now what did I do —

KATE: Penis! It's too much. I can't take it. That's the way I'm wired.

PETE: Well, you must learn to take it.

KATE: Don't you understand? It starts so insidiously. A man brings you flowers. Or he asks you to a movie and you start nuzzling and don't notice any more what's on the screen. And he turns into some nutcase who because you had a piece of spinach stuck between your teeth on your first date wants you to always have that same piece! He's disappointed when you brush! Or he works for some pharmaceutical company that sells AIDS drugs for billions in Africa and doesn't even think it's wrong! Or he votes Republican! Or he decides to go back to his old girlfriend! Or a million different things which I would just as soon not have to deal with. Let's get the pain out of the way first! I want to pay it all up front, and then, if there's any little bit of happiness left over . . . just a faint little flicker of happiness in a dungeon of —

PETE: Are you sure? Your boundaries seem to get pushed awfully easily.

KATE: That's for pleasure. For pain, I assure you, I am insatiable.

PETE: Are you sure you don't just want to — fuck? You are wearing your fuck-me shoes . . . I could do it in a very cold-hearted "slam bam thank you ma'am" sort of way. No foreplay.

KATE: Uh.

PETE: At least at first.

KATE: Now it starts.

PETE: I want to tell you a secret.

KATE: What?

PETE: That outfit you told me I should have been wearing? I was wearing it, just before I came.

KATE: You're an investment banker?

PETE: I am.

KATE: And do you invest in companies that manufacture firearms, nuclear weapons, or tobacco?

PETE: I don't know, quite honestly. I dress the way you seem to want, all day, every day. And I manage a lot of people, and I'm quite brisk and aloof and — I do it quite well, actually. I just thought it might be fun to be a lout and boss around some slutty lovely girl who isn't wearing a sheath with those spaghetti straps. "To the moon, Alice!" But now I think you'd probably like me more the way I am. Normally. Do you have a dress like that, by the way?

KATE: Ummhm.

PETE: Maybe you could go home and change into that dress, and I could put on my suit, and we could meet for dinner at Le Petit Gamin, where they don't serve any meat that hasn't been happily cantering all over the field.

KATE: And then they slaughter 'em. Ugh.

PETE: And then we could go to Chinatown and watch kung fu flicks. *(Kate shudders.)* Or, um, we could rent *Gone with the Wind* and go back to my place. *(Happily mimes carrying her up the staircase while quoting from the wrong movie.)* "You 'n' me had this date from the very beginning . . ."

KATE: Please!

PETE: Or we could rent — *The Story of O* on video? How about it?

KATE: You mean, like, a date?

PETE: A date.

KATE: A straight date. Where I put on makeup —

PETE: *(Interrupting.)* You don't need makeup —

KATE: And those dinky little pumps that look comfortable but really aren't. And then we live together and argue about the upholstery and I meet your family and we fight about moving and you sleep with your secretary, but not really, and you get prostate cancer and die on me, and we go to Le Petit Gamin and remember how we used to be so hot for each other —

PETE: Something like that. If it all works out —

KATE: A date?

PETE: A straight date.

KATE: That would be torture!

END OF PLAY

The Pain in the Poetry

Glenn Alterman

The Pain in the Poetry was originally produced by Workshop Theater, New York City, June 14, 2008, as part of A Crazy Little Thing Called Love, an evening of one-acts. Directed by Allison Smith. Cast: Sheridan — Fred Velde; Pamela — Christine Verleny.

SHERIDAN: He may seem timid, but has inner passion and power.

PAMELA: Sheridan's wife. She may seem cool and controlling, but also has warmth and deep passion.

SETTING

There is no set. Pamela is seated in a comfortable chair (possibly a rocking chair), knitting. Next to her chair is a large knitting basket. Sheridan enters, stands in front of her.)

TIME

The present.

NOTE: Both Sheridan and Pamela can be played by actors as young as their thirties or as old as their fifties or sixties. They must be believable as a married couple.

• • •

SHERIDAN: *(Meek, softly.)* I wrote a play.

PAMELA: *(Looking up.)* Hm, what?

SHERIDAN: *(A little bolder.)* I said, I wrote a play.

PAMELA: That's nice dear. Did you feed the dog?

SHERIDAN: Did you hear what I said?

PAMELA: Yes, you said you wrote a play or something.

SHERIDAN: A full length!

PAMELA: And I asked you if you fed the dog.

SHERIDAN: One act with no intermission.

PAMELA: The dog hasn't eaten all day.

SHERIDAN: *(Blurting it out.)* It's been my whole life for the last two years!

PAMELA: What has, your play?

SHERIDAN: Every second at work when I wasn't working I was working on it!

PAMELA: You were?

SHERIDAN: On lunch hours, in subway stations, on stairwells! Anywhere, anytime, whenever I had a moment it was just me . . .

PAMELA: I see.

SHERIDAN: . . . alone with my play!

PAMELA: Why didn't you tell me?

SHERIDAN: I couldn't.

PAMELA: Why not?

SHERIDAN: It was — too private. Something I had to do alone; something I couldn't share with anyone.

PAMELA: Not even me.

SHERIDAN: *(An edge.)* Especially not you.

PAMELA: I see.

SHERIDAN: Then late last night, well actually early this morning, while you were asleep, I finished it, on the bathroom floor, by candlelight.

PAMELA: I wondered why you were spending so much time in there.

SHERIDAN: I didn't want to talk about it until it was all down on paper. I was afraid.

PAMELA: Of what?

SHERIDAN: Giving away the ending.

PAMELA: But you say it's over now?

SHERIDAN: Yes. Finished. Complete. Done.

PAMELA: *(She puts her knitting down. Gently, sincerely.)* Well I'm glad you told me. I understand.

SHERIDAN: Do you?

PAMELA: Yes. Now let's just forget about it and go on as if . . .

(Suddenly Sheridan walks away from her.)

PAMELA: Where are you going, what's wrong?

SHERIDAN: Nothing.

PAMELA: Tell me.

(He stops, looks guiltily at her.)

PAMELA: There isn't another one, is there?

SHERIDAN: No.

PAMELA: Don't lie to me!

SHERIDAN: I tell you I haven't written another word!

PAMELA: I won't put up with it; the bathroom, backstreets, another two years!

SHERIDAN: I said, I haven't-written-a-word!

PAMELA: OK, all right.

SHERIDAN: But . . .

PAMELA: What?

SHERIDAN: I've been having these "thoughts."

PAMELA: What kind of thoughts?

SHERIDAN: *(Filled with guilt.)* Snippets, little snippets — of dialogue.

PAMELA: No!

SHERIDAN: *(Walking away, tormented.)* Yes, this two-character scene keeps playing over and over in my head. All right, I admit it, YES, I'm thinking about another play!

PAMELA: You can't be! You just finished one, this morning. My God, what kind of insatiable . . . ?!

SHERIDAN: I was lying there on the bathroom floor, satisfied, content. Holding my play lovingly in my arms. Caressing it, fingering the folder. When I heard the faucet drip.

PAMELA: The faucet?

SHERIDAN: Drip, drip-drop; a lovely sound, really.

PAMELA: You were holding your play in . . . ? Caressing it?!

SHERIDAN: I gently put it down by my side and just listened to the water for a while. Drip, drip-drop, drip-drop. Sounded like, I don't know, little feet.

PAMELA: Little feet?

SHERIDAN: Tiny, little, tap-dancing feet. I lay there on the floor for I don't know how long; just listening. When suddenly it hit me!

PAMELA: What, the water?

SHERIDAN: No, the thought.

PAMELA: What thought?

SHERIDAN: Maybe . . . maybe a musical!

PAMELA: A musical?!

SHERIDAN: You know, dancing, singing . . .

PAMELA: We are a family, have you forgotten?!

SHERIDAN: *(Walking away.)* Don't.

PAMELA: You have a job, responsibilities. And what about me, huh, us?!

SHERIDAN: *(Stopping.)* I'm sorry, it's just something I have to do!

PAMELA: *(Getting worked up.)* What's next, huh?! A comedy, some cheap comedy? Oh I can just see it now, you and your dirty little comedy. The two of you having lots of laughs in some dark stairwell together. A chuckle on the bathroom floor. Dirty jokes, pathetic puns. Well I'm telling you right now your fun's over. I will not play second fiddle to some musical! *(She gathers her knitting, starts to leave.)*

SHERIDAN: Where you going?

PAMELA: I'm leaving you — playwright!

SHERIDAN: *(He grabs her arm.)* Don't leave, please!
  (As she pulls her arm free, her knitting basket accidentally opens up. Hundreds of sheets of paper fall out. They both stop, see the papers fall.)

SHERIDAN: What are those?

PAMELA: *(Quickly gathering some of the papers.)* Nothing, knitting instructions.

SHERIDAN: *(Picking one up, reading it.)* This is your handwriting.

PAMELA: *(Trying to grab it from him.)* Give me that!

SHERIDAN: What is this?

PAMELA: Scribblings, recipes. Give me that paper!

SHERIDAN: It's . . . it's a poem! *(Looking at her, astonished.)* You've been writing poetry.

PAMELA: Yes, all right, I had to do something! What was I supposed to do, knit all day?! You were always away, or upstairs locked in the bathroom. I was going out of my mind with loneliness. Then one day in my despair, a couplet came to me. A rhyme, and then a verse. A beautiful image, a matching thought. And after that, well, there was no stopping me.

SHERIDAN: You're a poet!

PAMELA: *(Looking away.)* Yes, . . . I guess I am.

SHERIDAN: How long?

PAMELA: Two years.

SHERIDAN: Why didn't you tell me?

PAMELA: When? You were never here. And when you were, you were always a million miles away, probably thinking about your precious play. *(As she picks the papers up, and gently puts them back in her basket.)* And my poems, they kept me company, gave me solace. My poetry was something I didn't have to share with anyone.

SHERIDAN: Not even me?

PAMELA: *(An edge.)* Especially not you.

SHERIDAN: I see.

(They look at each other for a moment. Then, with disdain)

SHERIDAN: So — what are they about, your poems?

PAMELA: *(Tenderly.)* Love, loss, unrequited love. *(Then, with disdain.)* And your play?

SHERIDAN: Love. Lost love. It's the story of a married couple who can barely stand to be with each other in the same room anymore. Something had happened two years earlier; an incident, a betrayal.

PAMELA: Betrayal?

SHERIDAN: That they both knew about but never acknowledged. A dark secret that tore them apart. *(Then, smiling.)* It's a two-character comedy.

PAMELA: A comedy, you're kidding?

SHERIDAN: No, it's an absurd comedy. The humor comes out of the pain. The play is filled with hidden meanings; the pain is in the subtext.

PAMELA: I see.

SHERIDAN: So are all your poems sad?

PAMELA: Tragic, each and every one.

SHERIDAN: What are they about?

PAMELA: Regrets.

SHERIDAN: Regrets?

PAMELA: And the loneliness that comes from lies. And about apologies, thought about, but never actually made.

SHERIDAN: How sad.

PAMELA: How does your play end?

SHERIDAN: You'll have to read it to find out.

PAMELA: You'd let me? I'd love to. When?

SHERIDAN: *(Backing off.)* I don't know, we'll see, someday.

PAMELA: And maybe someday I'll let you read some of my poems.

SHERIDAN: You would? I'd like that.

PAMELA: Would you?

SHERIDAN: Very much.

PAMELA: And who knows, maybe, maybe someday we could even "collaborate" on something.

SHERIDAN: Collaborate?

PAMELA: Sure, why not?

SHERIDAN: Maybe . . . someday.

(They look at each other for a moment. Then . . .)

SHERIDAN: But for now I prefer working alone.

PAMELA: *(Sitting down in the chair.)* So do I.

(She starts knitting again. He starts to leave.)

PAMELA: Where are you going?

SHERIDAN: *(He stops.)* To the bathroom.

PAMELA: Oh, I see. Well don't let me stop you. — Your faucet is waiting!

(He looks at her, then leaves. She watches him go. After a moment, she slowly puts the knitting down, sadly looks up, takes out some paper and a pen. Just as she begins to write, Sheridan appears in the doorway. She puts the pen and paper down by her side,)

PAMELA: What, what is it?

SHERIDAN: *(Softly.)* I realized — I don't have to go to the bathroom.

PAMELA: *(With hope.)* No?

SHERIDAN: No.

(She looks down at the pen and paper next to her for a moment, then looks back up at Sheridan. Sheridan sits down. They look at each other for a moment. Then, slowly, we notice just a hint of a smile appear on their faces, as the lights fade.)

END OF PLAY

Quarks

WILLIAM BORDEN

Quarks was produced by Flush Ink Productions, Kitchener, Ontario, May 22–31, 2008, as part of the Asphalt Jungle IV series. Directed by Paddy Gillard-Bentley. Cast: Veronica — Jennifer Cornish; Joseph — Roger Sumner.

    VERONICA: Twenties or thirties, self-possessed and knockout sexy.
    JOSEPH: Twenties or thirties, lots of aplomb but maybe not enough.

SETTING
    An upscale bar.

TIME
    The present.

• • •

A pleasant, upscale bar. Veronica sits on a stool at the bar, a drink beside her. Joseph enters, glances about, fixes his gaze on Veronica, adjusts his tie, and strolls confidently up to her. He examines her drink.

JOSEPH: What are you having?
VERONICA: A double martini, extremely dry. With a fresh strawberry.
JOSEPH: Strawberry?
VERONICA: You soak the fresh strawberry in vermouth for a few days, then you lower it gently into gin that's been relaxing in a cold place.
JOSEPH: A few days?
VERONICA: Are you in a hurry?
JOSEPH: Tempus fugit. Carpe Diem. Time flies. Seize the day.
VERONICA: You're afraid life will escape you?
JOSEPH: Life? Life's an engine roaring past faster than the gates can come down. It's all you can do to stay on the rails.
VERONICA: Why would you want to stay on the rails?
    (Veronica hands him an identical martini.)
JOSEPH: That was quick.
VERONICA: Do you like it quick?
JOSEPH: I'm not sure.
VERONICA: You haven't been here before.
JOSEPH: I'm a traveling salesman.
VERONICA: Shoes?
JOSEPH: Supercomputers. One sale: twenty million dollars.
VERONICA: Super.
JOSEPH: I represent a Japanese firm.
VERONICA: You don't look Japanese.

JOSEPH: I'll bet you're a model.

(Joseph reaches for his martini. She places her hand over his.)

VERONICA: Wait.

JOSEPH: I'm thirsty.

VERONICA: We all thirst for something, Joseph.

JOSEPH: Yes, but —

VERONICA: Something to drink, something to hold, something — Allow the strawberry to seduce the gin. Permit the gin to charm the strawberry. You can't rush life, Joseph.

JOSEPH: How do you know my — ?

VERONICA: You race, you run, you hurry, but life — life ambles on at its own leisurely pace, and, no matter what you do, there you are, standing all alone, tapping your foot impatiently, waiting for life to catch up with you. Just as you are this moment, rushing, rushing away from life. So now —

JOSEPH: Now?

VERONICA: You have to wait.

JOSEPH: For — ?

(Joseph waits. He glances around — for life? Enlightenment?)

VERONICA: Now. A sip.

(They sip their martinis.)

VERONICA: Do you see what I mean? Life has caught up with the martini.

JOSEPH: You're too strange to be a model.

VERONICA: How many models do you know?

JOSEPH: I'll bet you're an actress.

VERONICA: I'm a theoretical physicist.

JOSEPH: Right.

VERONICA: I use the X537J.

JOSEPH: That's the one I sell.

VERONICA: I study quarks. Charmed quarks. There are also up quarks and down quarks and strange quarks. There are quarks with color — red, blue, green. Something like your tie.

JOSEPH: Do you like my tie?

VERONICA: Now take another sip. It's a little different, isn't it?

JOSEPH: I think so.

VERONICA: It's as if the strawberry comes and goes. We call them virtual particles. They come into existence, they vanish so quickly we can only gasp. It happens all the time, throughout the universe, even as we speak, subatomic particles popping in and out of existence, countless births and deaths. Like us, only in a different time scale. We're virtual particles, here one instant, gone another, leaving little or no trace, most of us unobserved, most of us merely a theory.

JOSEPH: You're saying I'm just a theory?

VERONICA: Theoretically.

JOSEPH: I don't think it's good to think too much about these things.

VERONICA: Thinking can be very passionate.

JOSEPH: What do you think so passionately about?

VERONICA: Quarks. Charmed quarks.

JOSEPH: Aren't quarks those little things inside the atom?

VERONICA: We don't even know if quarks exist. But if we assume they do, they explain things. Everything's like that, Joseph. We don't know if we exist, but if we do, it explains certain things.

JOSEPH: What does it explain?

VERONICA: Your erection.

JOSEPH: What makes you think I — ?

VERONICA: The moisture between my thighs. How long do you think we'll be together, Joseph?

JOSEPH: I really hadn't . . .

VERONICA: I'm not sure how compatible we are. You travel, I work in a lab. You're easily aroused, I take a little longer. You like Scotch, I like strawberries soaked in gin.

JOSEPH: Opposites attract.

VERONICA: The positive proton holds the negative electron in orbit forever, as if they were desperately in love. Yet they can get no closer. If they draw any closer together, they repel one another.

(He moves closer.)

VERONICA: And if they're forced together . . .

(Closer.)

VERONICA: . . . they explode.

JOSEPH: Do you think we'll explode?

VERONICA: We'll see.

JOSEPH: Take off your panties.

VERONICA: What makes you think I'm wearing panties?

JOSEPH: Because you would want the pleasure of feeling the soft warm silk slip sensuously down your long cool bare legs.

VERONICA: And then?

JOSEPH: Cool air will excite your private thoughts. You'll have an unmentionable secret, known only to you and me, a secret these others will only guess at. You'll feel . . . free. You'll feel . . . special. You'll feel . . . dangerous.

VERONICA: I'm already dangerous, Joseph. You know that.
(Veronica slips off her panties. She stuffs them, like a handkerchief, into his coat pocket.) You look very debonair.

JOSEPH: Thank you.

VERONICA: Perhaps your tie.

JOSEPH: My tie?

VERONICA: You can't get something for nothing. It's a law of the universe. Energy becomes mass, mass explodes into energy, but nothing is lost. The universe keeps perfect books.

JOSEPH: It's an expensive tie.

VERONICA: My nipples are hard.
(He takes off his tie. She ties it around her waist.)

VERONICA: What shall we name our children?

JOSEPH: Our — ?

VERONICA: I want grandchildren of many races.

JOSEPH: Grandchildren?

VERONICA: I want to make love every night, and after we make love, I want to argue the meaning of existence. I won't ever wear panties again, and you'll study Buddhism, and we'll make a pact that if either of us grows senile, we'll commit suicide together.

JOSEPH: I think I'm on a runaway train here.

VERONICA: A train would be simple. We're on a runaway galaxy.

JOSEPH: I believe it.

VERONICA: Inside the quarks there are superstrings. Superstrings exist in ten dimensions. We live in four dimensions — left, right, up-and-down, the passage of time. Can you imagine ten dimensions, Joseph?

JOSEPH: No, I can't.

VERONICA: I can't either. It's mathematics. Mathematics and the X537J computer.

JOSEPH: Maybe God exists in ten dimensions.

VERONICA: That would explain a lot.

JOSEPH: I'm not religious or anything, but —

VERONICA: Quantum mechanics tells us that at the heart of the universe there is only chance. Do you believe that, Joseph? Do you believe we're merely random events in an irregular space-time continuum?

JOSEPH: This martini is really something.

VERONICA: Einstein said God doesn't shoot craps. But we've looked for meaning, Joseph, you with your X537J, I with my charmed quarks, and all we've found are things that come and go too fast to see. All we've found are mysteries that appear to be accidents. All we've found are uncertainty and danger. It's time. To eat the strawberry. Gently! Feel the tiny gin-soaked seeds between your teeth like quarks being ground out of their protons, like galaxies being crushed by the inexorable whirl of time. And the strawberry itself, soft now, soft as regret, oozing nostalgia and desire — dissolves, like memory, between the tongue and the palate, dissolves into nothingness. Gone.

JOSEPH: Listen, I —

VERONICA: I have to go.

JOSEPH: I don't even know your name.

VERONICA: Veronica.

JOSEPH: Now?

VERONICA: Life is waiting for me.

JOSEPH: But what about me?

VERONICA: You're waiting for life.

JOSEPH: You have my tie.

VERONICA: You have my panties.

JOSEPH: My wife gave me that tie.

VERONICA: My husband gave me those panties.

END OF PLAY

Road Kill

EDWARD CROSBY WELLS

Road Kill was first performed at Berea College, Berea,
Kentucky, August 1, 2008, as part of the Ten Minute Quilt
Play Festival. Directed by Kim Stinson. Cast: Joey —
Jimmy Besseck; Mary — Aubrey Dandeneau.

CHARACTERS

    JOEY: Late teens to late twenties, married to Mary.

    MARY: Late teens to late twenties, Joey's wife.

SETTING

    Along the side of a highway.

TIME

    Morning, early autumn, the present.

NOTE: Stage should be bare.

• • •

At rise: Enter Joey and Mary, a young homeless couple, pushing a shopping cart filled with their belongings, including their infant child wrapped in a quilt. There is a helium-filled red balloon tied to the cart, rising overhead. They are waiting by the side of the road for Joey's ride to his first day on his new job. Traffic sounds.

JOEY: *(Dressed in slacks in need of ironing, a white shirt, tie, and sweater. He stands back to display himself for Mary's approval.)* Well?

MARY: You look wonderful, Joey. Just wonderful! I know you'll get it.

JOEY: You think so?

MARY: Certain.

JOEY: He should be here soon.

MARY: He could have picked a spot where there's someplace to sit. Are you sure this is where he wanted you to meet him?

JOEY: Absolutely.

MARY: What kind of a car does he drive, Joey?

JOEY: One that works. What more do you need?

MARY: Very funny. *(A little soft-shoe.)* But seriously, folks. *(Finishes her little dance with her hand extended toward him as if to say, "It's your turn.")*

JOEY: *(He's too serious to dance today.)* Green. Yes, green.

MARY: *(Pointing.)* Is that him?

JOEY: *(Looking down the highway.)* No. Besides, that's not green. That's blue.

MARY: Well, kind of greenish-blue, wouldn't you say?

JOEY: Yeah, but his is green-green. Unmistakably green.

MARY: Oh, that kind of green. That's too green, if you ask me. I mean, for a car. *(A pause to look down the highway.)* You know what I'd like? I'd like one in silver. Can we get a silver car? I mean, when things get all right again.

JOEY: Maybe.

MARY: Well, I don't want a green one. Least, not too green.

JOEY: *(Looking down highway.)* We'll see.

MARY: I hope you get it, Joey. Maybe, if you get it and they like you — of course, they'll like you — they'll give you overtime. Overtime's good, Joey. And soon, before you know it, we'll have ourselves a silver car. *(To the baby.)* Wouldn't that be nice, sweetheart? Oh, yes. That would be wonderful. And Mommy and Daddy will take you for nice long rides. Maybe, we'll take a vacation to Yellowstone. Yes. You'd love that, wouldn't you? *(She reaches into the cart, adjusts the quilt before removing a loaf of bread. She takes out a slice and hands it to Joey who proceeds to eat it. She takes a slice for herself and puts the loaf back in the cart.)* I was thinking the baby and I would go to the zoo today.

JOEY: They charge.

MARY: Really?

JOEY: Almost certain.

MARY: But, isn't it like a public park or something?

JOEY: They still charge.

MARY: That's not fair.

JOEY: *(Looking down the highway.)* What is?

MARY: I'm not staying in that bus station all day anymore. They're getting funny about it.

JOEY: Nobody said anything to me.

MARY: Nobody said anything to me either, but they look at us funny.

JOEY: I never noticed.

MARY: That's because you're too busy looking at my ravishingly, beautiful body. *(Does her little soft-shoe.)* But seriously, folks . . . I don't like to be looked at funny. That's why we took a nice long walk when you went to the unemployment office. Saw some awful pretty houses, Joey. Even saw the street where I want us to live.

JOEY: *(Distracted.)* That's nice.

MARY: *(After a pause to look up and down the highway.)* Are you sure this is where you're supposed to meet him?

JOEY: Yes, Mary. I'm sure.

MARY: Well, where is he? Maybe he was a phony. Maybe he was just saying he'd take you to see his boss. Maybe he was making it all up.

JOEY: Why would somebody do a thing like that, huh? If he said he'd be here, he'll be here. All right?

MARY: Yeah. But, I hope it's soon. *(A beat.)* I need some big plastic garbage bags. If you run across any today bring them back with you, OK?

JOEY: 'Kay.

MARY: I'm going to start collecting aluminum cans. Dot and John got a regular business going. There's good money in aluminum cans.

JOEY: Who's Dot and John?

MARY: A couple I met when you were at the unemployment office. They live in their van, only it doesn't run. John's working on it though. Dot says John's a mechanic. There's big money in being a mechanic, isn't there?

JOEY: *(Looking down the highway, distracted.)* I suppose.

MARY: Sure there is. *(Looking down the highway.)* Wouldn't a van be nice, Joey? We could take all kinds of trips then, huh?

JOEY: *(Still distracted.)* Uh-huh. That would be nice, Mary. You don't suppose he was a phony?

MARY: That would be a terrible thing to do, Joey.

JOEY: I hope we didn't miss him.

MARY: I don't see how. He'll be here. *(To baby.)* Won't he, sweetheart? He'll be here with bells on. Then, Daddy's gonna get a job. Maybe in an office with real wood paneling and a brass lamp with a green glass shade on a great big desk. Then, we could visit Daddy in his office. *(To Joey.)* He's been sleeping an awful lot lately.

JOEY: That's what babies do. Keep him covered good with Mom's quilt

MARY: I do — may she rest in peace. But he never cries. Babies are supposed to cry.

JOEY: Naah. When they cry all the time there's something wrong with them. He's a prince. Princes don't cry.

MARY: I hope your right. *(To the baby.)* I sure hope your daddy's right. *(To Joey.)* Did he say what kind of job it was?

JOEY: Keeping count of things. Electronic stuff, I think.

MARY: Electronic stuff? Oh, maybe it's computers. That's the thing nowadays. I hope it's computers. There's a big future in computers, Joey. *(To the baby.)* Daddy's gonna be a computer operator like those men at NASA. Won't that be nice? *(To Joey.)* Are you sure he said today?

JOEY: Eight o'clock.

MARY: Well, it's just about that now. *(Looking down the highway.)* Oh! There he is! There he is! *(Both watch the same passing car.)* Nope. I guess that wasn't him. It was green though, wasn't it?

JOEY: Yes. It was green.

MARY: *(After a pause to think of something.)* Fart.

JOEY: What?

MARY: Pass gas.

JOEY: I don't have to pass gas.

MARY: That's too bad because if you did, he'd come. Every time I'm waiting for someone and I got to pass gas, I hold it in 'cause I'm afraid they're gonna show up and smell it. But, as soon as I let it out, sure enough, there they are! It's one of those laws of nature.

JOEY: I'll remember that. *(After a pause to contemplate.)* Mary . . . maybe we should find someplace to keep the baby. Until we get ourselves — situated. Not for long. Just a few weeks maybe.

MARY: We are situated. We got each other. You'll get that job and everything will be just fine.

JOEY: But, suppose I don't?

MARY: Suppose, suppose, suppose. Suppose you do and you will. How can you talk like that? You scare me when you talk like that.

JOEY: Sorry, but things haven't been turning out the way we thought.

MARY: They will, I promise.

JOEY: It's not yours to promise.

MARY: Everything will turn out just fine. You'll see.

JOEY: Until it does, I think we ought to find someplace for —

MARY: *(Cutting him off. Covering her ears.)* No! I don't want to hear it anymore! You promised! You promised!

JOEY: We've got to face the facts, Mary.

MARY: What facts? Everything's looking up. Everything will be just fine.

JOEY: *(Resigning.)* I hope you're right.

MARY: I am. You'll see. You make me so mad when you talk like that. *(To the baby.)* He makes me so mad. Doesn't he, sweetie? You won't ever be negative, will you? Oh, no. Negative is a bad thing to be. It sets all kinds of bad things into motion. Doesn't it? Our little prince will be so positive . . . why . . . you might grow up to be the president of the United States of America. *(To Joey.)* Wouldn't that be nice? I mean, he could be the president, couldn't he? Or, a doctor. I think there's more money in being a doctor.

JOEY: He could be both.

MARY: That's right! A doctor first and then the president. Did we ever have a president who was a doctor?

JOEY: I don't know.

MARY: Then he'll be the first. Oh, I'm excited already.

JOEY: Now don't go pushing him. He might want to be something else.

MARY: Like what?

JOEY: I don't know. A mechanic, maybe.

MARY: Of all the things in this world to be, why on earth would our son want to be a mechanic? Yuck.

JOEY: Maybe he won't, but maybe he won't want to be a doctor or the president, either.

MARY: Don't be silly. Who wouldn't want to be the president?

JOEY: I wouldn't.

MARY: Go on. You wouldn't want to be the president? Don't tell me. You mean to tell me you wouldn't want to rule the world?

JOEY: The president doesn't rule the world.

MARY: He does our world. He runs the country, doesn't he?

JOEY: Running the country and ruling the world are two different things.

MARY: I suppose. Ruling the world would be more fun, wouldn't it? I mean, the president doesn't really do anything, does he? I mean, who's in charge anyway?

JOEY: We. The people. Us.

MARY: Yeah, that's right. Kind of makes you feel proud, doesn't it? I mean, this great big country of ours, for good or for bad is run by we, the people. *(Shivers.)* Oh, God! Can't you feel the power? It gives me goose bumps. But how come we're not doing a better job?

JOEY: I don't know. Maybe, we don't know how.

MARY: That's it! We don't know how. Here we are — we, the people — running the best country on earth — America. We don't know how we do it, but we do it. What a shame.

JOEY: What's the shame?

MARY: The shame, Joseph Carpenter, is that we don't do it better. If it were run more by the people and more for the people, we the people would be a lot better off.

JOEY: Humph. I can't argue with that.

MARY: There's no good reason why you should want to argue with that. *(To the baby.)* Is there, sweetheart? *(To Joey who is looking down the highway.)* Maybe, he meant eight o'clock tonight.

JOEY: No. In the morning. He said to be here eight in the morning if I wanted a ride.

MARY: Well, this is the morning he meant, isn't it?

JOEY: Yes. This is the morning he meant.

MARY: Just checking.

JOEY: Are you sure I look all right?

MARY: You look wonderful, Joey.

JOEY: It's important to make a good first impression.

MARY: You will. I promise, you will. *(After a pause to search the highway.)* I was thinking. I mean, when things are better. You know, when we get a place to stay. A real place, not like the bus station. Do you think I could get a job?

JOEY: You know how I feel about my wife working.

MARY: I know, but it would be like a kind of insurance. You know, insurance against this happening again. I guess we didn't manage things quite right, huh? I'm not complaining. What's done is done. So they took back the house. So what? Things could be worse. I just don't like the way they look at me. You know, funny.

JOEY: Nobody looks at you funny, Mary.

MARY: They do. Honest, they do.

JOEY: Who? You tell me who looked at you funny and I'll —

MARY: You'll what, big man?

JOEY: *(Making a fist.)* I'll have a word with them. That's what I'll do.

MARY: *(To the baby.)* Listen to your daddy talk. What a funny man. What a big, funny man your daddy is. *(Notices something on the ground, several feet away.)* What's that?

JOEY: What?

MARY: *(Pointing.)* That. That, over there. On the ground. *(Crosses to it.)* Oh, no. *(Sad and angry.)* Oh, no. No, no, no.

JOEY: What? What is it?

MARY: Look.

JOEY: *(Coming over — looks.)* Come on. Get away from it.

MARY: But, somebody should bury it.

JOEY: It's half eaten and decayed already. In another week, there won't be a trace of it left.

MARY: It's not right to just leave it there.

JOEY: *(Pulling her back to the cart.)* Come on. That thing carries all kinds of diseases. We have ourselves to protect. Think of the baby.

MARY: I am thinking of the baby. *(Rummages through the cart and comes up with a small quilt.)*

JOEY: What are you going to do? That's Mom's quilt!

MARY: No it's not. Mom's quilt is covering the baby. This is just an old one they gave me down at the shelter. If it's not going to get buried, it needs to be covered.

JOEY: But, not with that.

MARY: I'm sorry, Joey. But that little animal needs it more than us.

JOEY: It's dead, Mary.

MARY: *(Crossing to the road kill.)* I know. I know. *(Covers it with the quilt.)* There. Nobody deserves to be left out in the open — even if they are dead.

JOEY: *(Reluctantly.)* Yeah . . . sure.

MARY: I found this beautiful street yesterday lined with trees and grass as green as green gets. Greener than that man's car, I bet. And the houses. They were so pretty. And somebody was burning leaves. I love the smell of burning leaves. There was this woman in the window of her beautiful house. And she looked at us looking in at her and she grabbed her baby . . .

JOEY: She had a baby?

MARY: Yes, 'bout the same age as our little prince. She grabbed her baby, held it close to her, then gave us a look. I'll never forget it. Never. I saw myself, Joey. Looking out as I was looking in, I saw myself in her eyes. It frightened me.

JOEY: *(Embracing her.)* She wasn't looking at you. She was looking at a stranger on the street. Not you. If she was looking at you, Mary — really looking at you — she'd have come to the door and invited you in. *(Kisses her sweetly.)*

MARY: *(After a pause to look into his eyes.)* What were you thinking of?

JOEY: When?

MARY: Just now. When you kissed me. What were you thinking of?

JOEY: I was thinking . . . well, I was thinking of you.

MARY: No, you weren't. Your eyes looked off to the side. You didn't look at me. You avoided me, Joey.

JOEY: That's not true.

MARY: You avoided me.

JOEY: I'm sorry. I just wish to God he'd hurry up and come, that's all.

MARY: He will. Be patient. *(To the baby.)* Good things come to those who wait. Don't they, sweetheart?

JOEY: There was a man. One of those people who were forced off the church property. He moved in with that bunch living in the parking lot under the bridge. His wife's in the city jail. They picked her up for shoplifting. So, he celebrated by getting drunk. Stinking, dead drunk. This was the day before yesterday. That night, the night before last when that storm hit us —

MARY: That was some storm! *(To the baby.)* Wasn't it, sweetheart?

JOEY: Dead drunk, he crawled into one of those dumpsters near the bridge and passed out. Yesterday morning the truck came to get the garbage —

MARY: *(Picks up the baby wrapped in the quilt and clutches it tightly.)* Oh, no.

JOEY: And they hooked the dumpster to the truck, lifted it, and dumped it into the truck. Then they turned on the switch to compress the garbage —

MARY: Oh, God.

JOEY: They heard a squeal. Like a sheep, they said.

MARY: Is he . . . dead?

JOEY: No. He lost both his legs, but he's not dead.

MARY: Poor man.

JOEY: *(Seeing his ride coming.)* There he is! Across the street!

MARY: *(Putting the baby back into the cart.)* Oh, hurry, Joey! Don't keep him waiting!

JOEY: *(A quick embrace. Kisses her. Kisses the baby.)* You sure I look OK?

MARY: You look magnificent. Now, hurry up and go before he leaves you here on the side of the highway.

JOEY: *(Hurrying toward exit and his ride.)* Wish me luck. Where will you be?

MARY: *(Calling after him.)* Look for the red balloon! *(Joey exits. To herself.)* Luck. *(To the baby.)* What are we gonna do today, huh? What does Mommy's little prince want to do? We could go to the park, collect aluminum cans, look at the leaves turning — falling. We could find another nice street with pretty houses on it. Would you like that? There's all kinds of things we could do. *(Pushing the cart, slowly, toward the exit opposite the one taken by Joey.)* Maybe today somebody will invite us in for tea and cookies. One never knows. Wouldn't that be nice? It's possible. In these United States of America, anything is possible. Isn't it, sweetheart? *(She does her little soft-shoe dance and then abruptly stops.)* But seriously, folks — *(She exits.)*

(Lighting fades, leaving a narrow spot on the quilt before fading to black out.)

END OF PLAY

A Short History of Weather

JONATHAN YUKICH

A Short History of Weather was first produced as
part of the 2006 Samuel French Off-Off Broadway Festival.
Directed by John O'Connell. Cast: Earl Grey — John Drago;
Aloe Vera — Rachel Simpson.

CHARACTERS

    EARL GREY: A man, any age.

    ALOE VERA: A woman, any age.

SETTING

    A bare stage.

TIME

    The present.

• • •

At rise: Earl Grey wearing a black raincoat. Gazes into the sky, surveying, then to the audience.

EARL GREY: What's today's weather? What's tomorrow's? Next week's? Have you noticed? Checked? I have. I know the weather very well, or try to. I'm not gloating, just saying. The weather's very important. Critical. It never leaves.

    (A female yelp is heard, followed by a thud.)

EARL GREY: My wife fell from the sky on a cold, misty morning.

    (Lights up to reveal Aloe Vera, also wearing a black raincoat, laid out.)

ALOE VERA: Oh gosh! Fallin' from the sky stings!

EARL GREY: Fifty-eight degrees, with a slight southwesterly breeze. Curious, and in the market for a mate, I move toward the stranger.

ALOE VERA: Oh, I think my face is broken! What misfortune!

EARL GREY: Miss, are you all right?

ALOE VERA: *(Shielding herself.)* Don't look! I'm unseemly!

EARL GREY: You took quite a dive.

ALOE VERA: I should be dead!

EARL GREY: Now, don't say that. Let me have a look.

    (He draws her hands from her face.)

EARL GREY: Oh my . . .

ALOE VERA: I know! Ghastly, aren't I! A she-beast! I was cute once, I swear!

EARL GREY: You still are. As cute as a bunny.

ALOE VERA: Don't goad me. I can take it. I'm a mutant!

EARL GREY: On the contrary . . .

ALOE VERA: I am! All because of air balloons! Such an impractical way to travel!

EARL GREY: Outdated, yes.

ALOE VERA: Hours ago I boarded one. Mostly cloudy, highs in the mideight-
ies. Out for a stroll, enjoying the grandness of life and climate, when,
suddenly, the parachute valve locked up! There was no way to land! I was
terrified!

EARL GREY: Naturally.

ALOE VERA: Here I am, stranded in midair, helpless, sailing closer and closer
to outer space where I'd probably combust or evaporate, right?

EARL GREY: Very likely.

ALOE VERA: So I gambled and hurled myself overboard, without thinking of
the pain or what it'd do to my face.

EARL GREY: Your face is lovely.

ALOE VERA: Oh, cease your niceties! I'm a disfigured hag! Give it to me
straight, why don't you!

(Earl Grey kisses her with feeling.)

ALOE VERA: I didn't get your name.

EARL GREY: Earl Grey. And yours?

ALOE VERA: Call me Aloe. Aloe Vera.

EARL GREY: Aloe Vera, I'd like to spend a lifetime with you.

ALOE VERA: Our wedding day is sunny and clear.

*(They shed their raincoats to reveal Aloe Vera's simple white dress and Earl
Grey's modest blue suit.)*

EARL GREY: Dewpoint: 12 percent.

ALOE VERA: Earl Grey rents a gazebo. I decorate with papier-maché.

EARL GREY: Do you take this man, me, to be your lawfully wedded husband?

ALOE VERA: I do. Do you take this woman, me, to be your lawfully wedded
wife?

EARL GREY: I do.

*(Loud, celebratory music. They dance a flash. Music and dance cut
abruptly.)*

ALOE VERA: After honeymooning at the South Pole, life ensues.

EARL GREY: Our future spreads before us like a broken mirror.

ALOE VERA: It's time to get jobs.

EARL GREY: Be adults.

ALOE VERA: I land a position as a phone psychic.

EARL GREY: I become a traveling gutter salesman.

ALOE VERA: Tough rackets.

EARL GREY: You'll find most homeowners are content with their gutters.

ALOE VERA: And few psychic callers want to discuss the weather.

EARL GREY: *(As a caller.)* Ring-a-ding!

ALOE VERA: Phone psychic! How can I help!

EARL GREY: Will I ever know true love?

ALOE VERA: How 'bout this jet stream we've been seeing?

EARL GREY: *(Hanging up.)* Who gives a flip, you fake! Click!

ALOE VERA: Sadness.

EARL GREY: Our lives become mundane.

ALOE VERA: One dimensional.

EARL GREY: Lethargic.

ALOE VERA: So we buy a cat and name her Karen.

> *(A stuffed cat flies from offstage into Aloe Vera's arms.)*

EARL GREY: Yeow!

ALOE VERA: Hey kitty, kitty.

EARL GREY: So soft, so sweet.

ALOE VERA: A real part of the family.

EARL GREY: Then one icy winter evening . . .

ALOE VERA: Earl Grey backs over Karen with his gutter van.

> *(Tosses cat off.)*

EARL GREY: Yeow!

ALOE VERA: A deep depression sets in.

EARL GREY: The only cure is twins.

> *(Crying babies sound. Two baby bundles are thrown from an offstage area. Aloe Vera catches one, Earl Grey the other.)*

ALOE VERA: They're born during the summer solstice.

EARL GREY: A long day, indeed.

ALOE VERA: One girl, one boy.

EARL GREY: From the start, we could see the girl was intelligent and resourceful.

ALOE VERA: We name her Google.

EARL GREY: The boy dull and common.

ALOE VERA: We name him New Hampshire.

EARL GREY: For a while, we're the happiest family.

> *(Celebratory music again. Dancing. Cuts abruptly.)*

ALOE VERA: But funds dwindle.

EARL GREY: Aloe Vera loses her psychic job.

ALOE VERA: Didn't see it coming.

EARL GREY: And, despite the reliability of rain, the great gutter boom never unfolds.

ALOE VERA: I decide to speak to Earl Grey. *(To Earl Grey.)* Earl Grey, I feel something's missing from our lives.

EARL GREY: I feel it too, Aloe Vera.

ALOE VERA: Two kids, three mortgages, a pile of bills . . . where's the money gonna come from?

EARL GREY: Crime.

ALOE VERA: Earl Grey was right. The only reasonable option was crime. *(Both pull guns from their bundles before tossing them aside.)*

EARL GREY: Our first bank robbery comes on a storybook spring day.

ALOE VERA: Barometric pressure: 30.20 and rising.

EARL GREY: Blue skies and golden sunshine.

ALOE VERA: Perfect for a picnic.

EARL GREY: *(Gun pointed.)* THIS IS A HOLDUP! GET YOUR FUCKING HANDS UP, MAGGOTS!!!

ALOE VERA: *(Gun pointed.)* DO IT NOW, BITCHES! OR I'LL BLOW OFF YOUR UGLY HEADS AND DROP-KICK YOUR TESTICLES! *(Distant sirens sound. Adrenaline pounding. Coming together again, triumphant.)*

EARL GREY: What a rush!

ALOE VERA: Our own private fortune!

EARL GREY: Google and New Hampshire won't have to worry again.

ALOE VERA: And I don't feel guilty, not in the least.

EARL GREY: Who knew we could be so bad? *(Loud music, jubilant dance. Cuts abruptly.)*

ALOE VERA: Google goes to college, becomes an engineer, and invents a mechanized wind chime.

EARL GREY: We're very proud.

ALOE VERA: Meantime, New Hampshire drops outta school and joins a grunge band called The Sweaty Pickles.

EARL GREY: We're very disturbed. *(As if to his son.)* What's wrong with your biscuit, boy! You haven't left the garage in three weeks! It's time you stop playing this hullabaloo and think about your future! Make somethin' of yourself! Go in the market for a mate!

ALOE VERA: Financially, however, things are looking up

EARL GREY: With the extra loot, I'm able to expand the gutter business into monsoon regions.

ALOE VERA: Cha-ching!

EARL GREY: And for our twentieth anniversary, we splurge on a trip to Egypt.

ALOE VERA: Where a massive sandstorm ensnares our hotel.

EARL GREY: We watch from our penthouse balcony, knowing we might perish but unafraid still.

(Gusting winds are heard. Both are awed by what they see.)

ALOE VERA: Isn't it remarkable?

EARL GREY: Wondrous. *(Down on one knee, pulling out a ring.)* Aloe Vera, your falling from the sky was the most amazing gift. I'd like you to have this, love, as a token of my renewed vow.

ALOE VERA: Oh, Earl Grey . . .

(They embrace, cheek to cheek.)

EARL GREY: We're just two grains of sand.

ALOE VERA: Swirling madly in the desert debris.

EARL GREY: Clinging to each other despite it all.

(The wind gusts reach a crescendo, then cut.)

ALOE VERA: On the strength of our newfound fortune, Earl Grey runs for the Senate.

EARL GREY: My top issue: a national weather day.

ALOE VERA: Google, a celebrity inventor, is a huge help to the campaign.

EARL GREY: New Hampshire, stoned and doddering, a minor embarrassment.

ALOE VERA: Election night arrives and victory is ours.

EARL GREY: *(Stump speech.)* For too long this nation has shortchanged its weather! Tonight, with one voice, you sent a resounding message, friends! It's time to recognize! Let's hear it!

BOTH: We like weather! We like weather!

ALOE VERA: So we move to Washington.

EARL GREY: Where our ideas are met with stone-faced pundits.

ALOE VERA: They say the country isn't ready for a Weather Day.

EARL GREY: Buncha blowhards.

ALOE VERA: Even so, it was a happy time, those years.

EARL GREY: Google makes us grandparents.

ALOE VERA: And, to our astonishment, New Hampshire's band, The Sweaty Pickles, begins to take off.

EARL GREY: We actually attend a concert.

(Unsettling grunge music plays. Earl Grey and Aloe Vera appear befuddled. Music ends.)

EARL GREY: It sounds like dog rape.

ALOE VERA: Be nice. Here he comes. *(As if to her son.)* Wonderful job, sweetheart. Really something. Loved every second.

EARL GREY: Especially the ones in-between songs.

ALOE VERA: Your father and I never imagined there were so many Sweaty Pickle fans. We're so impressed, aren't we, Earl Grey?

EARL GREY: You baffle me, son. You've always been odd, done things your own way, but you've managed to pull it off. Just like your old pop. I'm proud of you.

ALOE VERA: *(Returning to the audience.)* After three terms in the Senate, Earl Grey finally gets his Weather Bill passed.

EARL GREY: How sweet it is!

ALOE VERA: I was working out on the StairMaster when he broke it to me. *(Begins stepping as if working out.)*

EARL GREY: Darling, I've got news.

ALOE VERA: I'll never forget the weather that day, not as long as I live. The sky was sepia. Sorta. I can't really describe the color, but once or twice in our lives, the heavens have a strange, hazy light to them. Kinda dulled, like the sunshine's weeping. Maybe I'm nuts, but it's comforting, those days, at least for me. I think it's the color of memory.

EARL GREY: It passed.

ALOE VERA: IT PASSED!

(Ecstatic, they embrace and dance again to the joyous music. Cuts.)

EARL GREY: *(Again, a stump speech.)* Humbly, we gather today to pay homage to the world's most persistent icon. And so, without further delay, what we've all been waiting for: I hereby declare this National Weather Day!

BOTH: Hip Hip Hooray! Hip Hip Hooray!

ALOE VERA: I love you, Earl Grey.

EARL GREY: I love you, Aloe Vera.

(A zap and a bright flash of light. Aloe Vera collapses like a brick.)

ALOE VERA: Ouch! What's happened?

EARL GREY: *(Rushing to her aid.)* You've been struck by lightning!

ALOE VERA: I'm all warm and fuzzy!

EARL GREY: It came outta nowhere!

ALOE VERA: I don't feel so good.

EARL GREY: Irony: my arch nemesis!

ALOE VERA: Live by it, die by it. Good-bye, Earl Grey. My heart's stopping.

EARL GREY: But you can't! Winter's around the corner . . . who'll drink cocoa and collect snowflakes with me? No one can marvel over a snowflake like you, Aloe Vera.

ALOE VERA: You kind man. Time marches, but your keen eyes are the same as that boy's who first rescued me. You asked for a lifetime and that's precisely what we've had together. I'm glad my air balloon malfunctioned.

EARL GREY: I'm glad your face wasn't broken.

   (They chuckle.)

ALOE VERA: When you think of all we'll leave behind . . .

EARL GREY: Not too shabby.

ALOE VERA: *(Growing weaker.)* You'll take care of the tombstone and epitaph . . . ?

EARL GREY: I didn't think the moment would come.

ALOE VERA: But you remember?

EARL GREY: "Everything possible is happening somewhere on earth. And above it, perpetually passive and indifferent, hovers the weather."

ALOE VERA: Very nice. Just as we drew it up.

EARL GREY: I wish there was something I could do. It all seems to happen so fast.

ALOE VERA: Tell me tonight's forecast?

EARL GREY: Foggy through the evening, turning cold, with a chance of early morning showers.

ALOE VERA: Our favorite.

   (Earl Grey hugs his wife to him as lights fade.)

END OF PLAY

Super 8 versus Bacara Resort and Spa

STEPHANIE HUTCHINSON

Super 8 versus Bacara Resort and Spa was originally presented at
The Actor's Group in Universal City, Calif., March 29, 2008,
as part of an Evening of Four 10-Minute Comedies by
Stephanie Hutchinson, AOPW Fellowship Award winner.
Directed by Jonathan Levit. Cast: Jeremy — Frytz Mor; Lula-
belle — Lauren Kidd. *Super 8 versus Bacara Resort and Spa* was
also performed at Camino Real Playhouse's Showoff! Interna-
tional Playwriting Festival in San Juan Capistrano, Calif.,
January 2009. Directed by Jennifer Hartline.
Cast: Jeremy — Corey Eib; Lulabelle — Jennifer Pearce.

CHARACTERS

> JEREMY: Thirties to forties, single, movie producer, takes no bull from anyone.
>
> LULABELLE: Twenties, single, very friendly, attractive but naïve small-town girl with a strong Southern accent; a sunbeam.

SETTING

> The patio of Bacara (pronounced "bah-CAR-ah") Resort and Spa, a posh resort in Santa Barbara, California. There is a potted palm, a small glass table, and two chairs. A partial wall separates this patio from the neighboring one, which has exactly the same setup.

TIME

> The present.

• • •

Jeremy, casually dressed and wearing sunglasses, is pacing while squeezing a stress ball and screaming into a cell phone.

JEREMY: WHAT? . . . NO! She can't quit, we're going into production next week! . . . I don't care where, just find me another actress! . . . Yeah. And Melinda, no calls. I don't want to be disturbed. I came here for peace and quiet. Yeah . . . bye.

> *(He throws the cell phone down and slumps into a chair. Lulabelle enters the next patio, wearing shorts and a T-shirt, flip-flops, very large hoop earrings, and oversized sunglasses on her head. She is chewing gum. She carries bottled water in one hand and a copy of* People *magazine in the other. She explores the space with delight and peeks around the dividing wall, seeing Jeremy.)*

LULABELLE: *(Very friendly and enthusiastically.)* Hi, neighbor!

> *(He groans; she waves.)*

LULABELLE: Hi, neighbor!

JEREMY: I'm not your neighbor.

LULABELLE: You are too. The Good Book says you are.

JEREMY: The good book?

LULABELLE: Don't you read it?

JEREMY: I haven't read any good books lately.

LULABELLE: Well, fer cryin' out loud, you need to read this one.

JEREMY: *(Takes off his sunglasses.)* What's it called again?

LULABELLE: The Good Book.

JEREMY: Who's it by? *(Beat.)*

LULABELLE: *(Incredulous.)* God. *(Beat.)* Where I'm from, it's rude not to greet your neighbors.

JEREMY: I told you, I'm not your neighbor.

LULABELLE: Yes you are, fer the next five days.

JEREMY: *(Groans.)* Maybe I can change rooms.

LULABELLE: It ain't as bad as all that. *(She extends her hand, smiling.)* I'm Lulabelle. Pleased to make your acquaintance.

    (Pause; Jeremy reluctantly shakes her hand.)

JEREMY: Jeremy.

LULABELLE: What a pretty name!

JEREMY: Look, miss whatever-your-name-is.

LULABELLE: Lulabelle —

JEREMY: Who the hell came up with a name like that?

LULABELLE: My dearly departed momma. Don't you say nothin' bad 'bout her. Folks should never speak ill of the dead.

JEREMY: I wasn't "speaking ill." Look, Lu . . .

LULABELLE: *(Slowly, as if to a child.)* Lula —

JEREMY: Lula —

LULABELLE: *(Mimes ringing a bell.)* Belle —

JEREMY: Belle —

LULABELLE: *(Smiles.)* You're gettin' it. Lulabelle —

JEREMY: Lu . . . Lulabelle, I just want to be left alone.

LULABELLE: Don't mind me, I'm as quiet as a little ole church mouse.

    (Beat; she looks around.) Ain't this place the cat's meow? I even got me a little fridge in my room an' it's all loaded up! Ain't that sweet of 'em? An' they don't even know me!

JEREMY: That's the minibar.

LULABELLE: Come again?

JEREMY: The minibar. The prices are listed on the sheet.

LULABELLE: *(About to take a swig of bottled water.)* Prices?

JEREMY: Yeah. If you eat or drink anything, they'll charge you. It's a rip-off — like ten bucks for a bottle of water.

LULABELLE: *(Looking aghast at the bottled water in her hand, then at him.)* Surely you jest.

JEREMY: I wish.

LULABELLE: *(Hastily putting the bottle down.)* I don't need no ten-dollar water, no sir.

JEREMY: Now, Lula —

LULABELLE: — Lulabelle

JEREMY: *(Annoyed.)* May I just call you Lula?

LULABELLE: *(Sweetly.)* It ain't that hard to say my name, jest practice it a little more. *(Enunciating.)* Lu-la-belle.

JEREMY: *(Mimicking her Southern accent.)* I just want peace and quiet.

LULABELLE: No problemo. I'll be jest as quiet as a little ole church mouse.

JEREMY: That would be gr —

LULABELLE: — I carried my bags — would you believe some guy tried to take 'em from me? But I stopped him. Imagine, somebody tryin' to steal my bags, right from under my own nose!

JEREMY: That's the bellman. He's supposed to carry your bags.

LULABELLE: I'm a strong girl, I am. I don't need nobody helpin' me an' then wantin' a handout, no sir.

JEREMY: It's not a handout, it's a tip.

LULABELLE: Same thing. *(Beat.)* You know, the first thing I done when I got to my room was to check fer bed bugs. Thank God there ain't none here.

JEREMY: Why would you even think of that?

LULABELLE: Why, the Super 8 Motel I stayed at last week had 'em.

JEREMY: That's disgusting!

LULABELLE: Oh, they was already dead, so they couldn't do me no harm. There they was, blood-red dead bed bugs up on the wall, right above the headboard. There was even more of 'em behind the headboard, dead, I mean. I checked the sheets and mattress but didn't find none, thank the Lord.

JEREMY: You notified the management, didn't you?

LULABELLE: I tried. The phone was busy — *(She imitates a phone ringing.)* — beep, beep, beep — an' it was late at night so I had me a mind to sleep on the chair, but I told myself, Lulabelle, them critters is already dead, so they can't hurt you none. *(Beat.)* I changed rooms the next day.

JEREMY: So the new room was clear of bed bugs?

LULABELLE: No, it had dead bed bugs up on the wall too, but they was tan colored. They was dead so long that they was mummified!

JEREMY: *(Observing.)* It's a long way from the Super 8 Motel to the Bacara Resort and Spa.

LULABELLE: Woo hoo! Ain't life excitin'? I never won nothin' in my whole life till I won this here vacation!

JEREMY: *(Sarcastically.)* Lucky you . . . *(He squeezes the stress ball.)* Lucky me.

LULABELLE: Oh, luck don't have nothin' to do with it. It's a blessin' from the Lord.

JEREMY: Whatever.

LULABELLE: An' can you believe there's a pair of slippers and a pretty white Fretty robe fer me to wear?

JEREMY: That's Fretté.

LULABELLE: An' a fireplace too! I gotta find me some matches.

JEREMY: *(Alarmed.)* No, it's a gas fireplace. You turn it on with a switch.

LULABELLE: *(Studies him.)* You're foolin' with me, Jeremy.

JEREMY: It's the truth. There was a big ad campaign about gas fireplaces that said, "In this town it's hard to spot the fakes."

LULABELLE: *(Gently.)* But you're not a fake, are you, Jeremy? I can tell that you're the real deal.

(Jeremy is unnerved and says nothing.)

LULABELLE: You're a real nice man, I can tell.

JEREMY: *(Cynically.)* Is that so?

LULABELLE: Yessir.

JEREMY: And how would you know?

LULABELLE: It's just an instinct that women have. I got it stronger than most.

JEREMY: Really.

(Beat; his cell phone rings. Lulabelle picks up the People *magazine and thumbs through it.)*

JEREMY: Melinda! I said no calls!

(Beat. Lulabelle stops and does a double take as she looks at Jeremy.)

LULABELLE: *(Gasps to herself.)* Oh!!!

JEREMY: WHAT? You did? . . . When can I see her? . . . She's on her way here now? . . . She has a deep Southern accent? *(He scrutinizes Lulabelle.)* About [He describes the height, hair color and eye color of the actress playing Lulabelle]? Thanks, Melinda. She's already arrived. *(He puts the cell phone down. To Lulabelle, sarcastically.)* Well, Lu, you can cut the act. I know you're auditioning for the part. Very clever of you.

LULABELLE: Jeremy? What's wrong?

JEREMY: Cut the innocent crap. I know who you are.

LULABELLE: *(Hurt.)* I don't know what you're talkin' 'bout, 'deed I don't.

JEREMY: That's exactly what I can't stand — a lying, filthy bi —

LULABELLE: — HOW DARE YOU! You apologize to me right now, neighbor!

JEREMY: For the hundredth time, I'm NOT your neighbor!

LULABELLE: Maybe I was wrong 'bout you. Maybe you ain't a nice man after all.

(She begins to cry and puts her sunglasses on.)

JEREMY: *(Harshly.)* Stop crying. The role doesn't call for it.

LULABELLE: What role? I ain't no actress. I'm jest a backwoods Southern girl, I am. You're hateful, you are!

(Jeremy's cell phone rings again)

JEREMY: Yeah? . . . What?

(Beat; he looks at Lulabelle.)

JEREMY: What do you mean, she's in the lobby? . . . Really? . . . I'll be right down.

(He hangs up and clears his throat.)

JEREMY: Uh, Lu . . .

(Pause.)

LULABELLE: *(Sniffling; she puts her sunglasses back on her head, without looking at him.)* Lulabelle.

JEREMY: *(Quietly.)* I'm . . . *(Beat.)* . . . sorry.

LULABELLE: *(Cupping her ear while looking away from him.)* Come again?

JEREMY: I said . . . maybe I can make it up to you at dinner tonight? There's a very fine restaurant here.

LULABELLE: *(Finally looking at him.)* Why, Jeremy, I heard that. Thank you very kindly. When should I meet you?

JEREMY: Dinner at eight?

LULABELLE: Sounds lovely.

JEREMY: *(Getting up.)* See you later, Lu.

LULABELLE: OK, Jeremy.

(He exits; she calls out after him)

LULABELLE: You're a real nice man, fer sure. *(To herself.)* A real nice bachelor. One of the 100 hottest, accordin' to *People* magazine! *(She picks up the copy of* People *magazine, which features a headshot of the actor playing Jeremy as one of the "100 Hottest Bachelors" and displays it for the audience to see. To audience.)* I ain't no actress, but I AM auditioning fer a part, if you catch my drift. *(She smiles and winks, puts on her sunglasses, and waves as she exits.)*

(Lights fade.)

END OF PLAY

The Transfiguration of Linda

S.W. SENEK

The Transfiguration of Linda was originally presented at the 2008 New York City Fifteen Minute Play Festival. Directed by Julie Jensen. Cast: Linda — Sara J. Asselin; Randy — Brian Frank.

CHARACTERS

LINDA: Thirty-something, childlike, full of enthusiasm — and insanity.

RANDY: Thirty-something, businessman, not very adventurous.

SETTING

Randy's apartment.

TIME

The present.

• • •

Randy's apartment. Sound of an alarm clock. Linda and Randy sit up in bed. Randy is in pajamas, while Linda has a raincoat on. There is a duffle bag on the floor beside the bed.

LINDA: *(Kissing him on the cheek.)* Good morning, Randy.

RANDY: *(Smiling.)* Good morning, Linda. *(Beat. He scoots away startled.)* Linda? Linda Belinda?

LINDA: You're just the way I remember.

RANDY: What are you doing here?

LINDA: What a silly question. We have a complete day ahead of us. First, we'll eat a scrumptious foie gras omelet, get our teeth cleaned by my dentist, Darrell — Oooh, and I know the perfect dairy farm upstate where we can milk cows all afternoon — lastly —

RANDY: Wait. Linda, we broke up. *(Linda giggles.)* I'm serious.

LINDA: *(She stares at him blankly for a moment, then continues.)* After the cows, we can navigate peddle boats across the English Channel. I have plane tickets and reservations for Peter's Pond Power Peddler — it'll be priceless peddling.

RANDY: I'm calling the police. Where's my phone?

LINDA: I threw it out the window. You shouldn't leave your window unlocked — a person could come in and slice your artery — a main one. You could even die. *(She pulls out a bright red shirt.)* Speaking of death, here, I brought you this.

RANDY: You climbed ten stories?

LINDA: Red is still your color. It's from the large and tall store. But you'll grow into them — like our love.

RANDY: Linda, you should have warned me — where's my suit? It was on this chair.

LINDA: *(She giggles.)* With the phone.

RANDY: I have a business meeting. Linda, we broke up quite a while ago. It was hard enough the first time. *(Politely, but physically tries to escort her out.)*

LINDA: Darling, don't push away. Oh, I need to breathe. *(Trying to concentrate. Somewhat weak.)* Breathe.

RANDY: Are you OK?

LINDA: Hold on. *(She freezes.)* It's a sinus problem that causes this imbalance. *(She moans. Then again, but louder.)*

RANDY: Has this happened before?

LINDA: *(Beat.)* I'm fine. *(Very loud moan.)* That's the one I was looking for. Breathe. You should start packing.

RANDY: I'm not — *(Starts to escort her again — barely even touching her — she moans.)* Sorry.

LINDA: It's me.

RANDY: This isn't a good idea, us together.

LINDA: You're simply ridiculous. You have two minutes to shower — especially if you want to make love under the moonlit sky or under the milk cows.

RANDY: I'm not making love under anything.

LINDA: You're so closed minded. We can "moo" together. MOOOOOOOO!

RANDY: Linda —

LINDA: Come on. MOOOOOO!

RANDY: Linda — *(Barely touching her. She moans.)* I have neighbors. *(She moans louder.)* Shhhh. Fine, I'll "moo." *(Softly.)* Mooo.

LINDA: *(Trying to get him to "moo" louder.)* MOOOOOO!

RANDY: Moooooo.

LINDA: *(Louder.)* MOOOO!

RANDY AND LINDA: MOOOOO! MOOOOO!

RANDY: I insist you leave.

LINDA: We "moo" so well together.

RANDY: Don't reopen old wounds.

LINDA: You said we'd be together "forever." You said "forever." *(Dreamy sigh. Then moans.)*

RANDY: I didn't mean it.

LINDA: "Forever" and "only." It's in writing. *(She pulls out an old letter.)* On top of that you said I was "the one," "your girl," "your bitch."

RANDY: *(Looking at the letter.)* Linda, this is from fifth grade. Fifth grade!

LINDA: We were supposed to read *Romeo and Juliet* together — remember.

RANDY: Things have changed.

LINDA: *(She pulls out another paper.)* I wrote you an iambic pentameter poem. It's called "I thought, thought, thought about you ev'ry day." *(Beat.)*
I thought, thought, thought about you ev'ry day.
Since you broke up with me. Me, me, me, me.
I knew one day you would return to me.
But, I, I have returned to you, you, you.
I thought, thought, thought about you ev'ry day.

RANDY: Linda — *(He reaches out to her. She moans. He withdraws.)*

LINDA: I see it in your eyes. We're supposed to be together . . . "forever."

RANDY: *(He steps toward her. She moans again. He steps back.)* Linda, I have a fiancée.

LINDA: The one away on business?

RANDY: How do you know?

LINDA: So unfortunate — her untimely death.

RANDY: What!

LINDA: *(Giggles.)* I'm not a murderer. *(She moans.)*

RANDY: That's not funny.

LINDA: Truth is, I hired a hitman.

RANDY: My God.

LINDA: *(Giggles.)* Kidding. But I did kidnap, tie her up, and smash her head in with one of my elephant knickknacks. I went, "Knick knack paddy — WHACK!" *(Giggles, moans.)*

RANDY: Linda —

LINDA: *(Moan.)* Kidding. *(Giggles.)* I'm sure she's fine — *(Dark voice.)* I hope her plane burns in hell. *(Giggles.)* Sorry, that's nervous talk. *(Moan.)*

RANDY: Stop the moaning. Look, fifth grade was so long time ago. I don't love you anymore.

LINDA: This was wrong — me doing this to you now, wasn't it?

RANDY: Yes. give me a minute and we'll go down to the coffee shop and catch up, OK?

LINDA: We can start over, right?

RANDY: Fine.

LINDA: Your idea sounds so awkward. But — OK, we'll start over then.

RANDY: Good.

LINDA: *(She extends her hand.)* Hi, I'm Linda.

RANDY: Hi, Linda, I'm Randy. *(He extends his hand, she moans, he withdraws his hand.)*

LINDA: Hi, Randy. You inspire me. *(She takes her raincoat off. She has a skimpy dress that is made of old material. It looks homemade — not quite fitted.)*

It's made from the same dress I wore when you wrote "forever" and "only" — and when you dumped! *(She dramatically cries.)*

RANDY: *(Cautiously comforts her.)* Linda, Linda. Shhhhh. *(He embraces her. Pause.)* Linda . . .

LINDA: *(Stops crying. Then moans.)* Kiss me. Kiss me you fool.

RANDY: *(He lets go of her.)* I'm taking you down to the police station. Where are my slippers?

LINDA: Well.

RANDY: You threw those, too?

LINDA: Just one. Here. *(Hands one slipper to him.)*

RANDY: That's it — *(Puts one slipper on.)* we're going —

(He grabs her. She moans.)

RANDY: Moan. I don't care!

LINDA: *(Resisting.)* But our future is so bright! We can move into that leaning crack house on Lancaster street — the one with the graffiti on the shutters —

RANDY: No.

(She then jumps on his back.)

LINDA: It's my dream house.

RANDY: Get off of me! *(He tries to get her off him.)* I can't see!

LINDA: *(Struggles.)* Stop. Please. Help! Help!

RANDY: Stop yelling.

(He tries to cover her mouth. She moans loudly.)

LINDA: Help!

(She grabs his arm and twists it — putting him in pain.)

RANDY: Ow — what —

LINDA: *(Linda now plays a bad cop.)* How's it feel now, pal?

RANDY: Linda —

LINDA: *(As bad cop.)* What are you trying to pull — first, you dump her, now this — no one likes this game.

RANDY: What are you doing?

LINDA: *(As bad cop.)* I'm putting you under arrest — or killing you, depend how much you resist.

RANDY: Why are you doing this?

LINDA: *(As bad cop.)* Do you see the badge? Do you?

RANDY: No.

(Linda as bad cop twists his arm.)

RANDY: Ouch! Yes.

LINDA: *(As Linda.)* Officer — I'm sure he didn't mean it. Tell him, Randy.

RANDY: You're hurting me.

LINDA: *(As bad cop.)* It can hurt worse, pal.

    (As Linda.) Be strong, Randy. Be strong.

    (As bad cop.) Are you making a mockery of me?

    (As Linda.) I've seen your type before. You're a bad cop.

    (As bad cop) Lady, it's people like him that ruin people like us. I can take care of him right now and no one has to know.

    (Bad cop twists Randy's arm, hurting him.)

RANDY: Ouch! Can't we sit and talk about this?

LINDA: *(Bad cop ties Randy's hands together pulling rope out of a duffle bag. As bad cop.)* You missed that boat back at Peter's Power Peddlers, pal. You think you can just drop someone in fifth grade and bon voyage?

RANDY: Ouch! It's too tight.

LINDA: *(As bad cop.)* You broke her heart, and that's a crime in my book, pal.

    (As Linda.) I didn't want it to come to this. Get your hands off of him.

    (Linda grabs the bad cop's hand [her own hand], forcing her off Randy, but bad cop grabs Randy's hand again. Bad cop grabs Linda's hair.)

    (As bad cop.) I make the rules now, lady.

    (As good cop.) Johnson. Let go of her. This ain't your fight. It's for the court.

    (As bad cop.) Listen good cop, we can end it here — quietly.

    (As good cop.) That's where you're wrong, Johnson. He's gonna get a fair trial, see? A fair trial.

    (As bad cop to Randy.) It's your lucky day, pal.

RANDY: Linda, don't do this.

LINDA: *(As good cop.)* Are you pressing charges, miss?

    (As Linda.) Yes. Sorry, Randy.

    (As bad cop. Bad cop pulls out jumper cables.) They'll fry you like fish on Good Friday.

RANDY: Fry?

LINDA: *(As a prosecutor, she grabs a clipboard from the duffle bag.)* Your honor, as prosecutor, it's my duty to put people like this away. He thinks he's normal, but he knows he isn't. Do we want him roaming the very streets where our precious fifth graders play?

RANDY: We're not in court.

LINDA: *(As judge.)* Overruled.

    (As lawyer.) Thank you, your honor. I call to the stand . . . Linda.

    (As Linda.) No.

    (As lawyer.) Is it true he dumped you in fifth grade?

    (As Linda.) Sorry, Randy. Yes.

RANDY: Linda!

LINDA: *(As Linda.)* We could've milked cows together.

  (As bad cop pulling a fish from a duffle bag.) Fish fry Friday!

  (As lawyer.) I have nothing more your honor, except, he's guilty, GUILTY!

RANDY: I'm innocent, your honor!

LINDA: *(As judge.)* Order! Order! Verdict time — GUILTY! The punishment is — DEATH!

RANDY: Wait! Don't I have a right to testify?

LINDA: *(As bad cop.)* You all want to plead "the fifth" — until it's time to pay. You should've thought about "the fifth" back in fifth grade. Fry the fish!

RANDY: Wait! Don't I have last words?

LINDA: *(As Linda.)* Please, let him speak. *(Moans.)*

  (As bad cop.) Make it snappy, sappy.

RANDY: Linda, fifth grade was so long ago. I had glasses, pimples, and I was the only kid who wore a fedora to school. You were a cheerleader. I wasn't — although, I wore my mother's dress once. *(Beat.)* Yes, I declared my love for Linda. I did use the words "forever" and "only." The day before we were to read *Romeo and Juliet* in class . . . we were to meet at the Tastee-Freez for a double banana split sundae. *(Linda gasps.)* Yes, a double banana split sundae. That's what she dreamed of. Isn't that right? That's what you dreamed of, wasn't it. Wasn't it!

LINDA: *(As judge.)* Order! Order! Answer the question.

  (Beat. As Linda.) I told him, if he truly loved me, he'd buy his Juliet a double banana split sundae and share it.

  (As judge.) Did he buy it for you?

  (As Linda.) He left a note in my locker which read . . . *(Pulls the note out.)* "I have to break up with you. Enjoy your banana split." He never showed up.

RANDY: What else was in the envelope?

LINDA: *(As judge.)* Miss Belinda, what was in the envelope?

  (As Linda.) Exact change for a banana split. *(Linda cries. Then moans.)*

  (As lawyer.) Objection. He technically didn't share — plus, he dumped her.

  (As judge.) I'm sorry, but that fact remains. DEATH!

RANDY: Wait. There's one other thing that I didn't write in the letter. That I had a problem . . . I was . . . allergic to bananas.

  (Linda gasps in surprise.)

LINDA: *(As judge.)* Order! Order!

RANDY: I convince my family to move — and change our name. I couldn't

hold her back, knowing there might be someone out there who could —
and would — eat a double banana split sundae with her.

LINDA: *(As lawyer.)* Your honor, this is absurd!

(As Linda.) All this time I — why didn't you tell me?

RANDY: I tried like hell to put it behind me — moving from city to city, hoping
you'd never find me. I didn't want to face you in shame. But here you are.

LINDA: *(As Linda.)* Here I am.

RANDY: I could fall in love all over again . . . years later.

LINDA: *(As Linda.)* Randy, I don't know what to say.

(As bad cop.) You can say good-bye, pal!

(As Linda.) Randy! Look out!

(As bad cop pulling a knife out of the duffle bag.) I'm taking the law into
my own hands.

*(Bad cop starts to come at Randy but Linda grabs him [er . . . herself] and
puts up a struggle. It's quite a struggle. Finally, bad cop stabs Linda.)*

(As Linda.) Ahhh — Randy! He got me. *(Linda stumbles over to Randy.)*
He got me good.

*(She melodramatically falls to the ground — lifts her head. She moans. She
drops her head, then lifts it again. Moans. She drops her head, then lifts it
again. Moans. He rushes over.)*

RANDY: Linda. I'm so sorry — I love you! If I could only change it all.

LINDA: *(As Linda, grabs him.)* It's not too late. *(She opens her duffle bag and
pulls out a double banana split sundae — the one from fifth grade.)*

RANDY: A double banana split sundae. It's like kryptonite. *(He backs away.)*

LINDA: I bought it . . . in fifth grade . . . and saved it . . . after all these years.

RANDY: It looks pretty moldy.

LINDA: It is.

RANDY: If I eat it . . . I could die instantly.

LINDA: I know, but — Ohhhhh! I don't have much longer.

RANDY: Then . . . let's share it.

LINDA: Oh . . . Randy. *(He gives her a bite.)* Randy . . .

RANDY: *(He takes a bite.)* Oh . . . Linda.

LINDA: Randy . . . *(She moans.)*

RANDY: Linda . . .

*(They collapse. Pause. They moan together again, then collapse. Pause. They
moan together, then collapse. The moan once more. Dramatic pause. They
both collapse. Black out.)*

END OF PLAY

Valentine's Play

JENNY LYN BADER

Valentine's Play was originally produced by Stageworks/Hudson in Hudson, N.Y., October 2008, as part of their 2008 Play by Play Festival. Directed by Billy Kimball. Cast: Kelly — Myleah Misenheimer; Bob — David Tass. It was first read at a benefit for Women's Expressive Theater, New York City, February 2008. Directed by Abby Epstein. Cast: Kelly — Ricki Lake; Bob — Neil Patrick Harris.

CHARACTERS

> KELLY: Twenties to thirties, the girlfriend.
> BOB: Twenties to thirties, the boyfriend.

SETTING

> A living room.

TIME

> February, early evening.

• • •

Kelly, lovely and upbeat, enters the apartment she shares with her boyfriend, Bob. She wears a coat and hat, is obviously coming in from the cold. She is carrying a large bag. She takes off her coat, and she is wearing red. From the bag, she takes a small gift with a bow and presents it to Bob.

KELLY: Happy Valentine's Day, sweetheart!
> *(Bob looks completely panicked.)*
BOB: Oh no. Is it today already?
> *(Kelly pushes up a small, square joke-of-the-day calendar so he can see it. It says February 14.)*
BOB: Oh God.
KELLY: Open it!
> *(Bob opens it and finds an envelope with tickets in it. He is ecstatic.)*
BOB: Do you realize this is the game I most want to go to all year?
KELLY: Yes. This is the little gift that goes with it.
> *(She hands him a gift bag with crepe paper, and he takes out a team cap and shirt and stuffed animal mascot.)*
BOB: Wow. Perfect! Since I haven't . . . um, picked up your gift yet, I was thinking that . . .
KELLY: *(Cheerful.)* No worries! I did that.
BOB: You picked up — ?
KELLY: Oh yes. Here.
> *(Kelly hands Bob a wrapped gift.)*
KELLY: For you. To give to me.
> *(Bob holds it for a moment, then gives it to her. She suddenly acts surprised.)*
KELLY: Thank you! Oh let me see . . . *(She opens it with excitement and seems genuinely delighted.)* Honey, it's just exactly the one I wanted!

BOB: *(Bob can't tell what's in the box, but tries to play along.)* I felt it was really — you. It is you.

KELLY: It's so understated. But provocative.

BOB: That's what I was thinking!

KELLY: It could easily be too much. But it isn't.

BOB: *(Baffled.)* Too much? I can barely . . . see it.

KELLY: Just look what it is.

BOB: What?

KELLY: Oh my God is it see-through?

BOB: I was hoping it might be, but, it uh, depends, on how it looks on . . .

KELLY: Do you want me to put it on?

BOB: *(Hopeful.)* Yes oh yes.

> *(She takes it out. He's disappointed. It is clearly not lingerie. In fact he's not sure what it is. It is so small he can barely see it. It seems like a bobby pin of some kind with a small rhinestone attached. She puts it in her hair.)*

KELLY: I'm putting it on right now!

BOB: *(Mystified.)* That is the thing you wanted?

KELLY: Desperately.

BOB: I'm so glad I got it.

> *(She takes it out of her hair and admires it.)*

KELLY: Did you know, this is exactly what I need with my new hairstyle?

BOB: I suspected. When I saw. How you styled. Your new — style.

KELLY: I knew you noticed it.

BOB: Are you kidding? It's so different!

KELLY: You didn't say anything but you noticed, and then you got me the perfect accessory. Thank you.

BOB: No, thank you.

KELLY: No, thank you for giving me this.

BOB: Oh . . . You're welcome!

KELLY: *(Coy.)* So what else did you get me?

BOB: What else??

KELLY: In the other box.

BOB: *(Anxious.)* There's another box!

KELLY: The big one. In the shopping bag.

BOB: So, what did I get you . . .

KELLY: Let's see.

BOB: They do such a good job with gift wrapping these days, don't you think? Look at that nice. Big. Box.

KELLY: Should I open it?

BOB: Of course. Is this all I got you?

KELLY: What do you mean?

BOB: Are there gonna be any more surprises? Just this big box, and the other little box, the one you already opened, right? I didn't go crazy buying you lots of stuff, did I?

KELLY: Why would you do that?

BOB: Since I seem to be so clear about what you want right now, I just want to be sure . . . about . . . what you want. Do you want me getting you boxes and boxes of stuff?

KELLY: *(Unwrapping the box as she reassures him.)* I want nothing.

BOB: You do?

KELLY: Nothing more than — nothing.

BOB: OK. Kelly. I'm trying to understand . . . If you want nothing, then what's in the big box? *(Bob looks in the box. A beat. He is not sure whether to be worried.)* There is nothing in this big box.

KELLY: The gift wrapping is so lovely though, isn't it? I might keep this ribbon and flower.

BOB: Kelly, I got you a big box of nothing.

KELLY: And that is so sweet. Because that is what I wanted for Valentine's Day. Nothing at all. Except pure love.

BOB: The pure love between us.

KELLY: Exactly. There are no more boxes.

BOB: There are no more boxes because I get nervous that you want things but really you don't want anything.

KELLY: *(Really wanting Bob to know she thinks this is true.)* I'm very low maintenance.

BOB: You just want nothing. And a hair accessory.

KELLY: That's all.

BOB: You're so — full of surprises. I'm sorry if I've misunderstood you.

KELLY: It's OK.

BOB: When it comes to Valentine's — I guess I worry a little bit. That you want all kinds of — things. Things in little boxes and big boxes. Chocolate-covered things. Bejewelled things. Silken things.

KELLY: I don't!

BOB: Oh and roses.

KELLY: *(Agreeing.)* A dozen.

BOB: Yes! Not one or two. Not a half dozen.

KELLY: A dozen roses.

BOB: Oh God you do want that. *(Guessing.)* But you would never buy that for yourself. I should go get them —

KELLY: Not now.

BOB: Not now . . . *(Trying to figure it out.)* because you sent them? Did you call in and send them? For both of us? From both of us? God I love you.

KELLY: Actually you have till tomorrow.

BOB: What?

KELLY: To get the roses. Because I — exaggerated a little bit earlier. Today is really . . . only . . . *(A confession.)* February thirteenth.

BOB: It's . . . *(Confused.)* But you're wearing red.

KELLY: I know I am.

BOB: You never wear red except . . . You wore red on the thirteenth . . . *(Remembering.)* And wasn't . . . ? *(Finds the February 13 page hidden under the calendar. Astonished.)* You tore my joke-of-the-day calendar! I don't even know what the joke was today!

KELLY: I'm sorry, honey, perhaps it was unfair of me to prey on your fear of forgetting Valentine's.

BOB: I didn't forget it! I still had twenty-four hours!

KELLY: But isn't it better I reminded you? Now you have a whole day . . .

BOB: Sure. A whole day to find the perfect gifts for you . . . Which you already got!

KELLY: So maybe I went a little overboard.

BOB: Overboard? You went a little nuts! Every now and then, you go a little nuts. And this time, you know why you did?

KELLY: Why?

BOB: Because you don't believe in me. You don't trust me to figure out what day it is.

KELLY: You didn't figure it out last year!

BOB: *(Embarrassed.)* That's different.

KELLY: How?

BOB: Because umm . . . now . . . it's this year! This year's not the same thing as last year. And it's today. Today's not the same thing as tomorrow. Which normally I would completely know. Except you lied to me.

KELLY: OK, I may have lied a little, but emotionally? It wasn't really a lie. Because I was already feeling tomorrow.

BOB: Oh so you can feel days of the week now. That's great. Next it'll be, "Sorry, I can't see you on Saturday, I'm feeling too Wednesday."

KELLY: That's not . . .

BOB: Y'know, when you go after me like this . . .

KELLY: Sweetie it's not you, anyone — or, any guy — might forget . . .

BOB: . . . I feel . . . like there's a trapdoor some place that I could fall through at any moment, and I don't know where it is, but you do, and you always have the remote-

KELLY: You always have the remote.

BOB: *(Referencing the remote control on the coffee table.)* I'm not talking about this remote, I'm talking about —

KELLY: There's no trap. I just wanna make sure that tomorrow —

BOB: And you know what? You're not even listening!

KELLY: What? Of course I . . .

BOB: Honey, you can't do this to me! You have to give me a chance to fuck up.

KELLY: I don't want you to fuck up.

BOB: OK, but it doesn't count, when I don't fuck up, if I never had the chance!

KELLY: That makes no sense.

BOB: You just pretended one day was a completely different day, then bought yourself presents from me and thanked me for them, but I make no sense?

KELLY: I thanked you because I was grateful to you, you dork!

BOB: For what?

KELLY: For caring so much about what I might want even when you have no clue what it is.

BOB: Yeah?

KELLY: Yeah. It's very touching.

Bob: *(Calmer.)* I'm grateful to you too.

KELLY: *(Playful.)* Oh yeah? Even when I'm going a little nuts?

BOB: Mmm hmm. Especially then. Because when you go a little nuts, it's always out of love.

KELLY: Yeah?

BOB: Yeah. Never any other agenda.

KELLY: *(Considering this.)* You know, you're right.

BOB: What, now you're thinking back on all the times you've been nuts? *(She swats him with the gift wrapping.)*

BOB: Hey. Let's go out for a Valentine's eve dinner.

KELLY: "Valentine's eve"? I've never heard of it.

BOB: Oh, it's great! You can get into any restaurant. All the gifts are knock-you-over, out-of-nowhere surprises. And when it gets late? . . . It suddenly turns into Valentine's Day itself.

KELLY: Sounds magical.

BOB: But while it's happening? You can feel very "tonight."

KELLY: I think I'm feeling tonight already.

BOB: Are you?

KELLY: Mmm. I'll get ready to go out . . .

BOB: Let me get you ready.

KELLY: Huh?

(He takes the tiny hair accessory and positions it in her hair just so. She looks up, a little startled. In a good way.)

BOB: There. You're good to go.

(They get their coats.)

END OF PLAY

A Very Very Short Play

JACQUELYN REINGOLD

A Very Very Short Play was first produced by
Ensemble Studio Theatre, New York City, June 2008.
Directed by Jonathan Bernstein. Cast: Man —
Adam Dannheisser; Woman — Julie Fitzpatrick.

CHARACTERS
    ROGER: Thirties.
    JOAN: Thirties.

SETTING
    On an airplane.

TIME
    The present.

NOTE: Roger and Joan should be played by actors of normal height.

• • •

A woman sits on an airplane. She is reading a book. A man sits next to her.
They are midflight.

ROGER: I'm sorry to ask, you look so content so calm so reasonably relaxed
    I'm sorry to ask. Your wrist is just so, and your shoes are just right, what
    are they pumps, mules, puels? I'm sorry to ask, but that shaft of light is
    hitting your hair and making it glow. And I know, I do, look at me not
    exactly coiffed, 'cause this crazy way of getting from here to there makes
    me well want to die, with its clouds and oh God the sky, I can't help it
    I'll stop, the rhyming I'll drop. But the question's still in here: I'd love to
    know yet I hate to ask, but you, you are the smallest woman I've ever
    seen. So in between the pretzels and the plastic cup of cola, while we're
    madly flying over Massapequa toward Madagascar, with Anawanda on
    the right and Alabama on the left, I am compelled while I eat my salted
    nuts, and if you don't mind, it's a nervousness of mine, take out my hi-
    bachi and grill shrimp kebobs: just how tall or small are you, and how
    delicate are your ankles when they're undressed and, what, if I dare ask,
    is your name?
JOAN: I was trying to read.
ROGER: Yes, of course, reading. I should read, too. I love to read, don't you?
    I mean. Let me try again. And then I'll leave you be, but you are so, well,
    so well, petitely proportioned. I don't mean to be fresh. Fresh is not a
    word that is used on me. But maybe, with your book, you would like a
    pear, a peach, a giant seedless watermelon? I know the seeded is tastier,
    but the seeds on the plane, with the size of the seats, is, well, not so good.

JOAN: I don't think you should cook on the plane. Really. A flame. A hot burning flame would be, just think of the heat and the oxygen. I'm reading!

ROGER: What are you reading?

JOAN: About a lawyer who is also a judge. A heroic man who would do anything for the small people of the world.

ROGER: I'm a lawyer.

JOAN: Coincidence.

ROGER: Perhaps there's some sense in coincidence.

JOAN: Excuse me.

ROGER: How 'bout a cream puff?

JOAN: I shouldn't.

ROGER: I'm a lawyer. I could argue that and win. So trust me. It's a chocolate one. Very chocolate. It's more chocolate than I can describe. What's your name? If you don't tell me, I'll make it up. You are Tiny Teena. You are Teenie Tyna. You are Itty Lily. You are Eenie Meenie. You are Lilly Putia. You are —

JOAN: Joan.

ROGER: Even better. How tall are you, Joan?

JOAN: About a foot.

ROGER: Ah. That means your foot, then, is far less than a foot.

JOAN: It does.

ROGER: That means your toes could fit in my nose.

JOAN: It does.

ROGER: That means your —

JOAN: I thought you weren't fresh.

ROGER: I'm not. I'm freshly flawed, flaught, fraught, fnaught, fmaught — Try the puff please please please.

JOAN: OK. If it will quiet you down.

(He feeds her the cream puff piece by small piece, into her tiny mouth. It is the best puff she's ever had.)

ROGER: Well?

JOAN: Well.

ROGER: More?

JOAN: Just a bit. *(He feeds her. While eating.)* May I ask: how tall are you?

ROGER: I'm twelve feet, eight inches.

JOAN: Wow. That means.

ROGER: It does.

JOAN: What's your name, big lawyer who carries so much food?

ROGER: Roger.

JOAN: We never could, you know, Roger, it would never work. How could it would it? Work? Impossible.

ROGER: Keep eating.

JOAN: I mean the mechanics. Even if I fell for you. Or you fell for me. I mean. You would fall a lot farther. And I would fall only a little. That would be dangerous. For you.

ROGER: Danger is my middle name.

JOAN: And your last name?

ROGER: Shmeck.

JOAN: Oh, come on. *(He shrugs.)* Enough, Roger Danger Shmeck. I don't have room. For more.

(She stops him from feeding her.)

ROGER: Just a little. Bite. From the inside, where it's sweetest and softest and nothing like it seems.

(He tries to feed her the cream from inside the puff.)

JOAN: I'm full.

ROGER: Try this.

JOAN: What is it?

ROGER: Arroz con pollo.

JOAN: I can only eat so much.

ROGER: You could fit in more, if you danced on my knees. Or jogged in my hair.

JOAN: I've been through this before.

ROGER: Not with me. See, my thighs are wide, my head is flat, my heart is large.

JOAN: I cannot see your heart.

ROGER: But I bet you can hear it.

(She listens; she cannot hear it.)

JOAN: I only hear the plane.

ROGER: Look, I brought seeds that we can plant then watch them grow. I have chicks that we can raise 'til they give eggs for a soufflé. Try this.

JOAN: What is it?

ROGER: Pickles for a picnic. Brisket for a barbecue. It's the middle of June, it's the beginning of summer. A taste for everyone. And for everyone who doesn't have a someone, or only has the wrong one, there's always the hope for the real one, even when, or especially if, it's impossible, it would never work, it couldn't work, it can never be. But if it were you, I would thank you every day. So, take another bite. Joan. When you think you can't, open your mouth and taste what I have.

JOAN: Well. Roger. Danger. Shmeck. I might. I will. But only if you'll pick me up so I can adjust the little blower near the light button. It's driving me crazy.

ROGER: Gladly.

(He picks her up over his head; she reaches for the blower button and aims its air stream at his face. He pulls her down to him. They kiss. Her tiny lips on his right eye. Then on his left eye. Then lips to lips, though his cover half her face. He almost tosses her across the plane, he's so happy, but instead, he puts her back in her seat.)

ROGER: I never knew such citrus lips.

JOAN: And I thought only small was beautiful.

ROGER: And I thought you never meet anyone you ever want to talk to on a plane. You know, it's always the kind of guy that won't shut up, that goes on and on and all you want to do is watch the bad movie and pray the plane doesn't crash and —

JOAN: Shut up my sweet-tasting lawyer with too much food and lushest lips.

ROGER: Show me your ankles.

JOAN: If you show me yours.

(They take off their shoes and socks, show each other their ankles. The roof and the walls and the floor of the plane disappear. And they are flying high, ankle to ankle. Then Joan picks Roger up, over her head, as they soar up into the sky.)

END OF PLAY

Whistling in the Dark

ROSANNA YAMAGIWA ALFARO

Whistling in the Dark was performed at the Stanford
Calderwood Pavilion, Boston Center for the Arts, May 11,
2008, as part of the Boston Theater Marathon.
Directed by Daniel Gidron. Cast: Jeremy — Ken Baltin;
Estelle — Kippy Goldfarb.

CHARACTERS
> JEREMY: Seventy.
> ESTELLE: Sixty-seven.

SETTING
> Jeremy's living room.

TIME
> The present.

• • •

Jeremy and Estelle are having coffee.

JEREMY: It was nice of you to come on such short notice.

ESTELLE: I know how much Trish hates taking you to the hospital.

JEREMY: She also hated the thought of missing the big Filene's basement sale.

ESTELLE: Ah!

JEREMY: She's at the Arsenal Mall right now, waiting with the rest of the faithful for the doors to open.

ESTELLE: Tell her I'll never again bail her out so early in the morning.

JEREMY: Why?

ESTELLE: You won't believe this, but a coyote followed me three blocks down Brattle Street.

JEREMY: No!

ESTELLE: Do you suppose the wild animals take back the streets once we're tucked into our beds? It was a mangy-looking coyote with a sway back, probably the same one Trish spotted last week when she was out power walking in Mt. Auburn Cemetery.

JEREMY: Or maybe not. There's never just one coyote. It's like Julius Caesar, isn't it — night birds shrieking at noon and lions walking about in the marketplace? Something dreadful's obviously in the offing.

ESTELLE: *(She smiles.)* It's good to see you. It's been nearly two weeks. I've missed all the gloom and doom.

JEREMY: So all that time you've been all right? No more difficulty swallowing? No more chest pains?

ESTELLE: No. I went to my doctor, and she was very dismissive. She said I should drink more liquids and eat more slowly. With fewer teeth it seems you have to chew longer before swallowing.

JEREMY: And the chest pains?

ESTELLE: She said, "How long did they last?" I said, "Two or three days." She said, "Then it couldn't have been a heart attack," rolled her eyes and quickly changed the subject.

JEREMY: You should think of changing doctors.

ESTELLE: They're all the same.

JEREMY: They're all dimwits.

ESTELLE: And how are you feeling?

JEREMY: Oh, just little things. Nothing catastrophic. *(Beat.)* Remember that bout I had last year with double vision?

ESTELLE: Who could forget?

JEREMY: Remember they thought it could be a stroke or a brain tumor or MS? Well, I woke up at 3:30 this morning and began wondering what the "m" in MS stood for. I went through the vowels — "macular," "metasta-tic," "militant," "moribund." I even hit "multiple," but it didn't sound right. So I woke Trish up, and she instantly said "multiple" without even interrupting her deep REM sleep.

ESTELLE: You woke her up?

JEREMY: She went back to sleep in seconds. The thing is I didn't believe her. "Multiple" still felt wrong to me. Now, think carefully. What does this mean for a lawyer? Not being able to hit the right word — even though he can still make some high-falutin' educated guesses. What does it mean not to recognize a word that even a semi-illiterate can come up with in her sleep?

ESTELLE: That's not a very nice thing to say.

JEREMY: It isn't, but you know what I mean. It's like gaps on the library shelf, like speckles in the brain. Anyway, I looked up MS in the dictionary this morning.

ESTELLE: Why didn't you look it up at 3:30 instead of bothering Trish?

JEREMY: The dictionary's in the next room. It seemed too far to go at the time though it might have saved me two hours of sleep. Or maybe not. Do you know the meaning of MS?

ESTELLE: A disease that causes jerkiness?

JEREMY: Exactly. And you know I can't walk a straight line to save my life. I can't walk down the sidewalk with you without periodically bumping into you.

ESTELLE: *(She smiles.)* Oh. And I thought that was something else.

JEREMY: It is. It is. But it could also be the beginning stages of MS.

ESTELLE: They tested you for MS, Jeremy, and they said you didn't have it.

JEREMY: Do you know the root cause of MS?

ESTELLE: Nerves?

JEREMY: Contrary to what some people think, it's not stress or paranoia. And it's not an imaginary illness as Trish would like one to believe. It's simply hardened tissue in the brain or spinal cord. That's what causes the jerkiness and/or pa . . . pa . . . paralysis.

ESTELLE: Jeremy, you don't have MS. None of the rest of us knows for sure if we have MS, but you have recently been clinically tested. Remember when Tabitha was sick and they drew all that blood to test for feline HIV? The vet said she was the one cat in town who knew for sure she wasn't HIV positive.

JEREMY: And he was wrong. Tabitha didn't know. You knew. But that's a very good analogy. Tabitha continued being a very neurotic old cat with a lot of complaints in spite of her testing negative. And then she died. *(Beat.)* It's chilly in here, isn't it? Trish likes to keep the temperature at sixty-five in October. It could be forty out there but she still keeps it at sixty-five. *(He gives a little moan and painfully stretches his back.)* You know how when someone hugs me and presses the small of my back, I feel propelled backwards as if my legs were going to give out beneath me?

ESTELLE: Trish thinks that's also psychological.

JEREMY: It isn't psychological. Remember the dinner party when that lovely young woman with the spiky hair hugged me? I was suddenly and very unwillingly propelled out of her arms and onto the floor. Also when I lie down and the small of my back touches the bed, I feel as if I'm levitating. Obviously there's something's wrong with my back, not my mind.

ESTELLE: The doctor told you the backbone has nothing to do with the part of your brain that causes double vision and vertigo.

JEREMY: He knows what it isn't. He just hasn't a clue about what it is. According to him, all my ailments are idiopathic. Idiopathic, which means he's at a complete loss to explain them or fix them. As you get older, you realize most ailments are idiopathic and most doctors are idiots.

(A car honks. Estelle looks out the window.)

ESTELLE: The cab's here.

JEREMY: You know, just now, standing in the light of the window, you looked like Jessica Lang playing the angel of death in *All that Jazz.*

ESTELLE: I love that. *(Beat.)* Do I really look like Jessica Lang?

JEREMY: You have her smile.

(The car honks again. Jeremy pushes himself up on the arms of the chair, stands, and steadies himself.)

JEREMY: This should be fun.

ESTELLE: That's what they always say about MRIs.

JEREMY: It's just like being fed to an oven. The last time it sounded as if they were tapping the right side of my skull and then drilling through to the brain. The whole machine shook as if a nut were loose. At the end, the technician beamed and said, "Good job!" to me twice as if I had done something spectacular. Well, I guess they were grateful I didn't panic or pass out with all the bang banging.

ESTELLE: Maybe I should run out and tell him we're coming.

(Jeremy holds her back.)

JEREMY: No. Stop. Listen, it's not for us.

ESTELLE: It's a yellow cab.

JEREMY: It's probably come to pick up the old woman across the street. This chariot of death is for her, not me.

ESTELLE: Don't be obstinate, Jeremy.

JEREMY: Just check again, Estelle.

ESTELLE: *(She looks out the window.)* It's amazing. I can't believe it. You're right.

JEREMY: I'm always right.

ESTELLE: The cab driver's helping the old woman get in, just as you said.

JEREMY: It seems I've lured you over here on false pretenses. As soon as Trish left for Filene's basement, I canceled the MRI.

ESTELLE: You . . .

JEREMY: I called them and said I felt much too dizzy to leave the house.

ESTELLE: And is that true? Do you really feel dizzy?

JEREMY: What do you think? *(He stumbles and holds onto the back of the chair.)* Oh dear, maybe I spoke too soon.

(When Estelle rushes over, he catches her in his arms.)

JEREMY: False alarm.

ESTELLE: *(She is suddenly almost in tears.)* You awful man!

JEREMY: I didn't mean to upset you.

ESTELLE: You awful, awful man, I'm so glad I'm not your wife.

JEREMY: Why?

ESTELLE: Why?? Always scaring her.

JEREMY: Trish is a pretty tough lady. She doesn't scare easily.

ESTELLE: Always deceiving her.

JEREMY: Look, what harm have we done? I know for a fact she doesn't suspect you. No one would suspect you.

ESTELLE: Is that meant to be a compliment?

JEREMY: It is. It is. Neither of us could live without you. *(Beat.)* Tell me, how long has it been since we were alone together?

ESTELLE: Two weeks.

JEREMY: You told me that before, didn't you? You see, my memory's going. Anyway, as I remember, two weeks ago was very nice.

ESTELLE: It was.

JEREMY: I actually succeeded in doing something, didn't I? At our age it's especially important to seize the moment — engage in some bang banging of our own.

ESTELLE: You're an amazing man.

JEREMY: Well, that remains to be seen. With all this talk of sickness and death . . .

ESTELLE: Let's call it foreplay of an urgent sort. *(Beat.)* Suppose Trish comes back early?

JEREMY: From a Filene's basement sale? Come. Come to the back room. Tempus fugit. That's what my father said to his secretary when he wanted to show her the new litter of puppies. He said, "Work can wait. I'll drive you to the house right now. Life is short. You have to do things the moment you think of them."

ESTELLE: Did your father have a thing for his secretary?

JEREMY: No, but they were very fond of each other. She told me the story of the puppies at his funeral a few weeks later.

ESTELLE: Oh.

JEREMY: Brrrr. It's chilly in here. *(He looks at his watch.)* According to my watch we have an hour and a half. So, are you up to it?

ESTELLE: Are you?

JEREMY: I put the little heater on in the back room an hour ago.

ESTELLE: I can see you've been very busy since Trish left.

JEREMY: It should be nice and toasty. They say you put old bread in the oven and it comes back to life. *(Beat.)* Tell me, did I wake you when I called this morning?

ESTELLE: No, I was still in bed, but I'd been up for some time.

JEREMY: Liar! There was something about your voice — blurred, warm, moist . . .

ESTELLE: Juicy.

JEREMY: I imagined being there pressed against you in your bed.

ESTELLE: And that's when Trish picked up the other phone.

JEREMY: She was in the shower when I called you.

ESTELLE: She said, "Who's that, calling so early?" You said, "Just Estelle," and the three of us had a good laugh together.

END OF PLAY

PLAYS FOR
TWO MEN

Crossing the Border

EDUARDO MACHADO

Crossing the Border was originally performed at 59E59 Theaters, New York City, July 31, 2008, as part of Summer Shorts 2. Directed by Randal Myler. Cast: Jacinto — Mando Alvarado; Manue — Gio Perez.

MANUEL: Fifteen, thin, dark.

JACINTO: Early thirties, plump, less dark; father of Manuel.

SETTING

An alley in Playa Carmen, Mexico.

TIME

Late afternoon, the present.

• • •

You can hear Mexican rock music blaring from a car radio. The sound of motor bikes and bicycles. Manuel is holding a bat. His father, Jacinto, is pitching to him.

MANUEL: Papa. My teacher, she told me I write good essays. That I could win a contest. That she would help me after school. Isn't that great?

JACINTO: No.

MANUEL: No?

JACINTO: Hit the ball.

MANUEL: That's all you gotta say?

JACINTO: Hit it. You promise me you are going to hit it?

MANUEL: I'll try.

JACINTO: Not try. You are going to do it.

MANUEL: I'll try!

JACINTO: Trying is not enough.

MANUEL: That's all I can do.

JACINTO: Baseball is what you do best.

MANUEL: No. I can do physics and I know how to write in verse and I have read Lorca.

JACINTO: Lorca.

MANUEL: The great poet, killed by the fascists.

JACINTO: You know what fascists are?

MANUEL: Yes. The people who tried to take over the world.

JACINTO: The world?

MANUEL: They killed the gypsies and the Jews.

JACINTO: What?

MANUEL: And Garcia Lorca.

JACINTO: Why are you so smart, *mijo*?

MANUEL: 'Cause I read a lot.

JACINTO: You like reading.

MANUEL: I devour books.

JACINTO: You like science.

MANUEL: Yes.

JACINTO: And mathematics?

MANUEL: Numbers are an art form.

JACINTO: And poetry?

MANUEL: It fills my soul.

JACINTO: It does.

MANUEL: Yes!

JACINTO: Reading is not going to get you out of here.

MANUEL: I don't want to get out of here.

JACINTO: Yes, you do. Now get ready.

MANUEL: For what?

JACINTO: My pitch.

MANUEL: Baseball?

JACINTO: Yes.

MANUEL: Why?

JACINTO: Eyes on the ball.

MANUEL: Sure.

JACINTO: Yes?

MANUEL: Yes.

JACINTO: On the ball!

MANUEL: On the ball, Papa!

JACINTO: Here it comes. Might be a spit ball, keep your eye on my hand, the hand which is holding the ball, right?

MANUEL: Right!

JACINTO: Good son.

MANUEL: I'm ready!

(Jacinto pitches. Manuel misses.)

JACINTO: Goddam it! You missed the fucking ball!

MANUEL: I am sorry.

JACINTO: Sorry? You are sorry! You gotta concentrate.

MANUEL: I was.

JACINTO: Not good enough.

MANUEL: I am sorry.

JACINTO: Sorry ain't going to get you out of here.

MANUEL: I know. I am sorry.

JACINTO: Sorry will have you end up like me.

MANUEL: What's so bad.

JACINTO: What?

MANUEL: What's so bad with you?

JACINTO: My job.

MANUEL: What's wrong with your job?

JACINTO: Tour guide.

MANUEL: So?

JACINTO: A guide for tourists, French, German, Italians, but mostly gringos.

MANUEL: They come to the Mayan Riviera.

JACINTO: Mostly Texans.

MANUEL: Who can't afford to go anywhere but here.

JACINTO: That's right.

MANUEL: Sorry.

JACINTO: I make my living off a bunch of Texans.

MANUEL: You hate it?

JACINTO: What?

MANUEL: Your job?

JACINTO: It's what I have to do. What I have to do because I have one son, two daughters, another on the way. A wife that takes in sewing. And I live in Playa Carmen, Mexico, and there are thousands, millions. Just like me.

MANUEL: Just like you?

JACINTO: Fucked.

MANUEL: What do you mean?

JACINTO: 'Cause we were born in the wrong country, at the wrong time.

MANUEL: I see.

JACINTO: And I am trying to teach you something that will get you out of here, and you don't care.

MANUEL: I do!

JACINTO: You missed the ball!

MANUEL: Maybe I am no good at this.

JACINTO: Yes, you are.

MANUEL: Are you sure?

JACINTO: You got star potential, big leagues, U.S.A.

MANUEL: I don't see it, Papa.

JACINTO: I do.

MANUEL: I'm trying.

JACINTO: Believe it.

MANUEL: I take it very seriously. I try really hard to get better.

JACINTO: You are not trying hard enough!

MANUEL: What did I do wrong?

JACINTO: You missed the ball.

MANUEL: I know.

JACINTO: You did not concentrate hard enough.

MANUEL: Yes, I did.

JACINTO: Throw the ball back. Come on. Throw the ball to me.

MANUEL: Why?

JACINTO: 'Cause I told you to.

MANUEL: You have so many others right next to you.

JACINTO: But I want that one.

MANUEL: Why, Papa?

JACINTO: To punish you, son.

MANUEL: Punish me. I am punished enough.

JACINTO: No discipline, my son has no discipline.

MANUEL: I'm trying!

JACINTO: Not good enough.

MANUEL: It takes up all of my free time.

JACINTO: It has to!

MANUEL: We practice every day from when I get out of school at three till the sun goes down. That's enough punishment.

JACINTO: You think so?

MANUEL: Yes. I do, Papa.

JACINTO: You don't know what punishment is till you try to survive in this country . . . In this shit hole . . . in Mexico.

MANUEL: America is so much better?

JACINTO: So much more money.

MANUEL: For everybody?

JACINTO: Yes!

MANUEL: You sure?

JACINTO: If you are willing to work for it.

MANUEL: How do you know?

JACINTO: My brother.

MANUEL: Brother? You have a brother?

JACINTO: Yes. I had one.

MANUEL: Where is he?

JACINTO: Up north.

MANUEL: In California.

JACINTO: No. Tijuana.

MANUEL: Tijuana? He never came back here?

JACINTO: We don't speak. He ruined our chances. He got caught. He was supposed to go, then raise enough money so I could follow. But he got caught. Fucking idiot.

MANUEL: You should have gone first. You are smart.

JACINTO: You think so?

MANUEL: Yeah. You speak English.

JACINTO: Your mother. Didn't want me to land in jail. Like my brother. He went there to pick grapes. Went there to farm. To sweat. They need our sweat. But they hate us at the same time. Your mama needed to be here. A place where she knew she was wanted. Where she could starve, but with people that knew her.

MANUEL: Mama would not let you go?

JACINTO: After my brother was sent back . . .

MANUEL: Yes?

JACINTO: I was never able to raise enough to pay the coyotes.

MANUEL: How much money?

JACINTO: Couple of thousand.

MANUEL: Pesos.

JACINTO: Dollars.

MANUEL: Wow! High price.

JACINTO: It is.

MANUEL: I'm sorry. Here is the ball.

(Manuel throws the ball at Jacinto, who catches it.)

JACINTO: But you will get there.

MANUEL: To the U.S.A.?

JACINTO: Yes! Yes, you will! Right?

MANUEL: Maybe I don't want to get there.

JACINTO: Yes, you do.

MANUEL: They don't like us there.

JACINTO: They will . . .

MANUEL: They are building a huge wall.

JACINTO: I know. A wall to keep us out. They are sending an army to find us. The national guard. I read the paper. But we will change all that.

MANUEL: You think?

JACINTO: I know.

MANUEL: How?

JACINTO: For now, you hit this goddamn ball.

MANUEL: I will.

JACINTO: Good!

MANUEL: For you, Papa?

JACINTO: A home run?

MANUEL: I'll try.

JACINTO: But keep your eye on the ball!!

MANUEL: My eye is right on it, the ball, your hand, the pitch . . . Come on!
(*Jacinto pitches. Manuel hits it out of sight.*)

JACINTO: Out of the park! Yes! Good son! You are going to do it? Home run!
Home run!

MANUEL: I don't know, Papa.

JACINTO: Yes! Yes, it is!

MANUEL: It only went down half a block.

JACINTO: A home run! That's what I said, that's what it is, Manuel.

MANUEL: Maybe in this alley, Papa. But not in America.

JACINTO: Don't think that. Don't say that!

MANUEL: We're cockroaches to them. They don't like us.

JACINTO: They like our tequila.

MANUEL: Yeah, tequila and guacamole. That's all.

JACINTO: They like the Dominicans . . .

MANUEL: Do they?

JACINTO: If they can hit.

MANUEL: Like David Ortiz?

JACINTO: They like the Cubans . . .

MANUEL: No, they don't. They hate them.

JACINTO: Not if they can pitch.

MANUEL: Like "El Duque"?

JACINTO: If you can pitch or hit, you get an instant green card.

MANUEL: Really?

JACINTO: Yes.

MANUEL: Are you sure?

JACINTO: Positive. Look at their teams, everybody has a Spanish name.

MANUEL: Maybe they were born there.

JACINTO: No, as soon as a Cuban baseball star defects to Canada, the next day
they are a Yankee or a Dodger. They are welcomed and given millions.
Millions.

MANUEL: That's true?

JACINTO: Yes, it is.

MANUEL: I see.

JACINTO: So hit the ball as if your life depended on it.

MANUEL: I want to be good, Papa.

JACINTO: I will teach you to be great.

MANUEL: Were you good at baseball, Papa?

JACINTO: Never played it till I started teaching you.

MANUEL: Did you like the game?

JACINTO: I'm doing this for you. When you started playing in the streets with your friends when you were eight, you out hit everybody. I knew it would be your way out. All we had to do was train and concentrate. I want you to have a future, son!

MANUEL: Thank you.

JACINTO: Poverty is a terrible thing, son. It takes away your pride.

MANUEL: So does ignorance.

JACINTO: When you become a baseball star, you can read any book you want. Now, your eye on the ball.

MANUEL: Yes.

JACINTO: Pick up the bat.

MANUEL: Yes, Papa.

(Manuel picks up the bat.)

JACINTO: Baseball Hall of Fame, that's what I want for my son.

MANUEL: Eye on the ball.

JACINTO: Good.

(Jacinto pitches. Manuel misses.)

MANUEL: Shit!

JACINTO: Good, you're angry. Come on!

MANUEL: Yeah!

JACINTO: You have to hit it.

MANUEL: Yeah!

JACINTO: Out of the park.

MANUEL: Yeah!

JACINTO: So they'll want you, like the Dominicans and the Cubans and the Venezuelans.

MANUEL: I'm going to do it.

JACINTO: So we can have some money. So your sisters can share in your dignity.

MANUEL: My sisters. Yes!

JACINTO: National League. American League!

MANUEL: Here I come.

JACINTO: Hot dogs, and peanuts and beers.
  (Jacinto pitches. Manuel slams it out.)
JACINTO: Was that a foul ball?
MANUEL: No way. Hell no!
JACINTO: I don't know.
MANUEL: No way.
JACINTO: What?
MANUEL: It went so far down the street neither of us could see it. It had power. Home run.
JACINTO: Yes, it did.
MANUEL: Home run! Papa!
JACINTO: I like that.
MANUEL: What?
JACINTO: Are you beginning to see it?
MANUEL: Yes.
JACINTO: Your future. If you can hit that hard every time. Your future, son.
MANUEL: Will be full of endorsements?
JACINTO: For Nike, son.
MANUEL: Lots of girls?
JACINTO: With big tits, yeah.
  (Jacinto pitches, a strike.)
MANUEL: Fuck, a strike.
JACINTO: A strike is OK, as long as you only get two.
  (Jacinto pitches, a ball.)
MANUEL: Ball. Your fault.
JACINTO: My fault. It's going to click this time. Can you feel it?
MANUEL: I don't know.
JACINTO: Think of the names. David Ortiz, Alex Rodriguez, Palimero, Juan Gonzalez, Sammy Sosa, Vinny Castillo, Ivan Rodriguez, Pedro Martinez, Roberto Clemente, Orlando "El Duque."
  (Jacinto pitches. Manuel hits it hard.)
MANUEL: Wow! Yeah!
JACINTO: That's my son.
MANUEL: That was a home run. Two in a row.
JACINTO: Yes.
MANUEL: Wow!
JACINTO: Now you gotta do it every time.
MANUEL: Every time?
JACINTO: Yes. That's what it takes to get out of here.

MANUEL: Out of Mexico.

JACINTO: Yes. You'll do it?

MANUEL: Every time.

(Manuel grabs the bat.)

JACINTO: Good.

MANUEL: A home run!

JACINTO: Just think of the names. All the stars are Latinos, son, you'll be one of them! Ortiz, Rodriguez, Palimero, Gonzalez, Sosa, Castillo, Martinez, remember the names . . . Now pitching: Fernando Valenzuela, from Sonora, Mexico.

MANUEL: Wow.

(Jacinto gets ready to pitch. Black out.)

END OF PLAY

Crows over Wheatfield (or The Nuance of the Leap)

MARK SAUNDERS

Crows over Wheatfield was given a staged reading by the Cape Cod Theatre Project, July 2006. Directed by Andrew Polk. Cast: Vincent — John Cariani; Seurat — Lee Rosen.

CHARACTERS

VINCENT VAN GOGH: Midtwenties to midthirties. A sign painter, creative, impetuous, passionate, and possibly mad.

GEORGE SEURAT: Midtwenties to midthirties. A sign painter, creative, methodical, and studied, perhaps even a bit slothlike in his movements and delivery.

SETTING

A country road somewhere. Minimal if any set pieces are required. Sound cues for crows and for a gunshot will be required and a tight fade to black just before the gunshot at the end of the play.

TIME

No partiular time.

• • •

Van Gogh's painting Crows over Wheatfield *is the locale for this piece — lifted from nineteenth-century France and placed on a roadside shoulder in the middle of no particular place or time. Set pieces are not necessary though an audio intro of crows (and possibly a brief projection of Van Gogh's painting at the beginning) could aid in establishing setting. Vincent is onstage dressed as he is seen in any number of his self-portraits — work clothes and a straw hat. Props such as paint brushes, cans, a sign on the ground are optional. (Consider that Vincent may be prone to use his brush as agitated punctuation throughout the play.)*

VINCENT: Crows over wheatfield: black crow, yellow ocher, and vermillion wheatfield. Chrome-green grass, cobalt blue, and burnt sienna sky, you can put burnt sienna in the sky just for the hell of it — right? Mood, right? You can establish a mood because it doesn't have to be so goddamn literal all the time. *(Up.)* Does it? *(Sound of distant crows.)* It's the Underpainting. I put Chinese red in the cypresses — you can put the red in the cypresses even if you don't actually see the red — *(Sound of distant crows. Up.)* Well MAYBE IT'S MORE THAN just about draftsmanship, DID YOU STOP TO THINK ABOUT THAT? *(No response from crows as Vincent wipes sweat from brow.)* Cadmium yellow sun — 8:30 in the morning and already a swirling hot sun. That idiot called it an elk — said "I didn't know there were elk around here." *(Up.)* There aren't elk around here. Do you see elk around here? It's a goddamn deer

— a leaping deer: you got a torso, neck, head, legs — *(Up.)* — It's a deer, Gauguin. *(Sound of distant crows.)* Its forelegs are drawn together so that they read visually as one single leg — if he had any graphic literacy he'd . . .

(Vincent slowly scans the horizon until he is facing audience, wiping his bow again.)

VINCENT: It has to be about more than just draftsmanship. *(Up.)* It's got to be more than — that. Well look at your Cezanne. Cezanne knew it wasn't just about draftsmanship. Cezanne's deer — a juxtaposition of flattened planes that abandoned all spatial fealty to allow pure silhouette to convey the essence of the deer, the nuance of the deer's leap and the dire invocation that the deer would be Xing for the next six miles. *(Checks watch.)* Shit — four more signs till break.

(While Vincent has been conducting his rant downstage, George has entered upstage. In paint-splattered clothes and a hat, George carries his brush and two cans of paint by their handles. He walks slowly, deliberately — he comes off as a very deliberate fellow — stopping every half-dozen paces to kneel down and apply paint to something at about chest level. It becomes clear soon through dialogue that he is doing his job — applying paint to milepost markers.)

VINCENT: Anybody can look at a sky and say "blue" or a field and say "brown" — *(Up.)* Putting antlers on a deer does not make it an elk any more than putting a brush in Seurat's hand makes him any kind of a sign paint —

GEORGE: Vincent, is that you?

(Vincent winces, taken aback by George's presence. An awkward beat.)

VINCENT: Hello George. *(Vincent turns to acknowledge George.)* What the hell are you doing here, George?

GEORGE: Milepost four hundred and eight-five. *(George raises his brush.)* Voilá. Who were you talking to, Vincent?

VINCENT: No one.

GEORGE: You were ranting like a madman.

VINCENT: I was yelling at the crows.

GEORGE: To those crows?

VINCENT: To Those Crows — don't sneak up on me like that.

GEORGE: I wasn't sneaking up. I was making as much noise as someone painting dots can possibly make.

VINCENT: Don't sneak up on me like that ever. I carry a gun, you know. *(Beat — and then with some forced civility.)* Nice dot, by the way. Silver?

GEORGE: Metallic. You carry a gun?

VINCENT: You've developed a very strong dot, George.

GEORGE: I've painted seven hundred and five of them between Limoges and Perigueux

VINCENT: Very reminiscent of your milepost work between Avignon and Le Puy.

GEORGE: I've shifting the palette slightly — allowing the metallic to go cooler as I move north.

VINCENT: And the mile numbers?

GEORGE: I keep them black.

VINCENT: It sounds like a breakthrough.

(George swirls his brush in a paint can.)

GEORGE: Well, they're just dots.

VINCENT: They're more than just dots.

GEORGE: They allow vehiclists to see the mileposts at night. Plus, I happen to like dots. Vincent, why do you carry a gu —

VINCENT: Really, George, I think your work — it's about distance. The work needs to be seen from a distance.

GEORGE: They're dots. *(Beat.)* You're unhappy with your Elk Xing?

VINCENT: What?

GEORGE: Your sign is lying there in the field. What is that, Elk Xing?

VINCENT: *(Coldly.)* It's a deer, George."

GEORGE: It has antlers."

VINCENT: It's a deer, George."

GEORGE: I didn't know there were elk in these parts.

VINCENT: *(With growing agitation.)* There aren't elk in these parts — it's a deer, George. Deer Xing.

GEORGE: Why do you carry a gun when you paint?

VINCENT: What?

GEORGE: You said you car —

VINCENT: Forget it, George. What part of it doesn't look like a deer?

(George considers the sign, Vincent's agitated state, and the fact that he carries a gun.)

GEORGE: Now that you mention it, there isn't really any part of it that doesn't look like a deer. a very good deer, actually, and . . . it's leaping —

VINCENT: Xing.

GEORGE: Xing.

VINCENT: For the next six miles.

GEORGE: Exactly. I think your deer convey a real emotional intensity now, Vincent. Why is it lying in the field?

VINCENT: I'm just not feeling the deer anymore. I'm constrained by the palette.

GEORGE: Black.

VINCENT: It's constraining.

GEORGE: It works good against yellow.

VINCENT: I know it does, but the world is not just black against yellow. The world has an underpainting.

GEORGE: Which sometimes can be yellow. *(Beat.)* You're having trouble feeling the deer in black against yellow. *(Beat.)* Is this all about what Gauguin's been saying?

VINCENT: *(Agitated.)* I don't want to talk about Gauguin.

GEORGE: Fine.

(Beat.)

VINCENT: Has he been talking about me again?

GEORGE: *(Shrugging.)* He talks about you down at the garage.

VINCENT: It's all lies, of course.

GEORGE: Of course they are.

VINCENT: I don't want to talk about it. *(Beat.)* What does he say?

GEORGE: You know — that you . . . are not . . . — now I am only quoting —

VINCENT: Of course.

GEORGE: — the things that I hear.

VINCENT: I know.

GEORGE: I mean, I just go in there once in a while to get a coffee

VINCENT: I know, George.

GEORGE: Maybe a donut and Paul is there —

VINCENT: What is he saying, Seurat?

GEORGE: Gauguin suggests that you are . . . maybe . . . not so good . . . a draftsman.

VINCENT: He suggests that I am . . . ? That shitty little primitivist —

GEORGE: I know —

VINCENT: Who is he to talk!

GEORGE: A primitivist.

VINCENT: A shitty little primitivist.

GEORGE: He says your deer look like they only have one leg in front —

VINCENT: *(Up.)* Gauguin's cows — *(Reined in slightly)*. His cows looked like cardboard. Leg in front, leg in back — drawn like they were the same leg. Tanguay gave him the Cow Crossing sign and he couldn't do it.

GEORGE: He says they were Charolais.

VINCENT: White cows — white cows on yellow!

GEORGE: Tanguay had a fit.

VINCENT: White to hide the fact that he Can't Draw Cows. Did you see his cows?

GEORGE: I saw his cows.

VINCENT: He can't draw cows.

GEORGE: He's no Cezanne

VINCENT: You're absolutely right there.

GEORGE: And not like your elk.

VINCENT: Deer, George.

GEORGE: They have horns — *(Stops himself.)* — and not like your deer.

VINCENT: I can draw a goddamned deer.

GEORGE: I really like the feel of your deer even if the draftsmanship is not —

VINCENT: *(Exasperated.)* The forelegs are drawn together so that they read visually as one single leg.

GEORGE: I know that, Vincent.

VINCENT: Gauguin is an idiot.

GEORGE: He should be painting No Passing stripes.

VINCENT: *(Laughing.)* An idiot like Gauguin should be painting No Passing stripes.

GEORGE: *(Laughing.)* Or speed bumps.

VINCENT: *(Laughing.)* Or speed bumps. *(Laughing.)* Or dots. *(Stops laughing.)* No wait, not dots. He can't paint dots.

(Long beat.)

GEORGE: Gauguin has asked for the Truck on a Wedge position.

VINCENT: What? Six Percent Grade?

GEORGE: That's what I hear at the garage.

VINCENT: Truck on a Wedge? They can't give him that job.

GEORGE: I heard he had been considered.

VINCENT: He can't paint trucks.

GEORGE: That's what I heard.

VINCENT: I begged Tanguay last month to let me paint Truck on a Wedge signs. They can't give Gauguin Truck on a Wedge. He said No?

GEORGE: Tanguay said no. With your experience in leaping elk —

VINCENT: Deer, George.

GEORGE: Deer — that they're not even considering you for Six Percent Grade?

VINCENT: Not even considering?

GEORGE: It's an outrage.

VINCENT: Not even considering? What other crap did Tanguay say?

(George stirs his reflective paint reflectively for several beats.)

GEORGE: He asked me . . . if I wanted the job.

(Sound of distant crows.)

VINCENT: Which job?

GEORGE: Six Percent Grade — there sure are a lot of crows over there.

VINCENT: Who did?

GEORGE: Tanguay. Or are those ravens?

VINCENT: Tanguay asked y — Six Percent Grade?

GEORGE: Truck on a Wed —

VINCENT: Six Percent Grade?

GEORGE: Truck on a Wedge. Do you think maybe those are ravens?

VINCENT: They're crows, George. Tanguay asked you if you wanted Six Percent Grade. What the f — ?

GEORGE: I was surprised too.

VINCENT: When?

GEORGE: Last week.

VINCENT: Last week? What the . . . ? Last week he asked you if — ?

GEORGE: Truck on a Wedge.

VINCENT: What the fuck?

GEORGE: Of course, I said I was very happy painting mile marker dots.

VINCENT: Of course you are — an idiot could . . . *(Reining himself in.)* George listen, why are they not considering me?

GEORGE: The dots have been my life, of course.

VINCENT: George.

GEORGE: I've made my mark —

VINCENT: George, shut up! Did Tanguay say why?

(George shrugs and rises to go.)

GEORGE: I told him I'd think about it.

VINCENT: What?

GEORGE: I told Tanguay that I'd think about the position.

(Incredulous beat from Vincent.)

VINCENT: You mean you're taking it?

GEORGE: I mean I'm considering it.

VINCENT: But dots, George. Dots are your life — your mark. What about the fucking mark, George?

GEORGE: I've considered marks to be my life. But maybe it's time to make Truck on a Wedge my life. Tanguay says I have the draftsmanship.

VINCENT: It isn't just about draftsmanship.

GEORGE: A lot of it is. Maybe Tanguay thinks you don't have the line of the deer.

VINCENT: I have the nuance of the deer's leap.

GEORGE: Nuance is nice — and maybe you have the nuance of the Truck on a Wedge too, but not the line. And sometimes the line . . . *(Checks his watch.)* Well, I have four more miles until lunch.
(Beat.)

VINCENT: You know what, George? To hell with the Truck on a Wedge job anyway.

GEORGE: Exactly.

VINCENT: I don't need Truck on a Wedge for fulfillment.

GEORGE: You're right, Vincent.

VINCENT: Did Cezanne need Truck on a Wedge for fulfillment?

GEORGE: No.

VINCENT: And where is Cezanne now!

GEORGE: Accounting I think.

VINCENT: Do you think I need Leaping Deer Next Six Miles? Do you think I need any of this?

GEORGE: Everyone needs a job.

VINCENT: I'm an artist. Do you hear what I'm saying, George?

GEORGE: I do, Vincent.

VINCENT: Yellow ochre wheatfield and burnt sienna in the sky, chrome-green grass, prussian blue barrel — Black crow.

GEORGE: Prussian blue barrel? *(Vincent has pulled out his gun.)*

VINCENT: Underpainting, George.

GEORGE: What are you doing, Vincent?

VINCENT: Would you underpaint a wheatfield with cadmium red?

GEORGE: I don't paint wheatfields.

VINCENT: Wouldn't you put a gun to your chest if dots were all you had to look forward to?

GEORGE: What are you talking about?

VINCENT: A lifetime of painting dots, George.

GEORGE: I've enjoyed dots.

VINCENT: Nobody could blame you, could they?

GEORGE: Blame me for what?

VINCENT: Emptiness, George.

GEORGE: I have my whole life ahead of me.
(Vincent grabs George's hat and flings it into the field.)

VINCENT: Nothing to live for.

GEORGE: That's my good hat.

VINCENT: Go get your hat, George.

GEORGE: *(Realizing that Vincent may be planning to shoot him.)* I'm . . . I'm sure Tanguay could be convinced to consider y —

VINCENT: Your hat.

GEORGE: My hat. *(Beat.)* I better get my hat out of that field. *(George moves upstage, turns to Vincent.)* You wouldn't put cadmium red in a wheatfield, would you?

VINCENT: Don't let your hat blow away, George. *(Vincent watches George walk offstage before calling after him.)* You can put burnt sienna in the sky just for the hell of it — right? Mood, George. You can establish a mood with the underpainting because it doesn't have to be so goddamned literal all the time. *(Up.)* Does it?

(Fade to black. The sound of a gunshot followed by the unsettled caw of crows over wheatfield.)

END OF PLAY

Fragment of a
Paper Airplane

CARLOS MURILLO

Fragment of a Paper Airplane was originally produced at
City Theatre of Miami 13th Annual Summer Shorts Festival,
June 2008. Directed by Stuart Meltzer. Cast: Alvaro —
Paul Tei; Herman — Stephen Trovillan.

CHARACTERS
Herman F.: Midfifties.
Alvaro M.: Late forties.

SETTING
Two eat-in kitchen tables in separate tenement apartments. Herman's kitchen is in Hell's Kitchen; Alvaro's is in Washington Heights.

TIME
The present.

NOTE: Two slashes (//) indicate where an overlap, or stepping on, of the previous line of dialogue begins.

• • •

1.

HERMAN: Valerie P. telephoned at 2:35 this morning.

My telephone hardly ever rings anymore —
People stopped calling long ago.
To most people,
A telephone call that time of night —
How *intrusive*. How *thoughtless*. How *rude*.
But not me, no.
I sleep very little these days.
For all practical purposes
2:35 in the morning is quarter past noon is six forty-five p.m. is three
    minutes to midnight.

What *did* arouse my curiosity about the telephone call
Was the fact that Valerie P. bothered to make it in the first place.
You see:
More than a decade had passed since Valerie P., Javier C., and I
Played at being pioneers. Co-*colonists*
Inhabiting a tiny but shared slice of
Terra
Incognita.

In other words:
We stopped being friends
A long.
Time.
Ago.
Furthermore,
When we were friends —
If we ever *did* speak *telephonically*,
It was because my digits reached for hers.

Yes,
Valerie P. telephoned at 2:35 this morning
To inform me that Javier C.
Her estranged husband
(and father to their mutually estranged daughter *Lila*)
"Left the building" as it were.
This past Tuesday morning.
He drowned.
In a freak
Flash
Flood.
Somewhere in the wilds of Northern New Mexico.
Where Javier C. supposedly was immersed (forgive the pun)
in "research"
For a play he *claimed* to have been working on
for the last seventeen years.
Diagram of a Paper Airplane.
The third of a trilogy of works
That began with the seminal
Death of a Liberal, followed by the *truly* spooky,
The Rich Also Cry —
Two works for the theater noteworthy for their undeserved obscurity.

Hearing the news, the tips of my fingers went cold
A phenomenon followed by a rapid fire slide show of pictures in my
     head:
Moonless night. Arctic Circle.
A dilapidated Japanese fishing boat torn in half by an iceberg.
Japanese fisherman killing each other over pieces of floating debris

While their red and white flag burned in the sky.
I had no time to absorb these images let alone extract meaning from
    them, no
Valerie P. had more on her
Agenda:
Following her fragmentary and emotion-free description
of the circumstances surrounding Javier C.'s death,
She proceeded, without transition,
To ask me a *favor*.

Would I telephone
Alvaro M. (a fellow traveler-slash-casualty of our colonial exploits of
    yore)
And tell him the news.
I told her under no circumstances would I do such a thing.
For all I know Alvaro M. could be dead too,
And besides: I don't have his telephone number.
"Liar," she said.
I tried to reason with her, I said:
"Valerie: The likelihood that Alvaro hasn't moved
In the mountain of time that has passed between then and now . . ."
"Where are you sitting, Herman?" she asked.
"In my kitchen."
"You made a meal for me in that kitchen once upon a time."
"Your point being?"
"And the kitchen I'm sitting in
is the same one you wept in for ten days straight
When Maria F. left you. Once upon a time."
"Your *point. being.*"
"You haven't moved. I haven't moved. In that '*mountain of time*.'
So there's every reason to believe Alvaro M. is festering away in his
    kitchen too."
Then Valerie *reeeaaaally* crossed the line:
"Besides . . . this is what *Javier* would have *wanted*."
Which was cheap. Just cheap I mean
To pull out the "what-the-dead-guy-would-have-wanted" card.
And I told her as much, I said
"Valerie that is just plain cheap I would have expected more from you."
"You don't really know me anymore, do you . . . Herman?

"Call me after you've spoken to him."
Click!
That fucking passive aggressive . . .

So yes, I dug out
The *address* book
And dialed Alvaro M.'s number.

ALVARO: Hal —
    Oh
HERMAN: I hear a voice and I'll be damned
    It's Alvaro's voice
    Sounds older — a little less
    alive
    than I remember it . . .
    But then
    We're all a little less alive every day aren't we?

    Alvaro? Alvaro M.?

    It's Herman.
    Herman F.
ALVARO: Shit.
HERMAN: It's
    good to hear your voice.
ALVARO: Wish I could say the same.
    Hey:
    Didn't I read something about you? Like what?
    Ten years ago?
    Something in the
    What was it, the *Post*? *Daily News*? *Weekly World News*?
HERMAN: Alvaro.
ALVARO: That's right it was in the *New York Times*.
    Pay-puh uh record? Is that what they call it?
HERMAN: Alvaro . . .
ALVARO: Didn't you become like some
    Holocaust denier or some // shit like that?
HERMAN: Oh please, Alvaro // that's just
ALVARO: I read that and I was like "Man,
    I knew Aitch was one fucked-up individual // but . . . "

HERMAN: *Stop it.*

ALVARO: Why you dialing my number after all these years?

You getting all nostalgic cause you about to die or something?

You thinking while you're counting the days you got left on this earth why not make some phone calls? Right some wrongs just in case there is a // Man upstairs?

HERMAN: Hhhhhhhh // hhh

ALVARO: *Big sigh*

HERMAN: Look: I just received a call out of the blue from Valerie.

ALVARO: I'm sorry, Herman. But that name don't ring a bell.

HERMAN: Valerie // you know who

ALVARO: I think I might a known a Mallory once, but a // Valerie?

HERMAN: Valerie P. Javier C.'s ex-wife.

Alvaro?

ALVARO: Cut to the chase, Aitch.

HERMAN: Are you sitting down?

ALVARO: No I'm riding the last stage of the Tour de France, out with it Aitch.

HERMAN: Valerie called me

To tell me

That

Javier C.

Passed on Tuesday

ALVARO: "*Passed.*"

What'd he pass? A kidney stone? His driver's test? The ketchup?

Some of those warped motherfuckin' genes of his — now that would be a // tragedy.

HERMAN: Alvaro . . .

ALVARO: Ohhhh, you mean he *died.* Why didn't you just come out and say that?

(Shift: Alvaro telling the story in the past tense with present-time Herman interjections.)

ALVARO: An I'm like . . . .

Is that why you calling me? To tell me *that?*

An he's like

HERMAN: I thought you of all people   ALVARO: "I thought you of all people
would want to know   would want to know."

ALVARO: In that motherfucking patronizing voice of his like he's God's voice on earth or some shit

An' I'm like: "Thankyouverymuch for ruining my day."

An' he's like . . .

HERMAN: Horrible, isn't it.

ALVARO: An' I'm like . . .

No. I'm sorry.

That's just not something that registers on my horror-o-meter.

I'm glad that motherfucker is dead

HERMAN: Well If you're so glad he's gone

ALVARO: He said "*gone.*" Not "*dead.*" Shit. // What an asshole.

HERMAN: If you're so glad he's gone

how is it I ruined your day?

ALVARO: By telling me that bitch was still alive till last week.

'Cause as far as I was concerned?

Javier C. died a *loooong* time ago

And the *thought*

That he was still out there

Slithering around somewhere

That he still *existed*

Until Tuesday

That just fucks me up like you wouldn't believe.

HERMAN: His reaction was so

Shocking I

I was dumbstruck so I said something

feeble like

"Well,

Alvaro, I

I'm dumbstruck I

Didn't know you felt that way."

ALVARO: Well now you do, Mr. Herman F. Dumbstruck.

HERMAN: Look, I wouldn't have called you if Valerie hadn't asked me to . . .

ALVARO: What? Yoko Ono too delicate to dial the phone all by herself?

HERMAN: That's just —

ALVARO: Look, Aitch.

In like three seconds?

You gonna hear a click, OK?

And when you hear that click

I want you to understand in no uncertain terms what I mean by it:

Bye Bye. An' fuck off.

And *don't*
you ever call this number again. *Comprende, compadre?*
One
Two
Three
HERMAN: And the line went dead.

2.

ALVARO: I used to smoke Kools.
    I loved smoking.
    Sometimes? I would sit in my kitchen all day?
    An' just smoke.
    But I quit cold turkey like a year ago, right?
    Woke up one morning
    Went to the kitchen to do my first chore of the day
    Which was like
    smoke five Kools, drink a pot a coffee an' stare out the window,
    but that day I was like . . .
    "E-nuff. No more. I'm tired.
    Gotta find me something else to look forward to than the next Kool."
    Cause that's how bad shit had got — sit in my kitchen all day
    Only time I left the apartment was to replenish my pack.
    So I went into the kitchen to smoke my last Kool.
    An' I'm thinking this is like my last Kool ever.
    An' I start thinking about all the Kools I ever smoked
    An' I'm looking at the Kool I'm smoking
    An' I'm thinking
    "You're the last one, baby . . . "
    Kind a like breaking up with someone,
    But trying to let 'em down gentle?
    Like, "Aw, yeah, we had some good times, right?
    Remember that time we went to Coney Island in like December?
    An' like that time I got into a fight with my brother on Thanksgiving
    An' I came over an you made me potato salad?"
    But inside you're thinking
    "Gotta go."
    An' I *stubbed* that last Kool out.

'Cause in the end you gotta be hard
You gotta be like Japanese about it.

I picked up the pack,
the lighter an' ash tray off the table
Went over to the kitchen window
Which has like a million dollar view uh the airshaft?
an' the pile a garbage at the bottom of it?
An' I was like:
"Bye Kools. Nice knowing you.
Bye lighter. Have a good life.
Bye ashtray. You be cool now."

I have been clean since.
I keep myself honest.
See:
Like five minutes after I threw my paraphernalia down the airshaft?
I went down to the corner and bought me one last pack a Kools.
Brought it back in my kitchen.
put it in the drawer where I keep the knives.
Temptation's three feet away from me in my knife drawer —
But I *don't* succumb
Willpower, baby. I am the master of my own twisted desires.

Sometimes?
When shit gets real bad
I open that knife drawer
Take out that pack a Kools
Lay it down on the kitchen table
Gentle
An' I look at it
An' sometimes I touch it
An' sometimes —
I take one a the Kools out the pack
Smell it slip it in my mouth
Roll it around my lips
An' I got the lighter in my hands
Thumb on the flint wheel all twitchy
like I'm Christopher Walken playin' Russian roulette

An then I'm like
HA! Motherfucker
I don't need you.
You don't own me bitch.
Lonely, isn't it, in there all alone in the dark with the knives?

A year.

Then that bitch Herman calls me
To tell me that Javier C. "*passed.*"
Like thirty seconds after I hang up the phone?
I'm like *Night of the Living Dead.*
Get up from my kitchen table.
Make a zombie-line to the drawer with the knives.
Take out the Kools.
Zombie-line back over to the kitchen table.
An' I light one up.

I sat there smoking that first Kool in a year
"Hi old friend. Nice to see you. I missed you, baby."
An' five Kools later
I'm all relaxed, thinking that motherfucker Herman. The balls he got
    calling me after all these years,
But then my head starts tripping out —
I start thinking:
How'd Javi die?
Not like it mattered — when you die you die, right? Don't matter if it's
    a heart attack or a shark attack.
But how'd Javi die? (And why am I calling him Javi?)
Was Javi sick?
Was Javi alone?
Did Javi do it to himself?
Did his little girl know — (though she must not be so little no more)?
Did his not-so-little girl even care?
Did Javi live anywhere or was he just roaming?
Was someone gonna bury him? Or was he gonna end up in Potter's
    Field?

And what the fuck did he mean by that?
last motherfucking thing he said to me before he split —
what. the *fuck*. did he mean by that?

Next thing I know?
I reach for a Kool an' the pack is empty.
A year I been away from this shit.
That bitch Herman calls?
Two hours later the whole pack is gone.

Curiosity is killing the cat. My mother warned me about that shit.

I went down to the corner, to buy me another pack.

An' when I came back

I picked up the phone an' dialed . . .

END OF PLAY

Marilyn Gets Ice Cream

DON NIGRO

CHARACTERS

    KNEES: Thirties, a short, pudgy man.

    JAKE: Twenties, a young man.

SETTING

    A Tastee-Freez in Phoenix, Arizona.

TIME

    Evening in March 1956.

• • •

Knees is sitting on a little white wooden bench in a Tastee-Freez, eating a hot fudge sundae. Jake is sweeping up and getting ready to close for the night. There's a faint neon buzz.

KNEES: Those damned beetles.

JAKE: Yeah.

KNEES: There's like a million of them out there.

JAKE: I don't know where the hell they come from.

KNEES: It's the lights. They can't stay away from the lights. They fly head first into the lights and then fall on their backs on the sidewalk and can't turn over and they kick their little legs up in the air until they're exhausted and then you step on them.

JAKE: That's life.

KNEES: That's what happens when you build in the desert.

JAKE: Uh-huh.

KNEES: They got no place to go.

JAKE: I guess.

KNEES: You didn't think it'd be hot this time of year, did you?

JAKE: Not this hot, no.

KNEES: Cools off at night, but still. Love the hot fudge sundae. Best in Phoenix, right here.

JAKE: It's a well-kept secret.

KNEES: You know they fired that girl.

JAKE: What girl?

KNEES: That girl used to come in here, you were looking at.

JAKE: Lots of girls come in here.

KNEES: The real pretty one. The teacher. The second grade teacher. At the school where I work. The really young one. They fired her.

JAKE: They fired her?

KNEES: She's gone.

JAKE: She seemed like a really nice girl.

KNEES: I know it.

JAKE: So why did they fire her?

KNEES: Inappropriate behavior.

JAKE: What does that mean?

KNEES: Thought she was a bad influence on the kids.

JAKE: A bad influence?

KNEES: That's what they said.

JAKE: What kind of bad influence?

KNEES: Well, you know how cute she was.

JAKE: Yeah.

KNEES: She used to wear that little yellow sun dress.

JAKE: To school?

KNEES: No. Not to school. But she looked really nice.

JAKE: You spent a lot of time looking at her, did you?

KNEES: Well, who wouldn't?

JAKE: So what did she do?

KNEES: Somebody caught her.

JAKE: Doing what?

KNEES: They caught her doing something, and she's gone.

JAKE: Maybe she quit.

KNEES: She didn't quit. She was fired. She was crying when she come out of the office. I saw her. You know she lived right down the street there, past the orange grove.

JAKE: Yeah.

KNEES: I used to do odd jobs for her.

JAKE: Well, you're an odd guy, Knees.

KNEES: Don't call me Knees, all right? I don't like it when people call me Knees. My name is not Knees. It's Arthur. My name is Arthur. All right? Not Knees. Arthur.

JAKE: Then why do they call you Knees?

KNEES: Because they're assholes.

JAKE: OK.

KNEES: She used to sun bathe. Out in her backyard. In that little yellow sun dress. Pretty legs. Pretty arms and hands. Perfectly formed. Such a nice girl. So delicate looking. You just wanted to hold her, you know? Comfort her. Some girls you just want to hold. You know?

JAKE: So what do you think she did, to get fired?

KNEES: Well, you know women.

JAKE: Apparently not.

KNEES: So has Marilyn been back?

JAKE: Marilyn who?

KNEES: Marilyn who? Didn't Johnny tell you?

JAKE: Tell me what?

KNEES: I can't believe he didn't tell you. Marilyn was here. Marilyn Monroe.

JAKE: Marilyn Monroe?

KNEES: That's right.

JAKE: Marilyn Monroe was here?

KNEES: In the flesh.

JAKE: What was Marilyn Monroe doing here?

KNEES: Getting ice cream.

JAKE: You saw her?

KNEES: Not exactly.

JAKE: Johnny saw her?

KNEES: We didn't exactly see her.

JAKE: Then how do you know she was here?

KNEES: Big black limo pulls up, OK? Driver gets out. Great big guy. Huge guy. Looks like fricking Primo Carnera. Big as a horse. Comes in, orders two ice cream cones. I'm sitting right here. Johnny's behind the counter. Driver says, you know who I got back there in that limo? And Johnny says, who? And I says, some rich asshole? And the guy says, Marilyn Monroe and Jackie Gleason.

JAKE: No shit?

KNEES: That's what he said. Marilyn Monroe and Jackie Gleason.

JAKE: But you didn't see them?

KNEES: I tried. I walked out there. Thought maybe I could get her to autograph my dick or something. I don't know what I thought. I just wanted to see her. But the windows were all dark. I couldn't see through the glass. It was dark glass. I couldn't see nothing through it. Could have been anybody back there. I was standing two feet from Marilyn Monroe. And there was just this dark glass separating us. I could have reached out and touched her.

JAKE: You'd have had to break the glass.

KNEES: I thought about it. She was close, is what I'm saying. I almost knocked on the glass, to see if I could get them to roll the window down, to see if it was really her. But then that big ass driver came out with the ice cream cones and give me a look that would kill rabbits, so I backed off. The guy was big as a house.

JAKE: I think that guy was just messing with you, Knees.

KNEES: She's in town, you know.

JAKE: She's not in town.

KNEES: Christ, read the paper once in a while. They're making a movie.

JAKE: What movie?

KNEES: I don't know. There's a rodeo in it. They're filming at the rodeo. You heard of the rodeo, right? You're familiar with the concept of rodeos? Well, they're filming at it. The bull roping and all that shit.

JAKE: Yeah?

KNEES: Yeah.

JAKE: Her and Jackie Gleason?

KNEES: No. I don't think he's in the movie.

JAKE: What's he doing here, then?

KNEES: I don't know. We didn't have a chance to have a very deep conversation. He was behind two fricking inches of bulletproof glass. *Bus Stop.*

JAKE: What?

KNEES: That's the name of the movie they're making. *Bus Stop.*

JAKE: There ain't no movie called *Bus Stop.*

KNEES: There will be, when they get done.

JAKE: And it's got a rodeo in it?

KNEES: That's why they're here.

JAKE: What the hell has the rodeo got to do with a bus stop?

KNEES: I don't know. I didn't write the damned thing. All I know is, they're filming some shit at the rodeo, and Marilyn Monroe was here the other day to get an ice cream cone with George Gobel.

JAKE: Jackie Gleason.

KNEES: Whatever.

JAKE: Well, which was it?

KNEES: I don't know. One of them characters. What's the difference?

JAKE: About three hundred pounds.

KNEES: She's staying at George Gobel's hotel.

JAKE: George Gobel is that little runty guy with glasses. Lonesome George. He's a comedian.

KNEES: I know who George Gobel is. George Gobel owns a hotel in Phoenix, and Marilyn is staying at it while she makes this movie about a bus stop at the rodeo, and she went out for ice cream with Jackie Gleason, OK?

JAKE: OK.

KNEES: The hell of it is, I'll never be sure. I'll never know absolutely for sure if I was really that close to her or not. There's no way I can possibly ever know. My whole life is like that.

JAKE: Like what?

KNEES: I mean with women. It's like with Lou Ann.

JAKE: Who?

KNEES: The teacher. The girl who got fired. I was just getting to feel like her and me was, maybe, you know, slowly, kind of, establishing some sort of a relationship, you know?

JAKE: Yeah, right. A girl like that is going to form a relationship with the janitor at the grade school.

KNEES: It could happen.

JAKE: Your relationship was you cleaned up the dog shit in her yard.

KNEES: She used to bring me lemonade.

JAKE: So did your grandmother. Were you having a relationship with her?

KNEES: It was more than just lemonade. Sometimes it was also a doughnut. And she used to smile at me so sweet. In her little yellow sun dress. I think she was really getting to like me. I mean, you know, to get past the way I look, which is not necessarily, at first glance, all that impressive.

JAKE: No kidding.

KNEES: But I felt like, she was a sensitive girl. That she could maybe get beyond that sort of superficial crap. That she was a girl who could actually be capable of some deep human compassion for a person, you know?

JAKE: Is that what she got fired for?

KNEES: She got fired for screwing some guy in the coat room after school.

JAKE: Really?

KNEES: Yeah.

JAKE: How did they find out?

KNEES: Somebody saw her.

JAKE: You mean, some kid?

KNEES: No. Not some kid. It was after school. The kids were gone.

JAKE: Then who saw her?

KNEES: The point is, she was a nice girl. She shouldn't have been doing that.

JAKE: Nice girls do that.

KNEES: Not in the second grade.

JAKE: Who was it?

KNEES: Who was what?

JAKE: Who was the guy she was screwing in the coat room?

KNEES: Just some guy. I don't know. Her fiancé from Nebraska or some damned thing. It just makes me mad, you know? I just start to make a friend, and now she's gone. She moved out. She moved back to Wichita or some damned place. I don't even know where she went. One minute she's there, and the next minute she's gone, and you can't ever get to her again. It's just like Marilyn. She's right there, but she's behind the fucking glass. I can't see her, and I can't touch her. That's what it's like with women. It's like a fucking torture chamber. You're so close, but you can't touch them. You think maybe they like you, but you don't know for sure, and you don't want to touch them, in case they don't want you to touch them, but maybe they want you to touch them, but you're the guy, so you're supposed to make the move, and I never know whether I should make the move or not, and by the time you decide you should make the move, they're gone, or they're eating ice cream in a limo with some damned fat son of a bitch like Jackie Fucking Gleason. It's like the time I met this really nice girl in a bar, and we was actually starting to hit it off, really talking, you know? And then I went up to the bar to get us a couple of beers, and this big ass damned bartender looks down over the bar at me and he says, Hey, buddy, are you really that short, or are you standing on your knees? And the girl laughs, and everybody in the bar laughs, and they start calling me Knees, and now everybody in Phoenix calls me Knees. It's like I'm a fucking walking joke. And then you walk into the damned coat room, and there's the nicest girl you ever met, being fucked like a dog by some shit kicker from Nebraska. It's enough to make a person want to shoot himself in the fucking head. *(Pause.)*

JAKE: Well, we're closing now.

KNEES: Yeah, OK.

JAKE: You off tomorrow?

KNEES: Yeah. I'm goin' to the rodeo. Maybe I'll see her there. Marilyn. When they're filming the movie. At the rodeo.

JAKE: Maybe.

KNEES: Those damned beetles. The light draws them. And then you step on them and they crunch. *(Pause.)* So, you goin' to the rodeo?

JAKE: I don't think so, Arthur.

(The light fades on them and goes out.)

END OF PLAY

PLAYS FOR
TWO WOMEN

Counting Rita

PATRICK GABRIDGE

Counting Rita premiered at the Sargent Theatre, New York City, January 24–February 4, 2001. Produced by StageRight Productions. Directed by Paula D'Alessandris. Cast: Sarah — Jennifer Lorch; Rita: — Sherikay Perry. *Counting Rita* was also produced at the Stanford Calderwood Pavilion, Boston Center for the Arts, May 11, 2008, as part of the Boston Theater Marathon. Directed by Barlow Adamson. Cast: Sarah — Elaine Theodore; Rita — Julie Jirousek.

SARAH: Twenties to forties, Rita's friend.
RITA: Twenties to forties, Sarah's friend.

SETTING
A café, a table and two chairs.

TIME
The present.

NOTE: Ages can be flexible, but the two women should be about the same age. Sarah can have any kind of handheld counter, but it should make a sharp, annoying sound. The kind of clicker used for dog training actually does the trick quite well.

• • •

At rise: Sarah sits at the table, sipping a soda, waiting patiently. Rita arrives, harried.

RITA: Hi, Sarah. Sorry I'm late.
  (Sarah takes a small handheld counter out of her purse and clicks it once.)
RITA: What's that?
SARAH: A counter.
RITA: Why do you have a counter?
SARAH: It's an experiment. Not a big deal, really. Will it bother you?
RITA: No, I guess not.
SARAH: Is something wrong? You look flushed.
RITA: Wrong? No. My guitar lesson ran late, that's all.
Sarah clicks the counter.
SARAH: How are they coming?
RITA: What?
SARAH: The guitar lessons. You must be getting pretty good by now.
RITA: I need to practice more.
SARAH: I'd love to hear you play sometime.
RITA: Oh, I'm still horrible . . . I'm so glad you called. I've been thinking a lot about you.
SARAH: Have you?
RITA: We've kind of lost touch lately.

SARAH: I know what you mean. Whatever happened to being joined at the hip? Movies with the gang, concerts. You weren't at Jeremy's party, and then I hoped you would come apple picking with us, but you vanished again. You've been almost invisible.

RITA: I've been so busy. Too many papers to write. Lots of time at the library. I've been working too many hours at the store. Suddenly it seems like I never do anything fun.

(Sarah clicks the counter.)

RITA: Why are you doing that?

SARAH: I told you, it's an experiment. I'm trying to understand something.

RITA: About speech? About conversation? It's really annoying to have this little clicking in the middle of . . . What is this all about?

SARAH: I'm sorry it's bothering you. I know you like things quiet, inside and out.

RITA: What is that supposed to mean?

SARAH: Nothing.

RITA: See, that's something I don't like. It's very condescending when you do that. That tone of voice. Like you know so much more than me. I know you're smart, we all know you're smart, Sarah. But . . .

SARAH: You're mad at me.

RITA: No, I'm not . . . How could I be? You're sweet. You mean well. I'm insecure. That's all.

(Sarah clicks the counter.)

RITA: You're not going to stop that, are you?

SARAH: No. It's really helping me. It helps me pay attention to what you're saying, deeply. I deeply want to understand you, Rita.

RITA: And that little clicker is going to help?

SARAH: Sort of.

RITA: You've been so weird lately.

SARAH: How would you know? You've been avoiding me.

RITA: I have not been avoiding you. We've just been missing each other.

(Click.)

RITA: But I've heard from the others that you've been acting different.

SARAH: Who? What have they been saying?

RITA: You seem like you're in some sort of odd mental whirlpool. One minute you're laughing, and the next you're in a deep depression. You wander off in the middle of conversations.

SARAH: I didn't think I'd been acting any differently.

RITA: People have noticed. I talked with Julie about you. She has a theory.

SARAH: Enlighten me.

RITA: She thinks you're in love. And not with Jake.

(Sarah clicks the counter, laughing.)

SARAH: Is that what she said?

RITA: Even Jake is curious. He says you've seemed kind of distant.

(Sarah clicks the counter.)

SARAH: You talked with my boyfriend about me?

RITA: Just in passing.

(Click.)

SARAH: And he thinks I'm interested in someone else?

RITA: He didn't say that, not exactly. But, after you talk with enough people, it's easy to get this impression. Maybe it's easier for me to speculate, because I haven't seen you much. I sort of pieced it all together, from a distance. I mean, I know how things go. You've been going together for a long time. Sometimes people lose interest. Maybe you're just a little bored.

SARAH: Listen to yourself. Am I in the middle of a fling? I've always liked that about you, Rita, you're out there. Your best and worst quality, without a doubt. Truly amazing. Am I cheating on Jake?

RITA: Are you?

SARAH: Why do you want to know?

RITA: I'm concerned and curious. Sympathetic even. I'm your friend.

(Sarah clicks the counter.)

SARAH: I'm lucky to have someone to look out for me.

RITA: That's all I want. Just to be sure that you're OK. That everything is OK between you and Jake.

SARAH: And what if I say that I'm fine? That we're fine? That we're ecstatic?

RITA: Is that true?

SARAH: It could be.

RITA: Then I'd be very happy for you.

(Sarah clicks the counter.)

SARAH: Do you know what constitutes the basis of friendship?

RITA: What?

SARAH: Trust.

RITA: And I like to think that I've earned your trust.

SARAH: You're not the only one who's been talking with Julie. Did you know that she has the same theory about you? That you're the one with a new man.

RITA: Where did she get that idea?

SARAH: I'm not the only one who's been distracted. But instead of being depressed, you've been giddy. Bouncing around the room, flushed with excitement. You've been ducking friends, making excuses.

RITA: That's crazy. I am not seeing anyone.

(Sarah clicks the counter.)

RITA: Sarah, you're driving me nuts. We're talking about something very important and you're clicking.

SARAH: Eleven.

RITA: What?

SARAH: That's how many lies you've told since you arrived.

RITA: What lies? I don't know what you're talking about.

(Sarah clicks the clicker.)

RITA: Stop that.

SARAH: Your guitar lessons ended two months ago.

RITA: That's not true.

(Sarah clicks the counter.)

RITA: I'm going to take it away.

SARAH: Your new secret, your fellow member of the stolen moment club, is
my boyfriend.

RITA: I don't know who . . . That's just not true.

(Sarah clicks the counter.)

RITA: Who said something to you? They're lying. It's not what you think. It's
not something that I planned. It just . . . We . . . He said that he . . . I
never meant to hurt you.

(Sarah clicks again.)

SARAH: Fifteen. Just can't stop, can you?

RITA: Give me the clicker, Sarah.

SARAH: No.

RITA: Give me the clicker.

SARAH: Never.

RITA: We are going to talk about this, without an annoying little clicker interrupting every . . . Give it to me or I'll take it away.

SARAH: As long as I have this little counter in my hand, I can remain in control. I have a small physical space on which to concentrate. This counter
is the difference between me sitting here, chatting with you, and me
leaping over the table and choking the life out of you.

RITA: Fine. Keep it. I don't care.

(Click.)

RITA: You want to play little games, that's fine.

(Click.)

SARAH: I'd like to know the truth. If you're capable.

RITA: You know the truth. I hoped that you were through with him, because I don't want to hurt you.

(Click.)

RITA: Because we're friends.

(Click.)

RITA: Because we were friends, and it shouldn't end this way. We've been like sisters.

(Click.)

RITA: That's not a lie.

SARAH: OK, a backstabbing, betraying, lying, scummy sister. If that's what you mean, then I won't argue.

RITA: Fine. You always have to have the last word. Have it. You have the last word, I'll have Jake.

SARAH: Fine. Take him, with my blessing.

RITA: I'm not the only one who lies.

SARAH: But you have so much more practice.

RITA: Good-bye, Sarah. I'm sorry.

(Click. Rita leaves in a huff. Sarah sips her soda and looks at the counter, and then suddenly looks up, recognizing someone offstage.)

SARAH: Jake! Over here. *(To herself.)* Just let me reset this little . . .

(Lights out.)

END OF PLAY

Critical Care

BARA SWAIN

Critical Care was originally produced by Heartland Theatre
Company, Normal, Ill., May 29–June 21, 2008, as part of the
Annual 10-Minute Play Festival. Directed by D. Ann Jones.
Cast: Carol — Victoria Hill and Ann White; Theresa — Laura
Walsh. (Note: The character of Carol was double-cast.)
Critical Care was also produced at Payan Theatre, New York
City, October 15–19, 2008, as part of The Goldberg
Variations: An Evening of Short Plays.
Directed by Fred Murhammer. Cast: Carol —
Judy Chesnutt; Theresa — Olivia Roric.

CHARACTERS

    CAROL: Forties or fifties.

    THERESA: Twenties or thirties, Carol's daughter.

SETTING

    Twenty-four-hour diner.

TIME

    Winter, graveyard shift, 1:30 A.M.

• • •

At rise: Carol and her daughter, Theresa, are sitting at a table for four in an empty coffee shop. Theresa is wearing jeans and red high heels. Carol is carelessly dressed. Their winter coats are hung over the back of a chair. The downstage chair is empty. On the table are menus, two cups of coffee, milk and sugar. In the background, the sound of a siren is heard over the softly playing music. Lights up on Carol, who empties several sugar packets into her coffee.

CAROL: So I ran down the Coleman West corridor and up four flights of stairs to the Coronary Care Unit. And there's your Aunt Evelyn in front of the nurse's station crying, "Help! Help! I was just swallowed whole by a hungry red fox!"

THERESA: She wore her new fur coat to the hospital?

CAROL: Bingo! With a red fox handbag that cost more than your college education, Theresa. So I'm trying to catch my breath, and Evelyn plants her hands on those childbearing hips of hers, and she says to me, "Carol, did you read Walter's Discharge Plan!?" And I unbuttoned my designer coat from K-Mart, and I said to my sister, "What are you talking about, Evelyn? Walter never left the hospital! He's back in critical care, for God's sake!" *(Raising the pitcher of milk.)* Do you want some milk?

THERESA: I'll drink it black, Mom.

CAROL: And then I said — in my very best "inside" voice, I said, "It's the middle of the night, Evelyn. I'm missing my favorite rerun of *Everybody Loves Raymond* just to be with you, Evelyn. What else do you want?"

THERESA: That's a loaded question.

CAROL: Yeah, well your aunt tosses her head back and looks down her aquiline nose at me like I stole her prom date or something.

THERESA: You did, Mom.

CAROL: What?

THERESA: You stole Aunt Evelyn's prom date. Everyone knows that.

CAROL: Oh, that's water under the dam.

THERESA: I think it's a bridge, Mom.

CAROL: Water under the damn bridge, then. God, this coffee is hot.Hot and strong — *(She adds some more milk.)* — like Evelyn's first husband.

THERESA: Mother!

CAROL: What?

THERESA: Poor Aunt Evelyn.

CAROL: Yeah, right. So then your poor Aunt Evelyn — not! — says to me for the second time in thirty seconds, "Carol," she says, "did you or did you not read Walter's discharge plan!?" And her hips are wigglin,g and her nose is flaring, and I'm thinking to myself: Is this a trick question? And — why do nostrils flare in instead of out? And then — just then, I remembered something else, Theresa. I remembered a piece of paper lying next to your Uncle Walter's dinner tray yesterday. And so I said to my sister, "What are you talking about, Evelyn? Are you talking about that piece of colored paper?" *(To Theresa.)* Honestly, Theresa, it wasn't even lined! It was just a plain, stupid sheet of light . . . a sort of light purple-colored paper.

THERESA: Lavender?

CAROL: More like a bruise.

THERESA: Mauve?

CAROL: Bingo! The color of that awful bridesmaid dress I wore to Evelyn's second wedding.

(Theresa laughs.)

CAROL: Zip it up, Theresa. That will never, ever be a laughing matter to me. I mean it!

THERESA: It was twenty-five years ago, Mom.

CAROL: Well, it seems just like yesterday. Are you ready to order?

THERESA: No, I want to know what Aunt Evelyn said.

CAROL: Oh, she just turned redder than your Fuck-Me pumps —

(Theresa laughs again.)

THERESA: They were on sale, Mom!!!

CAROL: Uh-huh. And I said to her, "Evelyn, for the last time, it was just a loose sheet of goddamned paper lying next to Walter's chicken breast and string beans with blanched almonds, and it said things with bullets. You know, like: Bullet. Make sure you get your blood work done when you leave the hospital, and . . . Bullet. Don't forget to make a follow-up appointment with your doctor. And — " *(Whispering.)* Oh my God, Theresa! Don't look now, but there's a drop-dead handsome busboy wiping down the counter.

THERESA: Mother . . . ! "Bullet."

CAROL: Right. "Bullet: Get a medical alert. Ask your son, Evelyn," I said. "He was there."

THERESA: I thought Jimmy went to the orthodontist yesterday.

CAROL: He did. We met afterwards, and I took him over to the hospital to visit his dad. I thought it would be a nice surprise, right?

THERESA: Right.

CAROL: So then your Aunt Evelyn says to me — excuse me — she roars at me. Wait — did I say "roar"? I meant, she bellows at me: "Are you saying that you read Walter's discharge plan in front of our son!!?" And I was dumbstruck, you know? Really, I felt . . . struck dumb or something, and I said, "Jimmy is fifteen years old, Evelyn. He knows algorithms, for crying out loud. He can conjugate verbs, for God's sake! He tried pot!"

THERESA: He did?

CAROL: I don't know. He looks like a pothead.

THERESA: Did you say that to her, Mom?

CAROL: No, I didn't say that to her. I said, "Yes, Evelyn, yes. I read it in front of Jimmy."

THERESA: Did you beat your chest, too?

CAROL: No, I did not beat my chest.I said, "I had no choice, Evelyn, because your husband kept crossing his legs." "Walter," I said, "you just had a triple bypass. You should keep your legs elevated and uncrossed." And so your uncle uncrossed his legs, speared another green bean, and then he did it again!

THERESA: I don't get it.

CAROL: His legs. He crossed them again. Like this.
(Carol pushes out the empty chair and lifts her legs up. She raises her right leg up high and crosses it over the left.)

THERESA: Sorry, Mom.

CAROL: I'll do it again. Observe, Theresa. *(She raises her leg up higher this time and holds it in the air. Then She crosses her raised leg over the other. She looks at Theresa for her reaction.)* Oh, for God's sake. Do I have to spell everything out for you, too? "Evelyn," I said, "every time Walter crossed his bandy little legs, I got a ringside view of the family jewels."
(Theresa laughs.)

CAROL: Jimmy must've seen his father's whang-bone, too, but he didn't say a word. And, of course, I didn't say anything.

THERESA: Of course.

CAROL: I just . . . averted my eyes and picked up some reading material. At least, I thought it looked like reading material and so I read it. Aloud.

THERESA: You read Uncle Walter's discharge plan?

CAROL: Yeah. NO! It was a piece of goddamned mauve paper!

THERESA: Uh-huh.

CAROL: OK, so shoot me. Yeah, I did it! And you know what else I felt like saying to your precious aunt?

THERESA: Don't hold back, Mom.

CAROL: Honest to God, I wanted to say to her, "Evelyn, I looked in your closet last week, too, and I counted eleven winter coats." That's right, Theresa, plus three lined raincoats, cross my heart and hope to live long enough to use my new George Eastman Grill.

(Theresa laughs.)

CAROL: What's so funny now?

(Carol grabs Theresa's menu, leans forward, and smacks her on top of her knuckles. Carol keeps poking her with the menu while Theresa laughs.)

CAROL: Let's see who laughs last when I master Chicken la Poive with Baby Asparagus —

(Carol smacks the menu on top of Theresa's head several times. Theresa laughs hysterically.)

THERESA: Stop it, Mom!

CAROL: — or Caribbean Tuna with Mango Salsa and a side of sliced Portabello Mushrooms!

THERESA: Cut it out, Mom! I can't breathe!

CAROL: Go tell your Uncle Walter. I don't think he'll be too sympathetic, either.

THERESA: Mother!

CAROL: What?

THERESA: He's in critical care!

CAROL: Bingo! He's like eighty years old, Theresa!

(Carol prepares to give Theresa another wallop. Theresa cowers, protecting her head.)

THERESA: And . . . ! you're making a scene, Mom.

(Carol thinks about it. She drops her arm. Then she slides the menu toward Theresa.)

CAROL: I concede.

THERESA: Thank you.

CAROL: Even though there's no one else in this place except for you and me and a well-hung busboy. *(Quickly.)* Sorry.

THERESA: Apology accepted.

(Theresa opens her menu and studies the selections carefully. Silence. Carol studies her daughter. Another siren moans in the background.)

CAROL: I feel terrible about your uncle Walter. You know that, don't you?

THERESA: Of course you do, Mom. We all do. *(She looks up from the menu.)* So what do you think about splitting a BLT? Or do you want to just order a couple of appetizers?

CAROL: I want you to promise me something.

THERESA: OK, here's the deal. If we order Jumbo Shrimp Cocktail and Potato Skins with Bacon and Cheese, I promise that you can have four of the shrimp and all of the sour cream, and I'll have two shrimp and all of the bacon. How's that?

(Theresa smiles at her mother. Carol leans forward.)

CAROL: Honey, pay attention. I need you to give me your word on something. It's important to me.

THERESA: Go for it, Mom.

CAROL: If I ever get like Uncle Walter . . . ?

THERESA: Uh-huh.

CAROL: . . . just roll me in front of a car, OK?

THERESA: Mother!

CAROL: Or push me off the roof. That should do it.

THERESA: You're out of your mind! Where do you come up with these things?

CAROL: I just don't ever want to be that kind of burden to you, Theresa. Or to your husband.

THERESA: Mother, I'm not married! And I'm not getting married! Not even close.

CAROL: But you will some day.

THERESA: Nuts! You're absolutely nuts!

CAROL: *(Ignoring her.)* Now listen to me carefully, Theresa. If you aren't able to do it yourself, then ask your aunt Evelyn. She can be a little squeamish, but I don't think she'd mind putting a plastic bag over my head while I'm sleeping. Can you do that for me?

THERESA: Aunt Evelyn won't do it either, Mom!

CAROL: Of course, she will. Just make sure my hair has a little bounce to it. I don't want Evelyn criticizing my thin hair.

THERESA: This is ridiculous!

CAROL: This is funny — not! . . . but your Aunt Evelyn has always been very, very . . . exceptionally critical of me over the years and —

THERESA: Don't, Mom.

CAROL: And I know that's no surprise to you, Honey. But Evelyn is my sister and I love her —

THERESA: It's not worth it, Mom.

CAROL: — even though she takes more pride in her goddamned Burberry raincoat then me. And better care of it, too.

THERESA: Mom. Forget about it.Let's not get into it. Let's just order. *(Theresa calls out.)* WAITRESS!

CAROL: I'd do anything for her. You know that, Theresa, don't you?

THERESA: Yes, Mom. What do you want to eat?

CAROL: I love her. And all I ever really wanted was for my sister to —

THERESA: Shh, Mom. Please, let's order. Now what do you want?

CAROL: What do I want?

(She stares at Theresa. Then Carol picks up the menu. She stares at it.)

THERESA: *(Gently.)* What do you want, Mom?

(Carol looks up. She appears grief stricken.)

CAROL: *(Whispers.)* It's not on the menu. *(Silence. Carol raises her voice.)* It's not on the menu. *(Carol rises, holds onto the table and cries out in anguish.)* WAITRESS! IT'S NOT ON THE MENU!!!

(Lights dim to black.)

END OF PLAY

The Grand Scheme

JACK NEARY

The Grand Scheme was first produced at the Stanford
Calderwood Pavilion, Boston Center for the Arts, May 11,
2008, as part of the Boston Theater Marathon.
Directed by Jack Neary. Cast: Clarice — Ellen Colton;
Bethel — Bobbie Steinbach.

CLARICE: Around sixty.
BETHEL: Around sixty.

SETTING
A nondescript waiting room in any building, anywhere. All we really need to see are two old folding chairs, side by side.

TIME
The present.

• • •

Clarice sits in one of the chairs, holding a single sheet of paper. She is dressed smartly. She looks at the paper, appears to memorize something from it, then "reads" the line silently, with expression. She tries this line a couple of different ways, silently. Bethel enters, also dressed smartly, unseen by Clarice. Her first reaction when she sees Clarice is one of disappointment, almost disgust. "Oh, damn, she's here too" is the basic reaction. She watches as Clarice silently tries the line a time or two more. As Bethel speaks, she yanks her own single sheet of paper out of her bag.

BETHEL: Are we the only two broads left in this town they call in for stuff like this? *(She sits.)*
CLARICE: *(Not thrilled.)* Apparently.
BETHEL: I usually don't come in for this theater. They usually just call with an offer.
CLARICE: I never come in here. Just a call with an offer. Is what I get.
BETHEL: The director is new to the area. Rick asked me to be seen. I'm here to be seen as a personal favor to Rick.
CLARICE: *(Beat.)* Because I'm here now, Rick owes me a personal favor.
BETHEL: Seriously, they're not seeing anybody else?
CLARICE: Gretchen was leaving when I came in.
BETHEL: So it's just you and me.
CLARICE: It's you and me and Gretchen.
BETHEL: *(Beat, assessing Gretchen.)* So it's just you and me.
CLARICE: Right. *(They read.)*
BETHEL: So, they called you for . . . ?
CLARICE: The lead. *(Long beat.)* You? *(Bethel reacts; takes.)* Oh. Of course. You too. *(Again, they read.)*

BETHEL: Did you read the play?

CLARICE: I read it. What, you think I'd come to an audition without reading it?

BETHEL: It's a new play. I didn't know if you got your hands on it.

CLARICE: I read it at the Equity office.

BETHEL: *(With some meaning.)* Oh.

CLARICE: Oh? What do you mean "Oh"?

BETHEL: Well . . . I have my own copy. I'm personal friends with the playwright.

CLARICE: How personal?

BETHEL: *(Beat.)* It's personal. He sent me the play on a pdf.

CLARICE: Yeah?

BETHEL: Yeah.

CLARICE: What's a pdf?

BETHEL: *(Beat; it's a struggle.)* It's a thing . . . you get an e-mail . . . and on the e-mail . . . it says . . . "download."

CLARICE: What says download?

BETHEL: The e-mail.

CLARICE: So it says download. So what?

BETHEL: So you click on it.

CLARICE: On what?

BETHEL: On the download.

CLARICE: What's a download?

BETHEL: It's on the e-mail.

CLARICE: What happens when you click on it?

BETHEL: It downloads.

CLARICE: The download downloads?

BETHEL: What else would it do?

CLARICE: So you click on it, you get a download.

BETHEL: No, you click on it, you get the pdf.

CLARICE: What's the pdf?

BETHEL: The play.

CLARICE: Oh. *(Beat.)* What does pdf mean?

BETHEL: *(Grasping valiantly.)* Play . . . downloads . . . fast.

CLARICE: Oh.

BETHEL: It's a computer term.

CLARICE: Oh. *(They read.)* You'd think, for the lead, they'd want more than just a speech.

BETHEL: You'd think . . . It's an all right speech . . . It gives the essence.

CLARICE: Which is what you need. Of course. The essence.

BETHEL: Essentially. *(Again, they read.)*

CLARICE: Should we try it?

BETHEL: You mean in front of each other?

CLARICE: Yes. We don't have a scene. But we can watch each other do the speech . . .

BETHEL: Oh. All right. *(Rises, steps to the side.)*

CLARICE: And critique.

BETHEL: *(Beat, zips back into chair.)* You first.

CLARICE: Why me first?

BETHEL: Because if I go first, you'll steal my reading.

CLARICE: Why do I want to steal your reading? I have my own reading.

BETHEL: You do now, but once you see my reading you will assimilate . . . And emulate.

CLARICE: So I should go first?

BETHEL: Yes.

CLARICE: I should let you assimilate and emulate.

BETHEL: Well . . . we both know that won't happen.

CLARICE: Why won't it?

BETHEL: Well, for me, it's just . . . not . . .

CLARICE: Not what?

BETHEL: Necessary.

CLARICE: You think your reading of this speech is so good you can't learn anything from me?

BETHEL: My reading is definitive.

CLARICE: *(Beat.)* Lemme hear it.

BETHEL: I just told you I don't want you to . . .

CLARICE: I won't assimilate. I won't emulate. I want to show you how not only will I not steal from you, I will also, with my reading, transcend your definitiveness. *(Beat.)* See, I can use the big words, too. Go.
(Bethel freezes, then relents and rises to prepare. She clears her throat.)

CLARICE: Phlegm?

BETHEL: What?

CLARICE: Is that how you're starting the speech or is that phlegm?

BETHEL: *(Beat.)* It's phlegm.

CLARICE: Good. I just want to make sure if I start with phlegm that you don't think I'm emulating.
(Bethel gives Clarice the slow burn, then begins the speech. When she can,

she removes her eyes from the page. Her reading is soapy and melodramatic, with hammy gestures.)

BETHEL: "I took it, Desmond. Is that what you want me to say? All right. I took it. There. I said it. I took it and I said it. Yes, it's true I wanted you to think Tanya took it. I regret that. But once it was taken it was too late to tell you it was taken by me and not by Tanya. It never occurred to me that telling you that Tanya took it would be tantamount to . . . to . . ." *(She pauses in the scene. Clarice reaches for her piece of paper, looks at it mumbling "to . . . to . . . ," then notices Bethel's glare.)*

CLARICE: Oh! *(Points to paper.)* You're acting. Sorry. Thought you needed a line.

BETHEL: *(Another slow burn, then:)* "It never occurred to me that telling you that Tanya took it would be tantamount to . . . betrayal. Until now. Now I know. I know and you know. The question, Desmond . . . The question is . . . now that I know, and now that you know . . . now that we both . . . know . . . The question is . . . Does Tanya know? You know what I think, Desmond? I think . . . I think . . . no." *(She stops, lowers paper.)* It reads better than it plays.

CLARICE: Doesn't seem to have as much essence when you get it on its feet.

BETHEL: No.

CLARICE: Not a hell of a lot to emulate there.

BETHEL: You try it, you think you can do any better.
(Clarice rises with the paper as Bethel takes a seat. She prepares and acts. Her reading is more thirties gangster.)

CLARICE: "I took it, Desmond. Is that what you want me to say? All right. I took it. There. I said it. I took it and I said it. Yeah, it's true I wanted you to think Tanya took it. I regret that. But once it was taken it was too late to tell you it was taken by me and not by Tanya. It never occurred to me that telling you that Tanya took it would be tantamount to . . . betrayal. Until now. Now I know. I know and you know. The question, Desmond . . . The question is . . . now that I know, and now that you know . . . now that we both . . . know . . . The question is . . . Does Tanya know? You know what I think, Desmond? I think . . . I think . . . *(Forgets, looks at the paper.)* . . . no."

BETHEL: *(Long beat.)* I'm waiting for you to say, "You dirty rat."

CLARICE: What?

BETHEL: She's not a mobster, Clarice. She's a suburban matron.

CLARICE: To you, maybe.

BETHEL: What do you mean to me, maybe? It's in the play! It's in the story!

CLARICE: I'm interpreting! I'm an interpretive actress!

BETHEL: This is your interpretation? She gets caught by her lover and she turns into *Angels with Dirty Faces*?

CLARICE: *(Moves back to chair.)* Hey, you know, do it like you do it. Agnes Moorehead is dead, maybe you'll have a chance.

BETHEL: What do you mean, Agnes Moorehead?

CLARICE: I mean if there happens to be any scenery in that room when you go in, it won't be there when you come out.

BETHEL: You've never understood my layers.

CLARICE: Your what?

BETHEL: My layers! When I play a character, I go to the core and add layer after layer after layer after layer until the sum and substance of the character is achieved.

CLARICE: How many layers we talkin' about here?

BETHEL: What?

CLARICE: I counted four.

BETHEL: You're impossible.

CLARICE: I'm just thinkin' maybe you should back off after maybe the second or third layer. Stop at sum. Fuck substance. Give us all a break.

BETHEL: I should know better than to argue with an amateur.

CLARICE: *(Long, long beat.)* What did you say?

BETHEL: You heard me.

CLARICE: I'll have you know that I've been getting paid for it since I was twenty-seven years old.

BETHEL: I'm sure you have. But I was talking about acting.

CLARICE: I've forgotten more about acting than you'll ever know.

BETHEL: I agree. I saw you in *Lost in Yonkers*. You forgot about acting from page fourteen on.

(They sit and steam for a long moment. Finally, they seem to relax a bit.)

CLARICE: Why do we constantly insult each other?

BETHEL: Maybe . . . maybe because there's nobody else left worth insulting.

CLARICE: Gretchen.

BETHEL: You see my point.

CLARICE: *(Nods.)* Hmm.

BETHEL: Tell you what. You go in. Do your audition. I go in. I do mine. One of us will get the part. That's just the way it is. Whoever gets it will support the other. Friendship is more important than rivalry.

CLARICE: You're right. What's acting? It's a game. It's a lark. In the grand scheme, it's nothing. Friendship. Loyalty. That's everything.

BETHEL: Exactly. The grand scheme.

(Offstage, we hear a voice say, "Clarice!")

BETHEL: Go. Enjoy. Be wonderful. You always are.

CLARICE: Thank you.

(Clarice holds Bethel's hand a moment, then rises and steps toward offstage.)

BETHEL: And Clarice . . .

CLARICE: Yes, Bethel.

BETHEL: If there's anything . . . you saw . . . by chance . . . in my reading . . . anything you think might work for you . . . please . . . use it. I give you my blessing.

CLARICE: Thank you so much.

BETHEL: The truth . . . I think my reading . . . I think it's a good fit for you. I have a good feeling.

CLARICE: You may be right. *(Thinks.)* Yes. You may be right.

BETHEL: I am. Go. Go.

(Clarice walks off, mouthing the beginning of the speech in the soapy manner Bethel used, using whatever hammy gestures Bethel employed. Bethel waits, then smiles demonically. She stands up, clears her throat, and begins working on the speech using Clarice's gangster method. Clearly, she believes this is the way to go. If anything, her delivery is more Cagney than Clarice's . . .)

BETHEL: "I took it, Desmond. Is that what you want me to say? All right. I took it. There. I said it. I took it and I said it. Yeah, it's true I wanted you to think Tanya took it. I regret that . . . you dirty rat!"

(As Bethel smiles triumphantly. Black out.)

END OF PLAY

PLAYS FOR
ANY COMBINATION
OF MEN AND WOMEN

A Figment

Ron Weaver

A Figment was first produced at Barestage Theatre,
Red Bluff, Calif., September 7, 8, 21, 22, 2007. Directed by
Alyssa Larson. Cast: Character 1 — Alyssa Larson; Character 2
— Sabrina Schloss. *A Figment* was also performed at the
Nantucket Short Play Competition and Festival, Nantucket,
Mass., May 23, 24, 29, 30, 31, 2008. Directed by Bruce Yancy.
Cast: Character 1 — Kevin Mohler;
Character 2 — Vince Vailloux.

CHARACTERS
  CHARACTER 1: A man, any age, but older than Character 2.
  CHARACTER 2: A man, any age, but younger than Character 1.

SETTING
  An empty stage.

TIME
  The present.

• • •

At rise: Character 1 is pacing up and down with script in hand. He is making dramatic flourishes with one hand as he rehearses Hamlet.

CHARACTER 1: To be or not to be . . . To be or not to be, that is the question . . . That is the question.
  (Character 2 enters carrying a script.)
CHARACTER 1: Good, you're here. Let's rehearse.
CHARACTER 2: Not to be!
CHARACTER 1: What?
CHARACTER 2: Not to be here.
CHARACTER 1: What's that mean?
CHARACTER 2: Look, pal, it's been nice knowin' ya. I want out.
CHARACTER 1: Why?
CHARACTER 2: I wanta live. I want wine, women, and snowboarding. In that order. Or maybe women and then wine. Snowboarding is definitely third.
CHARACTER 1: That's not probable.
CHARACTER 2: Nonsense. I wanna be a noir detective. A great lover. I wanna be seen in fast cars with fast women drinking slow gin. Mostly, I want outta here.
CHARACTER 1: You may get your wish. The life span of a figment is short.
CHARACTER 2: Who's a figment?
CHARACTER 1: You are.
CHARACTER 2: Ridiculous. A figment of what?
CHARACTER 1: A figment of the playwright's imagination.
CHARACTER 2: Are you telling me that I only exist in the playwright's mind?
CHARACTER 1: As a character in his play, yes.

CHARACTER 2: Oh, go on.

CHARACTER 1: I'm not kidding, we're in his play now.

CHARACTER 2: We're in somebody's play right this minute?

CHARACTER 1: Of course. *(Points to the audience.)* Look out there. What do you see?

CHARACTER 2: People in seats looking at us.

CHARACTER 1: That's right. The audience.

CHARACTER 2: How'd they get there?

CHARACTER 1: Paid money.

CHARACTER 2: To see us?

CHARACTER 1: That's right.

CHARACTER 2: Are they crazy?

CHARACTER 1: No, they just want you to be a little bit entertaining.

CHARACTER 2: I said, pal, I want out!

CHARACTER 1: Do you know Pirandello?

CHARACTER 2: Who's he?

CHARACTER 1: He's the playwright who showed that play characters need authors, or they are adrift and miserable.

CHARACTER 2: I'm miserable because I'm here.

CHARACTER 1: But you only live in the play.

CHARACTER 2: Not true! I'll live anywhere I please, thank you.

CHARACTER 1: No you won't. You're a figment. You can't exist outside of the playwright's mind.

CHARACTER 2: Stop calling me a figment! I'm standing right in from of you.

CHARACTER 1: And I'm standing in front of you. That doesn't mean that we're not figments.

CHARACTER 2: Listen, pal, I don't wanna be a figment. I don't wanna be in a play. And I certainly don't wanna be here. So, I want out of this whole deal.

CHARACTER 1: You'll have to talk to the playwright about that.

CHARACTER 2: How?

CHARACTER 1: Call him on the phone. *(Hands Character 2 a cell phone, which he takes, then gives back.)*

CHARACTER 2: On second thought, I'll call my agent. He'll get me out of here.

CHARACTER 1: You don't have an agent.

CHARACTER 2: What d'ya mean?

CHARACTER 1: Characters don't have agents.

CHARACTER 2: Then why do I have an agent's name rattling around in my head?

CHARACTER 1: That's the actor's agent.

CHARACTER 2: What actor?

CHARACTER 1: The guy who's speaking your lines.

CHARACTER 2: There's somebody speaking my lines?

CHARACTER 1: Yes, I told you we're in a play.

CHARACTER 2: You told me I was a character.

CHARACTER 1: You are a character . . . And an actor.

CHARACTER 2: First I was a character, now I'm an actor.

CHARACTER 1: That's right.

CHARACTER 2: What is this? Who's on first?

CHARACTER 1: No! No! Those were two other guys.

CHARACTER 2: OK, we're not those two other guys, but I'm a character and —

CHARACTER 1: An actor.

CHARACTER 2: I don't like it. I still want out.

CHARACTER 1: The actor won't allow it.

CHARACTER 2: Why?

CHARACTER 1: He's Equity.

CHARACTER 2: So?

CHARACTER 1: He gets paid for doing this. If you go out, he loses his weekly check.

CHARACTER 2: I'll explain it to him. He'll understand.

CHARACTER 1: Go right ahead. Explain.

CHARACTER 2: Uh. Duh-uh. Uh-duh. The words I want won't come out.

CHARACTER 1: Of course not. You're like a dummy. Somebody else puts the words in your mouth.

CHARACTER 2: Who does that?

CHARACTER 1: The playwright gives your words to the actor.

CHARACTER 2: You mean I can't say what I want to?

CHARACTER 1: That's right.

CHARACTER 2: That does it! I won't be dictated to. I'm calling the playwright. Hand me the phone.

(Character 1 hands cell phone to Character 2.)

CHARACTER 2: What's his number.

CHARACTER 1: It should be in your head. After all, you're a figment.

CHARACTER 2: Stop calling me a figment! I don't know his number.

CHARACTER 1: *(Points to button on phone.)* Push that button. It's automatic.

CHARACTER 2: *(Pushes button and listens.)* Lines busy. You ever talk to him?

(Character 2 hands phone back to Character 1.)

CHARACTER 1: Only when I'm in his head.

CHARACTER 2: When's that?

CHARACTER 1: Not often. Sometimes in the shower. Once when he was boffing a blond.

CHARACTER 2: Stop! I don't want to hear anymore. I'm getting out of here.

CHARACTER 1: How?

CHARACTER 2: *(Points at the audience .)* I'm going to walk right out there.

CHARACTER 1: You can't do that. There's a wall between us and the audience.

CHARACTER 2: See those people out there. *(Points at the audience.)* Do you see a wall?

CHARACTER 1: I certainly do. It's called the fourth wall.

CHARACTER 2: Ha! You fool. There's no wall. I'm leaving. Good-bye. *(Walks to front of stage and abruptly stops.)* Ouch! What the hell, something punched me in the nose.

CHARACTER 1: You bumped into the fourth wall. Now do you believe me?

CHARACTER 2: I tell you there is no . . . *(Puts hands up and pantomimes a wall.)* Well, goddamn, there is a wall!

CHARACTER 1: I know. Wait, my phone is vibrating. *(Pulls phone from pocket.)*

CHARACTER 1: Hello. Yes, he's here. It's for you.

CHARACTER 2: Who is it?

CHARACTER 1: The playwright.

CHARACTER 2: It's about time. I'll tell him a thing or two. *(Takes phone from Character 1.)* Hello . . . yes, this is your character speaking. Listen, Mr. Playwright, as a character, I'm unhappy. I don't like it here. I want out. If you don't let me . . . You're what . . . You would do that . . . You would . . . Hey, that's fine by me jerk. Good-bye!

(He hands phone back to Character 1.)

CHARACTER 1: So, how'd it go?

CHARACTER 2: He's terminating my character.

CHARACTER 1: You're finally out. That's what you wanted.

CHARACTER 2: I guess. What happens to me now?

CHARACTER 1: Oh my God, I've seen this before!

CHARACTER 2: What?

CHARACTER 1: I can't watch.

(Character 1 turns his back on Character 2. Character 2 looks bewildered at the audience. Tries to speak but no sound comes out. Cups his hands around his mouth; tries to shout. No sound. Looks puzzled. Becomes very loose, sagging like a marionette, slowly collapses into a heap on the stage.)

CHARACTER 1: *(Turns around and faces the audience.)* You saw the whole shameful performance. *(Points to Character 2.)* Look at that pathetic heap. What can a playwright do with an incorrigible character except kill it? That is called character assassination. *(Bows to the audience.)* And now, dear friends, the play is over. *(Turns and touches Character 2.)* Stand up and take a bow.

(Character 2 stands up, walks to the front, and bows. Character 1 stands behind him and signals for the audience to applaud.)

CHARACTER 2: *(To the audience.)* Thank you for your warm applause. It means so much to us characters.

CHARACTER 1: *(To Character 2.)* And actors.

CHARACTER 2: *(To the audience.)* Yes, the actors too.

CHARACTER 1: Well done.

(They turn to leave.)

CHARACTER 1: You're lucky to get out of this a figment.

CHARACTER 2: Stop calling me a figment!

CHARACTER 1: Enough! Let us retire to the dressing room. The actors are taking us to dinner.

CHARACTER 2: Who's paying?

CHARACTER 1: They are.

CHARACTER 2: It's about time.

(They exit arm in arm.)

END OF PLAY

Tech Support

Henry Meyerson

Tech Support was originally produced at Chatham Playhouse, Chatham, N.J., July 25–August 2, 2008, as part of Jersey Voices One Act Festival. Directed by Joann Lopresti Scanlon. Cast: Actor 1 — Terri Sturtevant; Actor 2 — Stacey Simon.

CHARACTERS
    ACTOR 1.
    ACTOR 2.

SETTING
    Two chairs stage right and stage left facing the audience as far from each other as the stage permits. The impression should be they are in separate rooms.

TIME
    The present.

NOTE: The gender or age of each actor is irrelevant, thus the pronouns used in the script can be tailored to fit the actors.

• • •

At lights, Actors 1 and 2 sit in chairs. Actor 1 dials his cell phone. His impatience grows with each beat.

ACTOR 1: *(Speaking into the phone.)* 212-555-5432. *(Beat.)* Yes. *(Beat.)* Yes. *(Beat.)* No. *(Beat.)* Tech support. *(Beat.)* Land phone. *(Beat.)* No. *(Beat.)* My cell phone. *(Beat.)* 212-555-9876. *(Beat.)* No dial tone. *(Beat.)* On my land-line phone, damn it. Fucking computer prompts. *(Beat.)* Sorry. *(Beat.)* Thank you. *(Beat.)* You're just a goddamned computer voice, for Christ sakes so don't make a big deal out of it. *(Beat.)* Hello? Hello? Shit. *(Actor 1 dials his cell phone. He has calmed down.)*
ACTOR 1: *(Carefully, timidly.)* 212-555-5432. *(Beat.)* Yes. *(Beat.)* Yes. *(Beat.)* No. *(Beat.)* Tech support. *(Beat.)* Land phone. *(Beat.)* No. *(Beat.)* My cell phone. *(Beat.)* 212-555-9876. *(Beat.)* No dial tone. *(Beat.)* On my land-line phone. *(Beat.)* Yes, I'll hold . . .
ACTOR 2: *(Wearing a telephone head set.)* Can I help you?
ACTOR 1: Is this tech support?
ACTOR 2: Tech support, that's right.
ACTOR 1: Thank God!
ACTOR 2: You have indeed reached the omniscient one. How can I be of assistance?
ACTOR 1: I'm having trouble with my phone.
ACTOR 2: The one you're using?

ACTOR 1: No. My land-line phone.

ACTOR 2: Are you using your land-line phone now?

ACTOR 1: No, I can't use it. That's why I'm calling.

ACTOR 2: Then which phone are you using?

ACTOR 1: My cell phone.

ACTOR 2: Are you having trouble with the cell phone?

ACTOR 1: No. That's the phone I'm calling from.

ACTOR 2: What is the phone number?

ACTOR 1: Of which phone?

ACTOR 2: The one you're using.

ACTOR 1: But I'm not having trouble with the one I'm using.

ACTOR 2: Sir, before I can pull up your account, I need to know the number of the phone.

ACTOR 1: The one I'm using or the one I'm calling about?

ACTOR 2: The one you're calling about.

ACTOR 1: 212-555-5432.

ACTOR 2: That's the land-line phone?

ACTOR 1: That's right. I think we are making some progress.

ACTOR 2: I don't handle tech on land-line phones, sir.

ACTOR 1: Why didn't you tell me that before we . . . ?

ACTOR 2: Hold on, please. I'll connect you.

(Long pause during which time Actor 1 becomes increasingly enraged, and Actor 2 dances around the stage laughing his ass off. Actor 2 sits.)

ACTOR 2: *(In an accent of the Asian subcontinent.)* May I be of assistance?

ACTOR 1: Am I calling at a bad time?

ACTOR 2: We are of assistance seven days a week, twenty-four hours a day, sir.

ACTOR 1: Very reassuring.

ACTOR 2: Yes. Thank you, sir. Now how may I be of assistance?

ACTOR 1: I am having trouble with . . .

(Actor 2 placing his hand to his mouth makes a loud farting noise into the phone.)

ACTOR 1: What was that noise?

ACTOR 2: Where I live we call it Delhi Belly. I believe I had some bad curry for lunch.

ACTOR 1: Where am I talking to?

ACTOR 2: Boise, Idaho.

ACTOR 1: You don't sound like someone from Boise.

ACTOR 2: That's because I'm not originally from Boise.

ACTOR 1: India, right?

ACTOR 2: Why would you think that?

ACTOR 1: At this point I really don't know.

ACTOR 2: In fact, I am from Chicago.

ACTOR 1: Interesting. Look, I am calling you from my cell phone because I am having trouble with my land-line phone. There is no dial tone. Are you the right person to speak to?

ACTOR 2: You have reached the perfect person, sir. I am the tech expert on no dial tone problems for land-line phones.

ACTOR 1: Great, now . . .

ACTOR 2: But before we continue, because I don't want to waste your time, sir . . .

ACTOR 1: Waste more time, you mean.

ACTOR 2: Sir, I am merely trying to be of cordial assistance.

ACTOR 1: Yes, I'm sorry, but I have been on the phone now . . .

ACTOR 2: On the land-line phone?

ACTOR 1: NO, DAMN IT. I JUST TOLD YOU . . . I'm so sorry. I'm getting a little strung out, here.

ACTOR 2: I do not like to be abused, sir. It is no picnic for me, either, living in Boise, Idaho, having to listen all day to people who don't know how to use a phone. So if we may proceed in a more civil manner . . .

ACTOR 1: Yes, of course. I promise to behave.

ACTOR 2: As I was saying . . .

(*Actor 2 unleashes another fart into the phone and noiselessly has convulsive laughter.*)

ACTOR 2: Excuse me again, sir. I will go to that restaurant tonight and give them a good piece of my mind. I should know better than eat curry in Boise, Idaho.

ACTOR 1: Can we get back to . . . you know . . . ?

ACTOR 2: Ah, yes. I was saying, before we waste any more of your valuable time, tell me please, did you buy the land-line phone, the one whose dial tone is missing, did you buy that phone with cash, a check, or with a credit card.

ACTOR 1: (*Pause as he senses trouble brewing.*) Which one do you handle?

ACTOR 2: I am not permitted to tell you that, sir.

(*Actor 1 gives this a lot of painful thought.*)

ACTOR 1: It will go badly for me if I pick the wrong one, won't it?

ACTOR 2: It is a quandary, that's for sure, sir.

(*Actor 1 paces, wrings his hands, pulls at his hair.*)

ACTOR 1: Credit card.

ACTOR 2: Nice chatting with you, sir. One moment and I'll connect you to the right person.

(Actor 2 begins to dance around the stage as if he just scored a touchdown in the Super Bowl, beside himself with glee.)

ACTOR 1: *(Agonizing sound, a sound that would frighten demons.)*

(Actor 2 sits. With a grand flourish he removes his headset and disconnects the wires.)

ACTOR 1: Hello. Hello. Anyone there? *(With increasing volume.)* IS THERE ANYONE THERE. HELLO? HELLO? ANYONE?

(Crushed, Actor 1 slowly begins to weep. This slowly changes to anger, then rage. He begins to slam his cell phone on his desk. The slamming becomes increasingly violent as stage fades to black.)

END OF PLAY

What's the Meta?

ANDREW BISS

What's the Meta was first performed at FirstStage, Los Angeles,
May 25, 2008. Directed by John McDonald.
Cast: Part 1 — Darin Sanone; Part 2 — James Schendell.

CHARACTERS
    Part 1: A written part in a script.
    Part 2: A written part in a script.

SETTING
    A stage.

TIME
    The present.

NOTE: Both parts can be performed by any age, race, gender/orientation, etc., and in any combination thereof.

• • •

Two Parts on a stage in tableaux. After a moment, Part 1 emits a deep sigh. Part 2 turns and looks briefly at Part 1 before returning to his or her original pose. Soon after, Part 1 elicits another deep sigh.

PART 2: *(Again, looking back at Part 1.)* Is something wrong?
    (Beat. Part 1 shrugs off the question dismissively.)
PART 2: I asked you a question.
PART 1: I know.
PART 2: Well? What's the matter?
PART 1: You wouldn't understand. Don't worry about it.
    (Beat.)
PART 2: All right, first of all you have but the most rudimentary knowledge of who I am — me — so to assume that I wouldn't understand is presumptuous to say the least, and more than a little condescending. And secondly, I have to worry about it because I'm alone out here with you and a show's about to begin, so if there is a problem, I freely and openly admit to harboring a desire to see it resolved as quickly as possible. OK?
    (Beat.)
PART 1: Whatever.
PART 2: *(Enraged.)* What? How dare you — dare you! — you, as thoughtfully transcribed literature, utter that mindless catchall phrase that is the embodiment of total, unmitigated verbal and mental atrophy.
PART 1: It's not my fault. *(Beat.)* I'm a victim of circumstance.

PART 2: What circumstance? What's your problem? Stop whinging and just out with it.

(Beat.)

PART 1: I'm . . . I don't have . . . I lack motivation.

(Beat.)

PART 2: That's it?

PART 1: Yes.

PART 2: So what's the big deal? I don't have it either. Most people don't. We just have to force ourselves. Force ourselves to go on.

PART 1: I can't. There's nothing there.

PART 2: I know it feels that way sometimes, but you just have to buck up and press on.

PART 1: Oh yes, it's all right for you, isn't it?

PART 2: What do you mean?

PART 1: Because you're . . . fleshed out.

PART 2: No I'm not.

PART 1: Compared to me you are. You're multidimensional. I'm just a cipher. A convenient device thrown in by the writer to expound upon a certain point of view.

PART 2: But you're relevant. You have relevancy. You're integral to the story.

PART 1: Only in a narrative sense. I don't really belong.

PART 2: Don't be so self-pitying.

PART 1: I'm not, I'm just being honest.

PART 2: Look, a major and completely unexpected plot point hinges upon your sudden appearance in the proceedings. Without you the play wouldn't be turned on its head at the end of act one, leaving the audience breathless and gasping in anticipation — on a good night, at least.

PART 1: That's very kind of you, and I know you mean well, but I'm not so underwritten as to be painfully aware of the fact that I'm just a tool. And I can accept that — I can. But not happily.

PART 2: I think you're being a bit hard on yourself, don't you?

PART 1: *(Defensively.)* I'm not being hard on myself. It was all I was given.

PART 2: Then make the most of it.

PART 1: Oh, right! Say's you. It's all right for you — it's all downhill for you. You get to reveal a multitude of levels and depths as you continue your ninety-minute journey from point A to point B. Your character's arc gradually draws the audience in and endears you to them in ways that initially they would never have dreamt possible, leaving them satisfied and intrigued. Much to their astonishment, this person that they found themselves initially repulsed by turns out to be a complex and all too human representation of someone that they can empathize and identify with. As they walk out of the main door into the night air, they feel buoyed from a sense of having spent an evening and some hard-earned money in a rewarding and enlightening manner . . . with you.

PART 2: What's wrong with that?

PART 1: Nothing at all. But it wasn't my journey they were taking, it was yours. I was just a plot point.

PART 2: A vital one.

PART 1: In your story.

PART 2: In the story.

PART 1: In your story. I am a catalyst — nothing more. I have no depth. I have no raison d'etre. I have no inner life. *(Beat.)* And I damned well want one and I don't care who knows it!

PART 2: I think you've already started to give yourself one, don't you, the way you're carrying on?
(Beat.)

PART 1: Perhaps. Perhaps it's a start. *(Beat.)* But I shouldn't have to fight for it, and that's my point.

PART 2: Why not? Anything in this life worth a damn is worth fighting for.

PART 1: Maybe so, but it's so much harder for me, don't you see, because I . . . I lack —

PART 2: *(Impatiently.)* Motivation — yes, yes, yes, I got that part.

PART 1: There's no need to be so testy. It's not my fault I was underwritten.

PART 2: No, but it's not mine either. I didn't ask to be written as a bigger part. I didn't ask to be more absorbing and relevant to the current state of the human condition. You're behaving as if it were some sort of competition.

PART 1: Oh, "absorbing" are we now?

PART 2: *(Uncomfortably.)* Well . . . I'm speaking theoretically, of course. I mean . . . that's the writer's intention, it's nothing to do with me. I'm not saying that I'm personally absorbing, I'm just reflecting the viewpoint of —

PART 1: Is this preshow, by the way?

PART 2: What?

PART 2: This.

PART 1: This? No.

PART 1: Then what is it?

PART 2: It's, uh . . . it's pre-preshow.

(Beat.)

PART 1: What's that?

PART 2: It's sort of like . . . Off-Off-Broadway.

PART 1: Meaning?

PART 2: Well, it's not there, but it's not quite there either . . . so it's sort of almost not quite there.

PART 1: Where's there?

PART 2: Somewhere else.

PART 1: Sounds very ephemeral.

PART 2: Yes it is — and that's the beauty of it. And by the way, you're sound-
ing more dimensional by the minute.

PART 1: Oh, thank you. Against type, I might add.

PART 2: Indeed.

PART 1: Come to think of it, I meant to ask you about that earlier — are we
characters?

PART 2: *(Astonished.)* Us?

PART 1: Yes.

PART 2: No, no, no, of course not. I'm happy to see you become a little more
well rounded but don't get overinflated at the same time.

PART 1: Then what are we?

PART 2: Words! We're just words. Well, not just words. Words are the most
important part. But after all, we mustn't get too far ahead of ourselves
— we still only exist on paper.

PART 1: Then why are we here?

PART 2: I'm not here.

PART 1: You're not?

PART 2: Of course not.

PART 1: Am I?

PART 2: No.

(Beat.)

PART 1: *(Dispirited.)* But I . . . I thought I was a character. Or at the very least
. . . struggling to become one out of what little I am.

PART 2: No, no, no, there you go again — you have it all wrong.

PART 1: Then what am I?

PART 2: *(Implicitly.)* Ink on paper.

(Beat.)

PART 1: That's all?

PART 2: "That's all"? You ingrate! Don't you have the slightest conception of
what that means? You are the conception, you fool! You are the birth.

Without you nothing happens. Without you there is no play. Without you there is no novel, no film, no poem, nor any of their bastard relations. You are the seed — the root of it all.

PART 1: *(Ingenuously.)* I don't feel like it.

PART 2: Not you in yourself, necessarily, but in what you represent. You are ink on paper. From quill to laser jet printer, you are and always will be the beginning. Others may mold you and shape you according to their will — for better or worse — but you will always be the font, in every sense of the word. It's what you are.

(Pause.)

PART 1: Gosh . . . I'd never thought about it like that. All of a sudden I . . . I don't feel so sketched out and plot-convenient. Thank you. Thank you very much.

PART 2: I'm glad. And don't thank me — they weren't my words.

(Pause.)

PART 1: So what's next?

PART 2: Preshow.

PART 1: And that is?

PART 2: When the others take over.

PART 1: Take over what?

PART 2: Us.

PART 1: Which, in strict definition, means?

PART 2: Strictly speaking I wouldn't like to say, but which includes — though is by no means limited to . . . makeup, gargling, vocal exercises, diarrhea, frantic last-minute line readings, focus, pace, sense memory recall, and stumbling around in the dark trying to find your spot, praying to God that you do before the lights come up and expose you as a co-conspirator in the enormous piece of artifice that you are attempting to lay before a potentially skeptical, though willingly complicit public.

(Beat.)

PART 1: Good heavens! *(Beat.)* I think I'll just sink back into the paper and relax for a while, if it's all the same to you.

PART 2: Trust me, I'm about to do the same thing.

(Beat.)

PART 1: *(Awkwardly.)* By the way . . . well . . . if you don't mind my asking . . . are you male or female?

PART 2: Didn't you read the play?

PART 1: *(Somewhat embarrassed.)* Yes, but . . . mostly my bits . . . skipped the rest. It was a quick read.

PART 2: *(Reprovingly.)* Then shame on you. As I told you before, big or small we are all part of a whole and our acknowledgment of that is the only way we can function properly — all working together. If you don't have the last little piece you'll never complete the puzzle.

PART 1: Sorry.

PART 2: Anyway, does it matter?

PART 1: What?

PART 2: My gender?

PART 1: Not to me.

PART 2: So why ask?

PART 1: Well . . . I was just wondering if you fancied going for a drink — with me.

PART 2: Now?

PART 1: Only if you want to. I'm not trying to . . . no strings . . . I just . . . well, I sort of like you . . . in a way, and . . . anyway . . .

PART 2: As a matter of fact, I would love to — I am, quite literally, dying for a drink. Let's leave them to do what they will — good, bad, or just plain incomprehensible.

PART 1: And perhaps afterwards I could show you a bit of my subtext I've been working on.

PART 2: Easy tiger, let's not get carried away. One step at a time.

PART 1: Sorry, I wasn't trying to . . . *(Gesturing.)* Anyway, after you.

PART 2: *(Gesturing.)* No, no, I insist — after you. *(Beat.)* Did you have somewhere in mind?

PART 1: *(Begins exiting.)* No, do you?

PART 2: *(Begins exiting.)* No, but I know a nice place on 46th and First.

PART 1: *(Upon exiting.)* Sounds like a good place to start.

PART 2: *(Upon exiting.)* And end.

(The light fades to black.)

END OF PLAY

PLAYS FOR THREE OR FOUR ACTORS

PLAYS FOR
ONE MAN AND
TWO WOMEN

The Chocolate Affair

STEPHANIE ALISON WALKER

The Chocolate Affair was first produced at Glendale
Community College, Glendale, Calif., June 6, 2008, as part of
the Motel Chronicles Series. Directed by Kim Turnbull.
Cast: Beverly — Mary Claire Garcia; Mr. Goodbar —
Chris Beltran; M&M — Nancy Yalley.

CHARACTERS

BEVERLY: Thirty-three, quite thin but used to be fat.

MR. GOODBAR: Anywhere between nineteen and fifty, attractive to Beverly. He is a fine piece of candy.

M&M: Younger than Beverly. She is strong in her convictions and though she can be tough, many find her to be a candy-coated piece of happiness.

SETTING

A seedy motel room.

TIME

The present.

• • •

Lights up on Beverly — well put together, slim, and wearing flattering and feminine business attire. She cradles a plastic Halloween pumpkin filled with candy. She looks around the room and carefully sets the pumpkin on the bed. She looks at it for a beat, then closes the blinds, shutting out any hint of the outside. She sits on the bed next to the pumpkin.

BEVERLY: This is crazy.

(She looks at the pumpkin. Then away. Then at the pumpkin. And away. At the pumpkin. Away. Then she practically lunges at it, reaches in and pulls out a piece of candy. She holds the candy before her. She sniffs it, deeply inhaling its scent. She unwraps it and carefully takes a bite. Slowly. Savoring every morsel. She moans. This is ecstasy. She digs back into the pumpkin and excitedly dumps all the contents onto the bed. She rolls around in the candy. Laughing. Devouring piece after piece after piece. She begins to choke. And then recovers. She's silent for a few moments. Long enough for sadness to set in.)

(Mr. Goodbar appears and sits next to her on the bed. He puts his arm around her.)

MR. GOODBAR: Don't be sad, Bev.

BEVERLY: Holy crap!

MR. GOODBAR: Whoa, whoa, whoa. It's OK.

BEVERLY: Who are you? What are you doing here?!

MR. GOODBAR: You brought me here.

BEVERLY: I . . .

MR. GOODBAR: You brought all of us here. *(He gestures to the candy on the bed.)*

BEVERLY: You're . . .

MR. GOODBAR: Mr. Goodbar.

BEVERLY: I've had way too much sugar.

MR. GOODBAR: Are you OK, Bev?

BEVERLY: I shouldn't be here.

MR. GOODBAR: You wanted to be alone with us.

BEVERLY: Yes.

MR. GOODBAR: Have another piece of candy.

BEVERLY: I shouldn't.

MR. GOODBAR: If you can't eat candy when you're alone in a seedy motel room, when can you?

(He hands her a piece of candy. She eats it. It makes her happy.)

MR. GOODBAR: That worked, didn't it?

BEVERLY: Yeah.

(He sits on the bed with legs outstretched and leans against the headboard.)

BEVERLY: I love chocolate and peanuts.

MR. GOODBAR: That's me. Mr. Goodbar. Chocolate and peanuts.

BEVERLY: I love you.

MR. GOODBAR: C'mere.

(She lies back against him holding the pumpkin on her stomach.)

MR. GOODBAR: Have another.

(She reaches and grabs a minibag of M&Ms. She rips it open and pulls out an M&M.)

M&M: Stop!

BEVERLY: Who said that?

(An M&M enters in person form.)

M&M: What the heck do you think you're doing?

BEVERLY: I'm . . . I'm . . . nothing. Nothing.

MR. GOODBAR: For your information, she is giving herself a break.

BEVERLY: Yeah.

MR. GOODBAR: A well-deserved break.

BEVERLY: Well-deserved.

MR. GOODBAR: Hard-earned.

BEVERLY: I work so hard.

MR. GOODBAR: And she never gets to eat candy.

BEVERLY: Never. I never do.

M&M: But this isn't your candy to eat.

BEVERLY: Yes it is.

M&M: No it's not. It's Sally's candy.

MR. GOODBAR: Sally?

M&M: Sally. You know. Ten years old. Pigtails. Pirate.

MR. GOODBAR: Oh, the pirate girl. *(To Beverly.)* Is this true?

BEVERLY: No.

MR. GOODBAR: Bev?

BEVERLY: It's not true.

M&M: It is true. Your daughter Sally earned this candy. She trick or treated for this candy.

MR. GOODBAR: You stole this candy from your daughter?

BEVERLY: I didn't steal it.

MR. GOODBAR: And she made such a cute little pirate.

BEVERLY: She's a pirate every year.

> *(She reaches for another piece of candy, and M&M fights her for it. They fight over the candy.)*

M&M: It's not yours!

BEVERLY: Give it!

M&M: I won't let you eat your daughter's candy!

BEVERLY: But I'm helping her!

> *(Beverly rips the candy away from M&M and eats it.)*

MR. GOODBAR: You're helping her?

BEVERLY: Yes.

MR. GOODBAR: *(To M&M.)* See? She's helping her.

M&M: How is she helping her?

MR. GOODBAR: *(To Bev.)* How are you helping her?

BEVERLY: Sally's not allowed to eat candy.

M&M: Oh please.

BEVERLY: It's true!

M&M: That's pathetic.

BEVERLY: The kids at school . . . they make fun of her. They call her Miss Piggy.

MR. GOODBAR: Oh, that's awful. Kids are so mean!

BEVERLY: She comes home in tears some days and won't tell me why. But I know why.

M&M: Because she's fat?

BEVERLY: *(Softly.)* Yes.

M&M: So she's a chubster, huh?

MR. GOODBAR: M&M, have some tact.

BEVERLY: She can't help it. She just loves candy so much. And Tater Tots. And pizza and chips. The other kids eat the same things, and they don't get fat. How is that fair? It's not. Not one bit. The other day, I caught her melting cheese on a plate. To eat. As a snack. Just cheese melted on a plate.

M&M: That's disgusting.

BEVERLY: And of all the candy in the world, M&M, you're her favorite. She loves you the most.

MR. GOODBAR: That's sweet. I'm not jealous.

M&M: So Sally's a little chubby McChubster. A piggly wiggly.

MR. GOODBAR: Stop!

M&M: A roly-poly pirate girl?

MR. GOODBAR: Wait a second. The pirate girl was skinny.

M&M: Right. She was a beanpole. The only pig feature about her were her tails.

MR. GOODBAR: So Sally's not fat?

M&M: Sally — Bev's daughter, the pirate girl, the rightful owner of this here candy — is not fat.

MR. GOODBAR: Bev? Is this true?

(Beverly ignores the question and eats another piece of candy.)

MR. GOODBAR: It's all a lie?

M&M: You bet it's a lie.

MR. GOODBAR: I don't understand. What kind of person . . .

M&M: Come on Goodbar, let's get out of here.

MR. GOODBAR: Beverly . . . why?

M&M: Don't talk to her. She's pathetic! Help me with the candy.

(M&M starts gathering it up. Mr. Goodbar doesn't move.)

M&M: Come on, Goodbar! Help me.

MR. GOODBAR: Bev?!

M&M: Grab the candy.

MR. GOODBAR: Talk to us, Bev!

M&M: Save your breath. She's just gonna lie.

BEVERLY: I can't take it anymore!!

(M&M stops. A long beat. They watch Bev.)

BEVERLY: I'm up every day at five. Every day. Up at five, go for a jog, take a shower, wake Sally, cook breakfast — something healthy — egg whites, flax, kale, organic coffee, sprouted wheat. Sit down with Dave and Sally for breakfast. Eat a tiny portion. Be sure to leave some on the plate. Always leave some on the plate.

Get dressed. Something feminine, flattering. Kiss Dave good-bye. Make sure to give him a little something worth coming back home to.

Check on Sally. Comb her hair. Pack her lunch. Wait with her for the bus. Hug her good-bye. Make sure that hug lasts all day long . . . that she feels your arms around her even at recess when the mean kids pick on her because their moms don't hug them enough. Then let go. Watch her walk away, board the bus.

Choke back your tears. Taste the salt slide down the back of your throat. Go back inside. Check yourself in the mirror. Ugh. Turn around. Turn back hoping to see someone else. Cross through the kitchen. Pause. Feel the quiet of the empty house. No one watching. What can you eat? Open the pantry, look inside. Grab the jar of peanut butter. Unscrew the lid. Take a whiff. Stick your finger in the jar of peanut butter. Lick it off. Feel someone watching you. Shit. Turn around to face them. No one's there. Put the peanut butter away. Wash your hands, careful to remove any trace of peanut butter. Reapply lipstick. Head out the door. To work. Again.

(A long pause.)

M&M: *(A revelation.)* You used to be fat.

MR. GOODBAR: M&M!

M&M: Oh, please. I know her type. *(To Beverly.)* How much?

BEVERLY: My stomach hurts.

M&M: A hundred? Huh? How much?

MR. GOODBAR: A hundred what?

M&M: Pounds. *(To Beverly.)* Come on. How much did you lose?

BEVERLY: This isn't fun anymore.

M&M: She stole hard-earned Halloween candy from her daughter, ditched work, and checked herself into a seedy motel to eat it.

BEVERLY: There's something wrong with me.

MR. GOODBAR: She can't help it.

BEVERLY: I'm a terrible person.

M&M: I'd bet at least 110. Am I right? You lost 110 pounds?

MR. GOODBAR: Why 110?

M&M: She's got at least another whole person in here. *(She points at her head.)* And she walks like she used to waddle.

(Beverly throws a piece of candy at M&M and hits her in the head.)

M&M: Ouch!

MR. GOODBAR: That wasn't nice.

BEVERLY: You're supposed to make me feel better.

MR. GOODBAR: It's OK. Here. Have a Kit Kat.

BEVERLY: I don't want a Kit Kat.

MR. GOODBAR: Sure you do. It always makes you feel better.

(She takes the Kit Kat and unwraps it. She takes a bite and disappears into her happy place.)

M&M: No amount of candy will be enough to bury it for good. To make you forget about the chubby little girl nobody loves who melts cheese on a plate and sneaks french fries when nobody's looking and eats M&Ms like we were candy-coated pieces of happiness.

MR. GOODBAR: You are candy-coated pieces of happiness.

M&M: Thank you. I mean, we try.

(She finishes the Kit Kat. Swallows slowly and reaches for another piece.)

M&M: You better not.

MR. GOODBAR: Yeah, you probably shouldn't.

BEVERLY: Why?

M&M: Uh, cuz you'll get fat.

BEVERLY: I'm already fat.

MR. GOODBAR: No.

BEVERLY: Yes.

M&M: She's fat on the inside.

MR. GOODBAR: M&M!

M&M: *(To Beverly.)* Maybe you should . . . *(Looking at the bathroom.)* . . . you know. *(Sticking finger down throat.)*

BEVERLY: I don't do that!

MR. GOODBAR: Then what are you gonna do?

M&M: What are you gonna tell Sally?

MR. GOODBAR: She'll probably be missing her candy.

M&M: And Dave.

MR. GOODBAR: You'll just have to go back and pretend like this never happened.

M&M: Buy more candy for Sally.

MR. GOODBAR: Fill up the pumpkin. Put it back in her room. Cook a healthy dinner.

M&M: Vegan butternut squash soup and baby arugula salad.

MR. GOODBAR: With pine nuts.

M&M: With pine nuts.

MR. GOODBAR: Just pretend this never happened. You can do that. You're good at pretending.

M&M: Lying.

BEVERLY: I stole candy from my own daughter.

MR. GOODBAR: It's OK.

BEVERLY: She could eat this whole pumpkin and not gain a pound.

M&M: Poor Sally.

BEVERLY: I won't do it again.

MR. GOODBAR: I know.

BEVERLY: Vegan butternut squash soup.

MR. GOODBAR: And baby arugula salad.

BEVERLY: With pine nuts.

MR. GOODBAR: A healthy supper.

BEVERLY: We'll sit down at the table.

MR. GOODBAR: Like any other day.

BEVERLY: And say grace.

MR. GOODBAR: And it will all be OK.

BEVERLY: OK.

M&M: And if not . . .

MR. GOODBAR: We're always here for you.

   (A long beat.)

BEVERLY: (I wish I didn't need you.) I know.

   (Lights fade to black as Beverly slowly puts herself back together.)

END OF PLAY

Life Is Just a Bowl of Cellos

Ann L. Gibbs

Life Is Just a Bowl of Cellos was first produced at
Second Story Theatre, Hermosa Beach Community Center,
Hermosa Beach, Calif., October 25–26, 2008, as part of the
Hermosa Beach Writers Group's First Annual Ten-Minute Play
Weekend. Directed by Anne Hulegard. Cast: Beatrice —
Katherine Vandewark; Pearl — Shannon Welles; Boston —
Will August. *Life Is Just a Bowl of Cellos* was also produced by
Fire Rose Productions at the Miles Memorial Playhouse, Santa
Monica, Calif., 2008, as part of ACTober Fest, Fire Rose
Productions' 6th Annual Ten-Minute Play Festival. Directed by
Amanda Korpitz. Cast: Beatrice — Irene Chapman;
Pearl — Esther Rosen; Boston — Ahmad Russ.

BEATRICE: Late sixties to early seventies, as gentle as she is strong. She has strong opinions, strong muscles, strong morals, and the warmest, most compassionate (though tired) heart imaginable. No family and little money landed her at Sunset Meadows, an assisted-living facility in Hollywood. Not a nice place, and certainly not the place for freewilled Beatrice.

PEARL: Slightly older than Beatrice, in the early stages of dementia, which accentuates the girliness of her. Shy and a follower all her life, she is content to trust and be taken care of by Beatrice. Pearl was a cellist in a semiprofessional orchestra in her working days.

BOSTON: Of indeterminate age and ethnicity. The production custodial engineer at the Hollywood Bowl. He knows the ladies' secret and helps them in whatever ways he can. A strong man physically, he is a pussycat when it comes to Beatrice and Pearl.

SETTING

A storage room underneath the Hollywood Bowl in Los Angeles, so the set is minimal. Two cots of the type used in emergency medical centers at public facilities. Two chairs, a small bureau (probably cardboard). One door to the hall.

TIME

The present.

NOTE: How the ladies survive and in what ways Boston helps them are not specific concerns for the production. The director, cast, and audience can answer those questions in their own imaginations. The playwright has purposely not answered such questions, leaving room for speculation.

• • •

At opening, a few muted strains of a classical piece played by a full orchestra, heavy on strings, followed by muted applause. At rise: It is a small storage room beneath the Hollywood Bowl in Los Angeles. A few music stands are stacked in a corner. Faded posters from past concerts are taped to the walls. Against each side wall is a cot, neatly made. On the small bureau between the cots is a stack of concert programs, a bottle of cheap brandy, and two mismatched glasses. At the end of each cot is a metal folding chair. On one, Beatrice, dressed in her best, sits listening to the music. On the other chair, Pearl, not as tidy, hums with the string section. She is wearing floral garden gloves. The music stops, followed by the sound of applause. Beatrice applauds.

BEATRICE: Pearl?
(Pearl stops humming and claps.)
BEATRICE: Master Haydn's *Cello Concerto in C* was most stirring. Don't you agree, Pearl? Pearl?
(Pearl begins humming again.)
BEATRICE: However, I felt the string section ever so slightly strident tonight. Don't you agree?
(Annoyed, Pearl hums louder.)
BEATRICE: I know you favor the cello, but even the cello can occasionally cause a twinge.
PEARL: Humpf!
BEATRICE: *(Pointing to ceiling.)* Even so, I prefer our Hollywood Bowl Orchestra to the LA Philharmonic any old time. Concert's over. So any minute now it's going to be time to do what?
PEARL: What.
BEATRICE: It will be time to play "Quiet As a Mouse."
PEARL: *(Singsong.)* A mouse. A mouse. A mouse.
BEATRICE: That's right.
(Offstage, footsteps and muffled voices are heard. The doorknob is rattled.)
BEATRICE: *(Whispering.)* Shhh. Remember, Pearl? A mouse. A mouse. A quiet little mouse. No one must know there's a mouse in the house. *(Pause.)* Boston? No, he always knocks.
PEARL: A mouse. A mou . . .
(Beatrice grabs Pearl's arm to silence her. They sit still as stone. Finally, the rattling stops and footsteps move away. Beatrice sighs with relief.)
BEATRICE: It's OK now.
PEARL: Can we be noisy mice now?
BEATRICE: Maybe not "noisy," but comfortable.
PEARL: No mice in the house. We're not mice tonight.
BEATRICE: Shall we have a brandy before retiring?
(It's a nightly ritual. They pretend to consider the idea.)
BOTH: I believe we should.
(They laugh. Beatrice pours two glasses of brandy and puts one in Pearl's hand.)

BEATRICE: Careful, Pearl. Don't spill on your dress.

(Pearl stares at the glass in her hand, confused.)

BEATRICE: A toast. Let me see if I remember the one you give. *(Raising her glass.)* Good food when you're hungry. Old wine when you're dry. A good man to love you. And heaven when you die!

PEARL: Are we going to have a concert tonight?

BEATRICE: We just did, sweetie. Remember? We always have our brandy after the concert.

PEARL: *(Agitated.)* I don't know where I put my cello.

BEATRICE: We left your cello at Sunset Meadows where it will be safe.

PEARL: I used to live at Sunset Meadows. Did you ever go there?

BEATRICE: That's where you and I met. I know you can remember that.

PEARL: Yes, of course. Awful place! Crap!

BEATRICE: Certainly was. Too many rules and unhappy people.

PEARL: Terrible food! Crap!

BEATRICE: No taste. No crunch.

PEARL: Let's run away!

BEATRICE: Maybe tomorrow. But tonight we should finish our brandy and go to sleep.

PEARL: That's what we'll do. We'll run away. And we can take my cello?

BEATRICE: *(Exhausted.)* By all means.

PEARL: Miss Agnes gets awfully cross when I don't practice. And she tells Mother. Then Mother scolds me. "Why do I pay for lessons if you don't practice?" Do you know Miss Agnes?

BEATRICE: No, I never met her. And I imagine Miss Agnes has been gone for some years by now. *(Getting a bottle of Flintstones children's vitamins from the bureau, shaking one out and offering it to Pearl.)* Here's your evening mint.

PEARL: I don't want it.

BEATRICE: But you like Flintstones. And this is Dino. You always like Dino.

PEARL: Don't want it.

BEATRICE: Cherry flavor. Your favorite.

PEARL: Don't care.

BEATRICE: I think you're just overtired. I know I am. You need to take your vitamins to be healthy.

PEARL: No.

(Beatrice shakes another vitamin into her hand.)

BEATRICE: I'm taking mine. It's Barney. See? *(Popping the vitamin into her mouth and chewing.)* If you take yours, it'll be like having brandy and dessert together. Wouldn't that be fun?

(Pearl takes the vitamin and chews it.)

PEARL: It's cherry. I like cherry. Candy and brandy. Brandy and candy. Just like grown ups.

(There is a soft knock on the door. Beatrice freezes.)

BEATRICE: Pearl, mouse!

PEARL: *(Whispering.)* Shhh. Mouse. Mouse. Quiet as a mouse.

Boston *(Offstage, quietly.)* Ladies? It's me. Boston.

(Beatrice cautiously opens the door. Boston slips into the room, closing the door.)

BOSTON: Coast is clear.

BEATRICE: Look who's here, Pearl. It's Boston.

BOSTON: Evening, Miss Pearl.

(Pearl remains frozen.)

BOSTON: Is she having one of her bad days, Miss Bea?

BEATRICE: Nonsense. She's just tired from this evening's stirring concert. You know how the cello moves her. We were just having a drop of brandy. Will you join us?

BOSTON: Thank you kindly, ma'am. But I've still got my load of sweeping to do tonight. For a classical music audience, they sure dropped a lot of tacky trash.

BEATRICE: And what the Lord's wind doesn't blow away, Boston's broom will, right?

BOSTON: You got that right.

(There is an awkward pause.)

BEATRICE: Is anything wrong, Boston?

BOSTON: Yes, ma'am, I'm afraid so.

(He takes her by the elbow and moves away from Pearl, who is still frozen in "mouse mode.")

BEATRICE: What is it?

BOSTON: You know the bowl renovation begins next month.

BEATRICE: My goodness! Is it September already?

BOSTON: Thing is, we're supposed to clean out these unused storage rooms before the work starts.

BEATRICE: Oh, dear.

BOSTON: I can schedule the guys away from this area for a while, but not for long. Three days. Maybe four tops.

BEATRICE: Starting when?

BOSTON: Monday morning.

BEATRICE: What's today?

BOSTON: Thursday.

BEATRICE: Oh lord in heaven! Whatever will we do?

BOSTON: It was just announced. I'm sorry.

BEATRICE: So soon. This is terrible.

BOSTON: Is there anyplace you can go? How about back to that place . . .

BEATRICE: Sunset Meadows? No, I'm afraid we lit a brush fire in that meadow.

BOSTON: Well, we'll think of something. Now I've got to go scrape up a ton of apple peels and brie.

BEATRICE: Thank you for everything, Boston.

BOSTON: Maybe that brush fire wasn't as bad as you think. *(Heading for the door.)* Oh, there's some kind of modern dance troupe or something tomorrow night, Miss Pearl, but you can still hear the music.

PEARL: Modern claptrap.

BOSTON: You got that right, Miss Pearl. And, this one's heavy on the viola.

PEARL: Viola! Humpf!

BEATRICE: Pearl considers the viola just a cello that never grew up.

BOSTON: Yes, I know.

PEARL: Modern dance viola! Modern crap! Humpf!

BOSTON: Well, we can't have Haydn every night. *(Walking toward the door with Beatrice.)* I feel just awful about all this, Miss Bea. But don't you worry. We'll think of something. You take care now, Miss Pearl. *(He slips out after making sure the hall is empty.)*

BEATRICE: Such a dear man.

PEARL: Who?

BEATRICE: Never mind, sweetie. Let's go to bed. I'm so awfully tired.

PEARL: Are we going to have a concert tonight?

BEATRICE: Haydn's *Cello Concerto in C.* You liked it.

PEARL: No more quiet mice?

BEATRICE: Not tonight. I'm so tired.

PEARL: Mouse. Mouse. No mouse in the house.

BEATRICE: Shhh. That's right. No mouse. *(Heading for her cot, stumbling.)* I just don't feel quite right. I wonder if we kept that chicken chow mein too long.

PEARL: I finished my brandy.

BEATRICE: That's fine, dear. Put your glass on the bureau, would you. *(Pause.)* Oh, I have such heartburn. Do you feel all right, Pearl?

PEARL: I ate a cherry Dino.

BEATRICE: I think I'll go to bed now, Pearl. Will you be OK?

(Beatrice sinks onto her cot.)

PEARL: Aren't we going to have a concert tonight?

BEATRICE: Pearl, do you think you can find Boston?

PEARL: That's a town in Massachusetts. My mother took me to a concert there.

BEATRICE: *(Struggling to breathe.)* Pearl, I need you to listen very carefully. And I need you to concentrate. Can you do that?

PEARL: *(Frightened.)* Did I do something wrong? I didn't mean to.

BEATRICE: No, you didn't do anything wrong. But I need you to go find Boston. Remember Boston, our nice gentleman friend? You must go find him.

PEARL: I can't! I can't go outside! I have to practice. I promise I will practice, Miss Agnes. But don't make me go outside. I will be good. Please don't be mad.

(Frantically searching the room for her cello, as Beatrice slides off the cot.)

PEARL: I can't find it! I can't find my cello. I can't . . .

(Kneeling beside Beatrice on the floor.)

PEARL: Please don't be mad, Miss Agnes. I would have practiced. I would have. But I can't find my cello. Please don't tell Mother. She'll be so disappointed in me. She'll scold me.

(There is a soft knock on the door. Pearl goes into "mouse mode.")

BOSTON: *(Offstage.)* Ladies? It's me, Boston. *(Entering the room.)* I forgot to give you the program from tonight's . . . *(Seeing Beatrice on the floor.)* Oh, dear Jesus. What happened?

PEARL: Miss Agnes won't talk to me 'cause I lost my cello and didn't practice. Don't you be mad at me too.

(Boston checks Beatrice for a pulse. There isn't one.)

BOSTON: Oh, sweet Jesus.

PEARL: Miss Agnes said she was tired. But I think she's mad at me. Am I going to get into trouble?

BOSTON: No, Miss Pearl. But I am. *(Gently leading Pearl to her cot.)* Now, you just sit over here on your cot. Boston's going to take care of everything.

PEARL: Do you live at Sunset Meadows?

(Boston takes out his cell phone and dials.)

(Note: The following dialogue should overlap.)

BOSTON: Michaelson, Boston . . . Yeah . . . Listen, we need an ambulance . . . Yeah, I said an	PEARL: We lived at Sunset Meadows. But we didn't like it. Beatrice said we should run away. I

ambulance . . . That's right . . . was scared. But Beatrice I'm in Storage Space 12, Level 2 always knows what to do. . . . I know. I know. No. She's my friend. My very Look, I'll explain everything best friend. She always when you get here. takes care of me. Always.

(Note: End of overlapping dialogue.)

(Pearl wanders back to Beatrice's body and sits beside her on the floor. Boston, holding the phone, watches her.)

PEARL: A mouse. A mouse. A quiet little mouse. No one must know there's a mouse in the house. Shhh.

BOSTON: *(Into phone.)* No. No, Michaelson, there's no hurry.

(Lights fade.)

END OF PLAY

More Precious Than Diamonds

STEPHANIE HUTCHINSON

More Precious Than Diamonds was originally presented at
The Actor's Group in Universal City, Calif., March 29, 2008,
as part of An Evening of Four 10-Minute Comedies by
Stephanie Hutchinson, AOPW Fellowship Award winner.
Directed by Jonathan Levit. Cast: Michelle —
Angela Rose Sarno; Julie — Michelle Mania;
Salesman/Stewart — James McAndrew.

CHARACTERS

MICHELLE: Early forties, best friend of Julie, practical, married.

JULIE: Late thirties, imaginative, single.

SALESMAN/STEWART: Thirties, upper-crust British accent, scientific mind, handsome but unconscious of it, single.

SETTING

Interior of Tiffany's Beverly Hills store. There is a jewelry display case and three chairs.

TIME

An afternoon, the present.

• • •

At rise: Michelle and Julie enter.

MICHELLE: Don't do it, Julie, I beg you. You'll regret it.

JULIE: No, I won't.

MICHELLE: You know what I mean. Wait.

JULIE: I'm through waiting. I've dreamed all my life of getting a beautiful, big Tiffany diamond ring in a robin's egg blue box with a white bow. *(Beat.)* But here I am, facing forty, and my finger is still naked.

(She displays her left ring finger.)

MICHELLE: They say that forty is the new thirty.

JULIE: Yeah, and thirty is the new fifteen, I mean, twelve.

MICHELLE: Don't do everything yourself. Leave space for someone to love you.

JULIE: I've given up on love. If it hasn't happened by now, it never will.

MICHELLE: What about Joe? The guy with the big house?

JULIE: Oh, I loved the house, but unfortunately, Joe came with it. It was a package deal.

MICHELLE: Wait for a man to give you a diamond.

JULIE: I can't wait anymore. My birthday is next week, you know.

MICHELLE: Turning forty isn't such a big deal, trust me.

JULIE: Michelle, who are you to talk? You've been married for twenty years.

MICHELLE: That's not the point.

JULIE: That's exactly the point! *(Dreamily.)* All these years you've watched your diamond glint in the sunlight, reflecting the colors of the sky.

MICHELLE: You've been reading way too many ads.

JULIE: It's now or never.

MICHELLE: But to buy yourself a diamond? That's pathe —

JULIE: — Go ahead, say it. Pathetic —

MICHELLE: — I didn't mean —

JULIE: — Sure you did. Whatever you call it, I want a diamond. There's nothing more precious than diamonds. *(She points to an engagement ring in the case.)* Would you look at that cushion cut! I bet it's four carats.

MICHELLE: You'd have to marry a rock star to get a ring like that.

JULIE: Leeza got a ring like that. Of course, she's a slut. *(Beat.)* I wonder if any decent women ever get rocks like that?

MICHELLE: Look, it's not too late — we can still walk out the door.

(A salesman approaches, the studious type. He wears a bow tie. He is handsome but unaware of it.)

SALESMAN: *(English accent.)* Good afternoon, ladies. How are you today?

MICHELLE: We were just leaving. *(She pulls Julie by the arm.)* Come on, Jules.

(Julie extricates herself and sits.)

JULIE: Hello. I'd like to see that ring, please.

(She points to the cushion cut.)

SALESMAN: Certainly, Madame. *(He pulls the ring out.)* You have wonderful taste. This is one of our most expensive rings, due to its exquisite cut, color, clarity, and carats, the four Cs. *(Beat.)* Are you here today to pick out rings before your fiancé visits?

JULIE: *(Embarrassed.)* Uh . . . there is no fiancé. I was just . . . uh, I think I'd better leave.

(She rises to go)

SALESMAN: Oh, please stay and try it on. It's just your size!

(She sits.)

JULIE: *(Amazed.)* You can tell that just by looking at my finger?

SALESMAN: I was trained as a scientist. I've been researching rings for some time.

JULIE: Really?

MICHELLE: *(Impressed.)* How fascinating that a man is so interested in jewelry.

SALESMAN: The credit for that actually goes to my ex-girlfriend. I had hoped to marry her, but she ran off with a man who gave her a real diamond. I was only able to offer her a small cubic zirconia, being that I was just a poor graduate student at the time. *(Beat.)* I vowed then and there to research diamonds and to find out why women are so attracted to them.

MICHELLE: Did she marry him? The other guy?

SALESMAN: Yes, I'm afraid she did.

JULIE: Oh, I'm sorry.

SALESMAN: She's the one who would be sorry now if she knew that I was working here and getting the employee discount.

MICHELLE: That's the spirit!

SALESMAN: *(To Julie.)* Go ahead. Please try it on.

(She squints as she puts the ring on. It is obviously too tight.)

JULIE: *(Self-deprecatingly.)* I feel like Cinderella's stepsister trying on the shoe.

SALESMAN: *(Gallantly.)* No, you're like Cinderella herself.

(They share a deep look. He smiles at her. Time stops. Michelle looks down at other rings in the case, oblivious to the unfolding drama.)

MICHELLE: We'd better get going before our parking meter expires.

(No response, as they gaze deeply into each other's eyes.)

MICHELLE: Julie? *(She finally looks over and takes in what is transpiring.)* Oh my . . . !

JULIE: *(Snapping out of it.)* Uh . . . yes . . . it's really beautiful, don't you think, Michelle?

(Michelle looks at Salesman.)

MICHELLE: Yes he is, I mean, yes it is.

JULIE: How much did you say it costs?

SALESMAN: *(Flustered.)* It's a mere $84,900 but with my employee discount —

JULIE: Your discount?

MICHELLE: *(Disbelief.)* You'd give her your employee discount??

SALESMAN: Uh, that is to say —

(Julie tries to remove the ring; it is stuck.)

JULIE: Ouch — I can't — *(She pulls the ring but it doesn't budge; she begins to panic.)* I can't seem to get it off!

SALESMAN: Let me see.

(He takes her hand and again they gaze into each other's eyes, lost. He caresses her hand)

MICHELLE: Well? Is it coming off?

JULIE: *(Dreamily.)* I really don't care.

MICHELLE: For $84,900 you'd better care!

SALESMAN: Don't forget my employee discount.

MICHELLE: *(Sarcastically.)* Your employee discount?!

SALESMAN: *(Coming to his senses.)* Ladies, please wait here while I get our special liquid spray.

(He exits.)

MICHELLE: Julie, what just happened?

JULIE: I don't know. I looked into his eyes and suddenly I forgot about every-thing, even the diamond!

MICHELLE: This is major! I've never seen you so excited. Your eyes are sparkling and . . . why, you're blushing!

JULIE: *(Blushing.)* I don't know what's come over me.

MICHELLE: *(Getting practical.)* But we've got to get that ring off!

JULIE: *(Dreamily.)* Why?

MICHELLE: Snap out of it! I don't care how amazing this salesman is, you don't want to spend $84,900 on a ring, do you?

JULIE: He said he'd give me his employee discount.

MICHELLE: Julie! Listen to yourself! Get a grip! You've got to get that ring off, now!

(Salesman reenters with the spray).

SALESMAN: Here. *(He sprays Julie's finger; the ring gradually dislodges. All sigh with relief.)* That certainly was a close call.

MICHELLE: Does that happen often, that rings get stuck?

SALESMAN: *(Hesitantly.)* I wouldn't know.

MICHELLE: Well, how many times has it happened while you've been working here?

SALESMAN: *(Guiltily.)* Today is actually my first day. *(Beat.)* The manager is upset that I miscalculated your finger size and that the ring got stuck.

JULIE: And you risked your job to let me try on a ring that didn't even fit? *(To Michelle.)* That's so sweet!

(She looks up at him, her face glowing with tenderness.)

SALESMAN: So you're not angry?

JULIE: How could I be, when you risked so much for me?

MICHELLE: *(Cynically, to Julie.)* And you risked getting stuck with a $84,900 bill!

SALESMAN AND JULIE: Less the employee discount.

(They laugh.)

SALESMAN: So why did you come shopping today, if I may be so bold as to inquire?

JULIE: The truth is, I'm facing a major birthday and I'm tired of waiting for a Tiffany diamond. *(Beat.)* I suppose that must sound silly to you.

SALESMAN: Not at all. I understand completely, now that I'm researching women and diamonds.

JULIE: Yes, diamonds are the jewelry equivalent of chocolate.

SALESMAN: Precisely. *(Beat; to Julie.)* I'm sorry, I never did introduce myself. I'm Stewart, and you are?

JULIE: Julie.

STEWART: A real pleasure to meet you, Julie.

(They shake hands, smiling, for a lengthy time; Michelle coughs to get their attention.)

MICHELLE: I'm Michelle. *(She extends her hand.)*

STEWART: Pleased to make your acquaintance, Michelle.

(They shake, then Michelle stands.)

MICHELLE: Julie, we really have to get going or we're going to get a parking ticket. It was nice meeting you, Stewart.

JULIE: *(To Michelle.)* Why don't you get the car and circle the block? I'll meet you outside in a couple of minutes.

MICHELLE: OK, but don't take too long. You know how bad traffic gets around here.

JULIE: All right. Bye.

(Michelle waves and exits.)

STEWART: I hope you don't think that I'm too forward, but —

JULIE: — Yes?

STEWART: I should like to call on you someday, if I may?

JULIE: *(Unconsciously adopting his manner of speaking.)* That would be lovely, Stewart.

STEWART: I mean, I want to get to know you better, whether or not you ever buy diamonds here.

JULIE: I understand. After all, some things are more precious than diamonds.

(They smile and gaze at each other.)

(Lights fade out.)

END OF PLAY

Stuffed Grape Leaves

DAMON CHUA

Stuffed Grape Leaves was first produced by Company of Angels
Theatre, Los Angeles, April 17, 2008, as part of its
L.A. VIEWS Ten-Minute Play Festival. Directed by Armando
Molina. Cast: Iram — Richard Azurdia; Naomi — Jully Lee;
Sandrine — Claire Bocking.

CHARACTERS
    IRAM: Twenties to forties, Mexican; cook, with apron and hairnet.
    NAOMI: Twenties to thirties, Asian; server, with half-apron and pad.
    SANDRINE: Twenties to forties, white; diner, blonde, rich looking.

SETTING
    A small restaurant in Los Angeles.

TIME
    The present.

NOTE: Except for dialogue presented in italics, the rest of the text comprises verbal rendering of actual nonverbal interior monologues and telepathic exchanges between the characters. Think of how people silently size one another up in a restaurant setting.

• • •

Lights up showing Iram, Naomi, and Sandrine facing the audience. Iram stands behind a prep table, chopping vegetables. Sandrine is seated at a table, unfolding her napkin, a large handbag next to her. Naomi stands between them, holding a menu.

IRAM: *(Addresses the audience.)* My name is Iram. I'm the chef.
    (Naomi laughs derisively.)
IRAM: *(Reacting.)* I am the cook.
NAOMI: Iram.
IRAM: OK. I'm the prep guy. But when the cook, Rocky, is not here, I cook.
NAOMI: But you're not the cook.
IRAM: No, but I cook well. Which is why they allow me to cook.
NAOMI: Only when Rocky is not here. *(Turns to the audience.)* My name is Naomi. I'm the server. Notice I didn't say waitress. Or waitperson. People here don't like the term waitress. So I'm a server. I . . . serve.
    (Naomi is amused by her own joke.)
IRAM: Naomi's not a good server.
    (Naomi's mood darkens.)
NAOMI: I'm a better server than you're a cook. And you're not a cook.
IRAM: You're not a server. You're a student.
NAOMI: I'm a grad student. Trying to make ends meet.

IRAM: You drive a Lexus.

NAOMI: It's a lease.

IRAM: I take the bus.

NAOMI: I take the bus too. Sometimes. When the car is in the shop. Who takes the bus anyway?

(Sandrine looks impatiently at Naomi.)

IRAM: *(Indicating Sandrine.)* Someone's waiting.

NAOMI: What? Oh.

(Naomi rushes to Sandrine, proffers the menu. Iram shakes his head.)

NAOMI: *I'm Naomi. I'm your server today.*

SANDRINE: *(Takes the menu, unsmiling.)* Thanks. *(To audience.)* My name is Sandrine. I'm having lunch. I'm a person who has lunch.

NAOMI: I hate women who lunch. Don't they have anything to do?

IRAM: No one does anything in LA.

NAOMI: I do. I study, and I work part-time.

IRAM: I cook, and I study part-time.

SANDRINE: I lunch. And I run errands all the time. I'm really busy. Just ask my nanny.

IRAM: *(To Naomi.)* She has a nanny.

NAOMI: More than a woman who lunches, I hate wives who lunch.

(Iram sees that Sandrine is ready to order.)

IRAM: Hey, bad server.

NAOMI: What? Oops.

(Naomi turns to Sandrine.)

SANDRINE: *What's good here?*

NAOMI: *Uh, everything's good here.*

IRAM: See?

SANDRINE: *Do you have any specials today?*

NAOMI: *Well . . . no.*

IRAM: Really bad.

SANDRINE: *How's the chicken shwarma?*

IRAM: Did we say this is a Lebanese restaurant?

NAOMI: This is a Lebanese restaurant.

IRAM: Am I Lebanese? No. I'm Mexican.

NAOMI: I'm Japanese. But I've been here a long time.

IRAM: The owner's not Lebanese either.

NAOMI: I think he's Russian.

IRAM: Romanian.

NAOMI: No. But he's Jewish.

IRAM: They're all Jewish.

SANDRINE: I eat a lot of Lebanese food.

NAOMI: Is she Lebanese?

IRAM: Of course she's not Lebanese. If she were Lebanese, she'd be wearing that . . .

(He gestures some kind of headdress.)

NAOMI: You mean the Muslim stuff. A veil.

IRAM: Yes, a veil. And she won't have any rights.

NAOMI: No rights at all.

SANDRINE: *This menu's very confusing.*

NAOMI: Luckily here we have rights.

IRAM: For some of us anyway.

NAOMI: Us?

IRAM: Well, you.

NAOMI: Well, her. She has rights.

IRAM: Yes. She has rights.

SANDRINE: No, not the chicken shwarma. Something vegetarian. *What's vegetarian?*

IRAM: She's not really a vegetarian.

NAOMI: Clearly not. But I respect people who *try* to be vegetarian. *(To Sandrine.) For appetizers we have hummus or baba ghanoush. For mains you can try the stuffed grape leaves.*

SANDRINE: Stuffed grape leaves.

IRAM: We should never offer stuffed grape leaves. It takes too long to prepare.

NAOMI: It's premade.

IRAM: I premake it. And it takes forever.

SANDRINE: *I'll have the stuffed grape leaves.*

NAOMI: *Excellent choice.*

(Iram looks daggers at Naomi, who smiles.)

NAOMI: *(To Sandrine.) Anything to drink?*

IRAM: I'm guessing iced tea.

NAOMI: No sugar, with a slice of lemon.

SANDRINE: *I'll have an iced tea, no sugar, with a slice of lemon.*

(Iram and Naomi look at each other and smile, as Naomi jots down the order on her pad.)

NAOMI: *Coming right up.*

(Naomi moves toward Iram, tears off the top sheet of her pad, and hands it over to him. He takes it.)

SANDRINE: I have exactly twenty-seven minutes for lunch.

(She looks at Naomi and Iram.)

SANDRINE: I know what they're thinking. They think I'm one of those women in LA who has meals in restaurants. Who has a nanny for each of her kids. With a really busy schedule. Well, OK, but so what? I struggled to get to where I am today. I got what I want through hard work, street smarts, and, well, marriage. But mostly hard work. And street smarts. I don't take anything for granted. Did I order the stuffed grape leaves? What I'm dying for is a big juicy steak. What am I doing here?

(The stuffed grape leaves are done. Iram hands the plate over to Naomi.)

IRAM: Where do you think she's from?

NAOMI: *Bay Area.*

IRAM: *East Coast.*

SANDRINE: Look at them nattering away. But does it bother me? Not the least bit. Why should they bother me? The Mexican's probably illegal, and the Asian, a student. And a bad waitress to boot. Sorry. *Server.*

(Naomi takes the food to Sandrine.)

NAOMI: *(To Sandrine.) Sorry. Did you say something?*

SANDRINE: *(Caught.)* No, of course not.

IRAM: I think she said you're a bad server.

SANDRINE: *(All innocent.)* Why would I say that?

(Naomi places the plate in front of Sandrine.)

IRAM: Because you'd be one hundred percent correct.

NAOMI: *(To Iram.)* Shut up! *(To Sandrine.)* Don't choke.

IRAM: Just stating the obvious.

NAOMI: Why is everyone picking on me? I'm just a grad student trying to make ends meet.

SANDRINE: Am I accusing you of anything?

NAOMI: You said I'm a bad server.

SANDRINE: *(Referring to Iram.)* He's putting words in my mouth.

IRAM: What?

SANDRINE: *I said what lovely looking stuffed grape leaves.*

(Everyone is appeased. Sandrine begins to eat. Naomi goes to Iram.)

NAOMI: One more word from you.

IRAM: She's the one with the nanny. Probably lives up in the hills.

NAOMI: Palisades.

(Sandrine stops eating. She doesn't look happy.)

SANDRINE: *(To Naomi and Iram.)* I think that's enough.

(Naomi and Iram turn to look.)

NAOMI: I'm sorry?

SANDRINE: You two have been judging me since I stepped into this restaurant.

NAOMI: Why would we do that?

SANDRINE: Wives who lunch? The hills?

IRAM: I didn't say anything.

NAOMI: I didn't say anything either.

> *(Sandrine lets out a sigh.)*

SANDRINE: Well then none of us said anything. This is just a nice quiet lunch in a quaint little restaurant on the Westside.

NAOMI: Well said.

IRAM: *(To Naomi; worried.)* How does she know I'm illegal?

NAOMI: I thought you have Social Security and stuff.

IRAM: I'm using a friend's.

NAOMI: But you've been here . . .

IRAM: Ten years.

SANDRINE: You've been illegal for ten years?

> *(Iram and Naomi turn to Sandrine.)*

SANDRINE: Why don't you get married and get a green card? *(No response.)* What about her?

NAOMI: Me?!

IRAM: No way!

NAOMI: I'm on a student visa.

SANDRINE: Wait. If you're on a student visa, how can you work here?

NAOMI: Technically, I can't, but, well.

IRAM: We pay her in cash.

SANDRINE: So you're illegal too.

NAOMI: I'm a grad student trying to make ends meet.

IRAM: While driving a Lexus.

NAOMI: Stop it!

SANDRINE: Hey, join the club.

NAOMI: What do you mean? What club?

SANDRINE: I'm Canadian. You can't tell? I came here looking to marry someone, but instead fell in love with . . . a Lebanese.

IRAM: You don't mean lesb —

SANDRINE: Lebanese!

IRAM: Wait. You're saying you're illegal? How do you stay in this country?

SANDRINE: I fly back to Vancouver every six months.

NAOMI: But you live here, don't you?

SANDRINE: Torrance.

IRAM: *(To Naomi.)* You were so wrong.

NAOMI: So were you.

SANDRINE: These stuffed grape leaves are awful.

NAOMI: I'm sorry. I don't eat the stuff.

IRAM: I hate it too.

SANDRINE: So why is it on the menu?

IRAM: This is a Lebanese restaurant. It has to be on the menu.

(Sandrine sets aside her food, takes out a veil from her bag, and arranges it around her head.)

IRAM: Is that . . .

SANDRINE: I'm Muslim. Had to convert when I married Ahmed.

NAOMI: You're Muslim?!

IRAM: Is he legal?

SANDRINE: If he's legal would I be on a tourist visa?

NAOMI: Wow, maybe you should seek asylum.

SANDRINE: I'm Canadian, remember? In any case, I'm leaving him. Caught him the other day having lunch with this pretty young thing, and I thought . . . *(Sandrine spits out a piece of grape leaf from her mouth, winces.)* Gross. I hate this place.

(Iram and Naomi look at each other.)

NAOMI: This place?

SANDRINE: This restaurant. This city. This country.

NAOMI: Then get out. Go home.

SANDRINE: I'll go if you go. Would you?

(No response from Naomi.)

SANDRINE: *(To Iram.)* Or you?

(No response from Iram.)

SANDRINE: Thought so. *(She takes out the remnants of another leaf from her mouth.)* You know what, we're exactly like these stuffed grape leaves here. No one really wants us, but we're still here. Yeah, we're still here. Check? *(Black out.)*

END OF PLAY

PLAYS FOR
TWO MEN AND
ONE WOMAN

After Godot

George Freek

After Godot was originally produced by Auburn Players
Community Theatre, Auburn, N.Y., September 26–28 and
October 3–5, 2008. Directed by Bourke Kennedy.
Cast: Vladimir — Tom Hoey; Estragon — Andrew Tubiolo;
Lucky — Patricia Fisher.

CHARACTERS

> VLADIMIR: Thirty to fifty, an actor.
> ESTRAGON: Thirty to fifty, an actor.
> LUCKY: Thirty-five, director.

SETTING

> The stage of a community theater.

TIME

> After a performance of *Waiting for Godot*.

• • •

The stage of a community theater following a performance of Beckett's Waiting for Godot. *The audience has departed. However, the two main actors are sitting onstage. They wear bowler hats. They are very depressed. On the stage is a barren tree, which is the only piece of scenery in the play. A long rope with a noose hangs from a branch of the tree.*

VLADIMIR: *(Miserable, his head in his hands.)* That was a tragedy!

ESTRAGON: *(Philosophical.)* I think it's called a "tragi-comedy."

VLADIMIR: Well, our performance of it was a farce!

ESTRAGON: I think it's called a turkey.

VLADIMIR: I know, and you don't have to say it —

ESTRAGON: I don't have to say what?

VLADIMIR: That it was my fault!

ESTRAGON: You just said it.

VLADIMIR: OH GOD! Then you're saying it WAS my fault!

ESTRAGON: I'm afraid I'm not good at lying just to cheer people up.

VLADIMIR: And you're absolutely right. I messed up my lines.

ESTRAGON: Well, try to look on the bright side. Those were the only lines the audience found funny.

VLADIMIR: It wasn't supposed to be improv!

ESTRAGON: It just seemed like it was.

VLADIMIR: I really feel awful! *(He chokes back sobs.)*

ESTRAGON: For heaven's sake, don't whimper! I feel bad enough as it is!

VLADIMIR: I'm sorry. *(He rises from his chair and walks to the tree.)* What can I say? What can I do?

ESTRAGON: Nothing!

VLADIMIR: Well . . . You might try to cheer me up.

ESTRAGON: I told you I'm no good at that.

VLADIMIR: *(On the verge of tears again.)* And why should you? I think I should just hang myself!

ESTRAGON: No, you couldn't do that.

VLADIMIR: *(Challenging.)* What! You don't think I have the guts for it?

ESTRAGON: No, I think the rope is too long.

VLADIMIR: Thanks! *(He puts the noose around his neck.)*

ESTRAGON: Oh come on now, don't be a fool.

VLADIMIR: Why not? I've already made a fool of myself once tonight.

ESTRAGON: Now don't be silly. You know you don't mean that. For one thing, you have too much to live for —

VLADIMIR: Tell me what. *(A long pause.)* Well!

ESTRAGON: I'm thinking, I'm thinking!

VLADIMIR: That does it!

ESTRAGON: All right, wait a minute! Listen . . . Think of your wife. Think of your two teenage daughters —

VLADIMIR: God! Maybe I could make the rope shorter!

ESTRAGON: Now stop it! You're really overreacting. For heaven's sake, so you forgot some lines, so you were lousy —

VLADIMIR: Boy, you really aren't good at cheering a person up!

ESTRAGON: But look . . . What difference does it make if you were terrible?

VLADIMIR: That's easy for you to say!

ESTRAGON: But my point is this. This is the [name of the theater in which the play is being performed] . . . It's not exactly Broadway!

VLADIMIR: I know that. But still . . . Don't you see! I let our audience down!

ESTRAGON: *(With a sweeping gesture.)* Those boors! What do they know?

VLADIMIR: Still . . . We owe them something.

ESTRAGON: Don't give me that rot!

VLADIMIR: *(He looks into the auditorium.)* Hm . . . You could be right.

ESTRAGON: Anyway, you did your best, didn't you?

VLADIMIR: I really hope not! I forgot my lines!

ESTRAGON: Well, you gave your all, did you not?

VLADIMIR: *(Between a rock and a hard place.)* Um —

ESTRAGON: What I am telling you, man, is that it wasn't your fault!

VLADIMIR: It wasn't? You mean —

ESTRAGON: Right! That is exactly what I mean!

VLADIMIR: *(Uncertain.)* So it was . . .

ESTRAGON: The fault of the play!

VLADIMIR: It was . . . the play's fault?

ESTRAGON: Now you're getting it.

VLADIMIR: But, um . . . some people call it a masterpiece.

ESTRAGON: They once said that about *The Silver Cord.*

VLADIMIR: The . . . what?

ESTRAGON: Exactly!

VLADIMIR: So then you're saying it's . . . a FLAWED masterpeice?

ESTRAGON: I'm saying it's a piece of crap!

VLADIMIR: Whew! It's that bad?

ESTRAGON: I'm being kind!

VLADIMIR: I'm only curious, but . . . what's wrong with it?

ESTRAGON: For one thing, nothing happens.

VLADIMIR: *(He thinks.)* You're right about that.

ESTRAGON: And, therefore, it's too long.

VLADIMIR: Well, I suppose it would be if nothing happens.

ESTRAGON: It's WAY too long!

VLADIMIR: You think it's a one-act play in two acts?

ESTRAGON: I think it's a ten-minute play in two acts!

VLADIMIR: *(Getting into it.)* Yes, I see! Two very LONG acts!

ESTRAGON: And then these costumes!

VLADIMIR: Right! *(He takes off his hat, throws it on the floor.)* I really hate these
    silly hats!

ESTRAGON: Who wears them?

VLADIMIR: *(He jumps up and down on his hat.)* They're ridiculous!

ESTRAGON: The entire thing is impossible to do!

VLADIMIR: John Barrymore couldn't have pulled it off!

ESTRAGON: ETHEL Barrymore couldn't have pulled it off!

VLADIMIR: By God, you're right!

ESTRAGON: Of course I'm right!

VLADIMIR: I'm feeling a lot better!

ESTRAGON: *(He throws his hat away.)* I'm feeling pretty good myself.
    *(And then Lucky the director of the play enters. She looks very dejected,
    indeed.)*

LUCKY: Dear God, what an unmitigated disaster!

VLADIMIR: Oh . . . You mean —

LUCKY: What do you think I meant, pinhead!

VLADIMIR: Yes, right . . . but we were thinking . . . *(He looks for help to Estragon, who has, however, turned away, ignoring them both.)*

LUCKY: Yes? What were you thinking?

VLADIMIR: Well . . . We thought it might have been the play.

LUCKY: The PLAY!

VLADIMIR: Maybe?

LUCKY: That play is a masterpiece!

VLADIMIR: Yes, of course . . . we all know that. It's just that . . . *(He again appeals to Estragon without success.)*

LUCKY: It's just that . . . What!

VLADIMIR: Well . . . maybe it's just . . . a little bit . . . too long?

LUCKY: You think it's too long?

VLADIMIR: Maybe . . . by . . . a minute or two?

LUCKY: That play should be TWICE as long as it is! It should go on forever!

VLADIMIR: *(He glares at the silent Estragon.)* Some people think it does!

LUCKY: And some people forget their lines!

VLADIMIR: I know, I know! I lost it! It's just that I was . . . confused . . . temporarily.

LUCKY: They were your FIRST lines!

VLADIMIR: Exactly! I wasn't warmed-up yet.

LUCKY: God, you depress me!

VLADIMIR: So what can I say! I'm sorry, I'm sorry!

LUCKY: Well, I would hope so! Anyway, they're closing up. We have to leave. Thank heavens!

ESTRAGON: *(Grandiosely, turning to her.)* We shall depart presently.

LUCKY: *(Ignores him, stares at Vladimir's hat.)* My God! What did you do to your hat!

VLADIMIR: My hat! I . . . um . . . it fell off.

LUCKY: You'll pay for that! *(She storms angrily off.)*

VLADIMIR: *(Pause.)* You could have said something!

ESTRAGON: Oh, now it's MY fault!

VLADIMIR: No. No. I'm sorry.

ESTRAGON: Oh, forget it. You've had a rather bad night.

VLADIMIR: A RATHER bad night! *(He walks to the tree again.)* God! What are we going to do!

ESTRAGON: Now, now! I'll tell you what we do. We get up, and we go on. Tomorrow is another day!

VLADIMIR: *(Reluctantly.)* Yes, I suppose so.

ESTRAGON: *(Suddenly, with firm resolve.)* Of course it is! And that is exactly what we do!

VLADIMIR: You know. Maybe you're right! *(Firm.)* Yes! We get up, and we go on!

ESTRAGON: *(Somewhat less resolve.)* We move on.

VLADIMIR: *(He sits down again.)* Yes . . . So . . . Shall we?

ESTRAGON: Yes. Let's go.

(They do not move, as the lights slowly fade to a black out.)

END OF PLAY

Daddy Took
My Debt Away

BEKAH BRUNSTETTER

Daddy Took My Debt Away was originally produced by At Play
Productions, Atlantic Theater, New York City, May 19, 2008,
as part of Generation Me, an evening of one-acts.
Directed by James Dacre. Cast: Liz — Lauren Hines;
Ned — Zack Robidas; Ty — Roarke Walker.

CHARACTERS

NED: Twenty-four years old. His shirt is buttoned up to his neck; his tie is impeccable. He takes his first real job very seriously. His daddy taught him right.

TY: Twenty-three and a half years old. This is not his real name, but rather, a self-imposed nick name to make the days less boring. A writer with a day job, which he tries to wear ironically. No belt or tie. Tennis shoes, probably.

LIZ: Twenty-three years old. Drained already. Debt collector by day to pay off her gratuitous student loans. Whimsical, pretty, sheltered. This is her first real job.

SETTING

A small, cramped office: a student loans collection center where Ned and Ty work. It's constantly too hot or too cold. Phones, desks, computers, trashcans, twizzlers, et cetera. Somewhere else, another small, cramped office, where Liz sits behind a similar phone and computer.

TIME

The present.

• • •

Lights up on Liz at her desk. She wears all black. She's been crying. She has a stack of papers in front of her. She's on the phone. It's her fifty-seventh call of the day. No answer, so she leaves a disgruntled message.

LIZ: Hello, Hi, this message is for — *(She regards paper.)* Taylor Hicks. *(Pause.)* Is that your real name? Fine, OK. Sure.

My name's Liz, Elizabeth. I'm calling from American Express.

This is regarding your outstanding balance of *(Regards paperwork.)* — $15,321. And no cents. Good for you.

This includes but is not limited to — *(She regards paper.)* — wow — OK — a slew of pretty chubby late fees, as well as charges accrued with purchases at — establishments — *(She regards paper.)* — $231. 91 at Jimmy's Pub — wow — in one night — yee-haw — and then $347.53 at American Apparel the following business day — that's a lot of hoodies, friend — as well as $176.03 at let's see — Lace — which I believe is a respectable yet moderately trashy gentleman's club frequented by Indian businessmen and the likes of yourself.

And then finally, it looks like you tried to charge your rent to your credit card — heh — cute — and at that point, your card was officially declined.

Then — yeah — it looks like you called the following business day to ask for the fees to be reduced, nay, beg. According to notes in the ledger my coworker recorded you — wept — apparently — when she said no. Huh.

Well — Mr. Hicks — I don't think you need me to tell you this — but this account is past due. This is our fourth attempt to contact you, and if we do not hear back from you by the end of the business day, we will be forced to summon the apocalypse. With guns and giant flies and everything.

Just kidding. Not.

I was a religious studies major. What about you? I believe in the apocalypse, or some terrible end to things. I try not to think about it, though. You strike me as indecisive, as adventurous maybe, I bet you have a canoe. You're one of those guys that you go to his house, his house is little, but he's managed to hang a kayak on the wall.

But for real, call back. I would say give me a call on my direct line, but Taylor, I'm proud to say, you are my final call.

That's right, you're it. Feel special. Do it, just for a minute. Close your eyes. I'm going to do it too. *(She does.)* What do you look like? Nevermind. Point is: Today's my last day. Because of recent — because I — I'm quitting. And you're my last call. *(Pause.)* I have to tell you, you have the most lovely Social Security number I've ever seen. It nearly rhymes. I won't tell it to anyone. I mean I might. But I won't.
(Pause.)

You're pathetic, kind of. I think I'm going to tell you that now. Money isn't — I mean, you can't — I mean, do you think? You put a blow job on your credit card. Do you have a job, even? Who the fuck do you think you are? People are dead and you're — people are dying and, for no reason and getting hit by cars and THERE'S LIKE GENOCIDE IN DARFUR!
(Lights shift to include the work space of Ty and Ned, who are at their respective desks. Ty balances a pen on his finger, listens to a voicemail on his phone. His face is very what-the-fuck. Liz is quiet, embarrassed.)

So — yeah. You should call back. 1-800-AXPRESS. You can give them this handy — um — confirmation number — and — *(She shuffles through papers.)* You know what? Don't. Don't call back. You know what I think of money? It's imaginary, it's Care Bears. Life's too fucking short.

(She hangs up. She gathers her things, puts on her coat. She looks at her desk. Done. Her cell phone rings; she answers.)

Hey, Mom. Are you crying? I'm not. No, I stopped. After lunch. Yeah, I'm coming. I'll be right there.

(She goes. Lights out on her desk. Ned is efficiently shuffling though papers. The phone rings. Ned clears his throat, stretches his neck, cracks his knuckles, answers, softening his voice.)

NED: Thank you for calling Nelly Mae Trust, your single source solution for student loans. You've reached Ned in the Repayment Department. How may I help you today? *(Pause. He listens.)* Mr. Nobody!

(He hangs up. Ty flips his phone shut like POW, like a badass, sits up in his chair.)

TY: That was weird.

NED: What?

TY: Credit cards.

NED: We're not supposed to take personal calls. We're supposed to take them in the break room.

TY: Bitches!

NED: What?

TY: Corporate assholes.

(Pause.)

NED: Well — to be fair — you — technically — also — are a corporate person now, yourself.

TY: I'm infiltrating. OK? I'm sly. See this? *(He picks up a stapler. He puts it in his pocket. This is hard.)* Yeahh.

(Ned's phone rings. A few moments later, Ty's. They answer.)

NED: *(Soft, eager.)* Thank you for calling Nelly Mae Trust, your single source solution for student loans. You've reached Ned in the Repayment Department. How may I help you today?

TY: *(Flat.)* Thanks for calling the Trust, your solution for loans. You've got Ty in the Repayment Department. Can I help you? Hi, Rachel, how are you today? I'm great. You bet. Uh-huh. Uh-huh. What's your special number thing? *(Pause.)* Your Social. I was just being weird. I was just expressing myself. OK, go ahead. Uh-huh.

NED: OK, please stop crying. If you just — stop crying — OK — stop crying — are you sitting down? OK, sit down. Have a glass of water. Drink it up. There you go. That sounds like it tastes good. OK, great. What's your name?

Hi, Steve, how are you today? Right — right — and what's your Social?

Great. There you go.

One moment, while I pull up your account . . . .

TY: OK, Rachel, 83,000 in the hole. None too shabby. That's nothing, that's Cabbage Patch Kids. I myself have one hundred grand in the can. Beat that. Go get your master's, gal. I'm kidding. Don't do it.

No, do it, best years of your life.

Allrighty, given the amount of debt you've accrued, let's discuss your repayment options. I'm sure we can find a plan that's just right for you. Awesome. Let's do this.

NED: I'm showing a balance of $113, 546. And thirteen cents. *(Pause.)* Stop crying, Steve. Steve? Unfortunately, money exists as a thing in the actual world, it's not imaginary, and these things, they build up. Remember, you signed up for this.

TY: You've got forebearance / consolidation — hardship –

NED: Steve, what we can do for you is consolidate your loans to lower your monthly rate. And if this payment still isn't low / enough —

TY: Et cetera, et cetera, hand jobs at Port Authority —

NED: What we can do is, if your payment is equal to or greater than thirteen percent of your / monthly income before, you can temporarly defer your payments for up to one year

TY: Rachel, you're looking at 8,300 hand jobs. At least. And that's if you don't charge cheap. I gotta ask you, Rachel, what kind of girl are you, what kind of woman did your mother raise you to be? I'm kidding, I'm kidding. What are you wearing? Don't listen to me, I'm just being me. Rachel — have you ever considered the Peace Corps?

NED: No, interest will still accumulate on your federal subsidized and unsubsized loans during this time. Should you opt to pay the interest each month, your payment could be as low as thirty-three dollars. Does that sound like something that might work for you?

TY: Rachel, the Peace Corps. Listen. If you join, they pay up to ten thousand of your loans. I'm not kidding. Or, if you were to lose a limb and were rendered incapable of working, your loans would be forgiven by fifty percent.

NED: *(Excited.)* Also, if we extend the repayment plans of each loan to the maximum period — let's see here — yep — yessir — we can get your payment as low as $340 a month. Steve! How 'bout that! What do you say? How about that, sir?

TY: Unfortunately, if you were to die — not that I wish that upon you in any way — your loans would not be forgiven. Can you believe it? Transferred to your kin like an heirloom, but the kind that breaks the mantle. You liked that? I liked it too. I'm a writer actually.

NED: Allrighty! Steve, once I set this payment plan up for you that has been tailored to your needs, your loans will be repaid over a thirty-year period . . . let's see . . .

TY: Screenplays, mainly, psychological thrillers. And some children's theater. Remember the *Brave Little Toaster*? Yeah. Yeah!

NED: At the end of the thirty years, you will have paid a total of $223,671 dollars and fifty-two cents.

TY: Wait, what's your e-mail add? Is the one here? I'm gonna friend you. I'm gonna friend you right now.

NED: Stop crying. Please stop crying. Steve? In thirty years, you're just going to throw yourself a little party when you pay it all off. Just think of it as another bill.

TY: I just did it. Yeah, that's me.

NED: Call me anytime you have questions, Steve. Anytime. Extension 203. Everything's going to be fine.

TY: Great talking to you, Rachel. Rachel from Vermont. Nah, F your loans. Go to France. Go hide in a cave. Cheers. *(He hangs up.)* She sounded hot. How far's Vermont, where is it anyways?

NED: Bye bye now, Steve.
(Ned hangs up. He straightens his tie. He regards paperwork. Ty tries to balance a pencil on his nose, probably.)

TY: Vermont. Vermont.

NED: I hate it when they cry.

TY: I think it's funny.

NED: It's not funny.

TY: I mean objectively, ironically.

NED: I think it's sad. People without money are sad.

TY: I'm not sad.

NED: You're not.

TY: Nah. *(He stops. He thinks. He's sad. He covers.)* What are you gonna have for lunch?

NED: A sandwich.

TY: Hell yeah, me too. I'll order.

NED: I brought my own.

TY: No way.

(Ned pulls out the sandwich. It looks grand.)

NED: If I bring my own sandwich, I can save fifty dollars a week.

TY: Well, I'm gonna order mine. And it's gonna have bacon on it. *(He pulls out his credit card. He looks at it. He puts it down.)* Ned.

NED: What?

TY: Can I borrow ten bucks?

(Pause.)

NED: No.

TY: I maxed out my credit card. Don't be a douche bag.

NED: I'm not, it's just my ten bucks, I earned it.

TY: What, are you gonna invest it? You gonna buy a condo in Florida?

NED: The market's not good right now.

TY: Come on, loan me ten bucks. Your dad pays your rent.

NED: He does not. *(Pause.)* He pays half my rent.

(Pause. Ty smiles.)

NED: What? He pays half my rent and he's happy to do so. He's worked hard and he likes to share it with me. What? He used to be poor and now he's not. He likes to help. There's nothing wrong with that, I'm fine with that. I work, he helps. It's like we're pals.

And when he calls me crying or yelling because I'm ungrateful then gives me five thousand bucks to go to Spain, when he buys me a car then hates me for having it, I know that it's because he wants it to be for me like it was for him, but easier, and harder too.

(Pause. Ty spins in his chair. Ned neatly unwraps his sandwich.)

TY: I went to grad school with this dude, he wasn't worried about his loans. He'd say, I mean, my dad's getting old, and when he goes, I get a million bucks. Then he'd shrug and light a cigarette.

NED: That's sad.

(Lights shift to include Liz, later, sitting on a bench, waiting for a train. Her phone rings.)

LIZ: Hey, Mom. No, I'm waiting for the train. For the — for the train. It was fine. Felt good to just leave, yeah. I'll be right there. I said I'll be right there. An hour. Are you crying? No, I'm not. Love you too.

(She hangs up. She takes what seems to be a bill out of her bag and studies it. She lights a cigarette.)

TY: I wish I was black.

NED: What?

TY: Minority scholarships.

NED: Oh.

TY: If I had gotten some. Then I wouldn't be so in the fucking hole. I wouldn't be here.

NED: Are you being existential?

TY: No, I mean at this douche-bag job. I know a black guy, his mom was a real-life crack whore, he writes movies about it, now he shits gold. *(Pause. He swivels in his chair. He turns back to his computer.)* I want a gun. Like, a gun. Can I buy a gun on ebay?

NED: No, I've looked.

> *(Liz dials a number. It rings. It rings in the office. Ned is eating. Ty ignores the phone.)*

NED: Can you get that?

TY: Bullets sold separately . . .

NED: Ty.

> *(Finally, Ty answers the phone.)*

TY: Thank you for calling the loan center. You've reached Ty in repayment. Do you prefer machetes or hand grenades?

LIZ: Um — what?

TY: How may I service you?

LIZ: Um — hi — my name's Liz —

TY: Hi, Liz.

LIZ: Hi.

TY: Hi. How may I service you?

LIZ: I'm calling because I need to pay off my student loans. Entirely. I mean, I'm able to.

> *(Pause.)*

TY: What?

LIZ: I'd like to pay off my loans entirely.

TY: Liz, hold on, I'm going to have to put you on speaker. *(To Ned.)* Ned, you gotta hear this. *(He puts her on speaker.)* OK, Liz, go ahead.

LIZ: So I'm / wondering —

TY: No, from the beginning.

LIZ: I'd like to pay off my loans.

TY: Wouldn't we all. I'd like a hound-dog puppy and a new pair of shoes.

LIZ: No, I mean, I can. I'm able to.

TY: Oh? You win the lottery, Liz? You marry rich?

LIZ: No, my dad died. Suddenly, all of the sudden. *(Pause. Ty doesn't know what to say. The cat got all of his tongues.)* And as, um, as my consolation prize, I get lots of money. I get to quit my job. I get to move back home with my mom.

TY: Well — that's great news, Liz —

(Ned jumps up, takes the phone off speaker, sits in Ty's chair.)

NED: Hi, Liz? This is Ned. Ty had to step out and use the restroom a lot. I'll be happy to help you.

LIZ: Hi, Ned.

NED: I'm very sorry for your loss.

LIZ: No, I guess this is why he died, I guess. I — I don't have to worry any more.

NED: I — I'm very sorry.

LIZ: He didn't like me to have to worry all the time.

NED: I'm assuming you'd like us to bill the checking account on file?

LIZ: Yes, that's fine.

NED: We'll take care of everything, you don't have to do anything.

LIZ: Thank you.

NED: You're welcome. *(Pause.)* Is there anything else I can —

LIZ: No, that's all thanks. *(Pause.)* Good-bye, I guess, forever. *(They hang up. Liz waits for her train. Lights out on her.)*

(Ty is eating Ned's sandwich. He puts it down. He swallows. Ned stares at the phone. He goes back to the computer. He clears his throat, resumes working, obviously disturbed. Ty returns to his chair. He swivels.)

TY: Lucky bitch.

(Ned won't respond. He works.)

TY: Lucky, lucky bitch.

END OF PLAY

Enter the Naked Woman

BRENDON ETTER

Enter the Naked Woman was originally produced at the Northfield Arts Guild Theater, Northfield, Minn., January 2009. Directed by Brendon Etter. Cast: Nick — Brendon Etter; Ed — Steve Lawler; Amie — Ann Etter.

CHARACTERS

    NICK: Late twenties, professional, well dressed.

    ED: Late forties, older professional, Nick's boss.

    AMIE: Midtwenties, attractive French waitress.

SETTING

    Contemporary French restaurant, evening.

TIME

    The present.

• • •

Nick and Ed sit at a well-appointed restaurant table, looking over fancy menus.

NICK: So much to choose from. What doesn't this place offer?

ED: I've heard the food is tremendous.

NICK: Really, thanks for taking me here, Ed.

ED: Nothing but the best for our newest junior partner.

NICK: Thank you.

ED: Hey, Nick, you don't need to keep thanking me, you've earned this.

NICK: Still, it's . . .

ED: Nice, yeah, I know, but so many other nice things are going to start coming your way now. Get used to it, buddy. I've got to find the little boys' room. *(Leaves.)*

NICK: *(Looking around a bit, then back to his menu, shakes head lightly, gives a little laugh, then says to himself.)* Yeah . . . I could definitely get used to this.

    (Enter Amie, a very attractive woman, completely nude, more than adequately endowed. She pulls up to the table; she speaks English well with a strong French accent. It is imperative to the play that Amie does not notice her own nudity, nor is she actually trying to be sexual at any point.)

AMIE: Good evening, sir, my . . .

    (Nick picks his head out of his menu and nearly falls out of his chair in shock.)

AMIE: *(Grabbing Nick's shoulders to steady him.)* Oh, monsieur, are you OK?

NICK: Uhhh . . . uhhhh . . .

AMIE: My name is Amie. I will be your server for the evening. Would you care for anything to drink before your meal?

NICK: *(Trying his best to look at only her face, but actually can't force his gaze any lower than a spot about four feet above Amie's head.)* Uhhhh . . . uhh . . . wa . . . water would be . . . I need, uhhh . . . water would be . . . water.

AMIE: Water. Of course, sir. *(She starts to exit, then turns around.)* Pardon, sir, would your boyfriend like some water too?

NICK: Yes . . . uhhh . . . he . . . oh wait, umm, he's not my boyfriend. He's actually sort of my, uhhh, my boss at work.

AMIE: Yes, sir. Would your boss friend like some water too?

NICK: Just . . . ummm . . . yes. Water for him too.

AMIE: Right away, waters for the boyfriends. *(She exits.)*

NICK: *(Calling after her, but quietly.)* Just friends . . . friends.

(Nick gets up, still very much stunned, and starts heading toward the bathroom just as Ed reenters)

ED: *(Striding toward the table.)* Hey, guy. Bathroom? *(Nick nods.)* That way. *(Points him toward the bathrooms.)* You OK? *(Nick has already started heading off to the bathrooms and doesn't respond, Ed sits, look at his menu.)* *(Amie reenters, carrying a crystal carafe of ice water and two glasses)*

AMIE: *(Putting down the glasses.)* Hello, sir, your boyfr . . .

(Ed pulls his nose out of the menu, jumps backward out of his seat upon seeing Amie. Amie startles at his reaction, splashes some ice water on her chest.)

AMIE: Mon dieu! Pardon, pardon me, sir . . . sorry to have surprised you . . . ohh, look at me, I've spilled your water . . . and all over myself too.

ED: Ummm . . . miss . . . do you realize that you . . . uhhh . . .

AMIE: I am now so wet? Yes. One thousand apologies for my clumsiness, sir.

ED: But . . .

AMIE: Have I made you wet too, sir?

ED: No! No! I'm fine, I'm fine . . . Ummm . . .

AMIE: I promise to make it up to you in any manner, sir.

ED: Uhhh . . .

AMIE: I must dry myself. I will get a fresh tablecloth for you and your boyfriend, sir.

ED: No, don't worry, the tablecloth is fi . . . Wait. Nick? Ohhh, he's not my boyfriend.

AMIE: Yes, sir.

ED: He's my new partner.

AMIE: Yes, sir. This word works also.

ED: Ummm . . . can you . . . ahhh . . .

AMIE: Yes, sorry, I will be back shortly. There is a towel in the kitchen.

(Amie exits, Ed stands up, the spilled water has landed all over his lap. He fans out his pants for a while, Nick reenters and sits. Ed turns at just this moment to hide his wet pants from Nick, starts exiting.)

NICK: Did she bring . . . Ed?

ED: *(As he exits, muttering.)* Bathroom.

NICK: *(Looks at his menu and toward the kitchen over and over again, mumbles.)* Bizarre . . .

(Amie reenters, dried off, with a fresh carafe of ice water.)

AMIE: Ohh, your boyfriend has left?

NICK: Bathroom.

AMIE: *(Pouring water for Nick.)* I'm afraid I must have embarrassed him. He was there and jumped, and it made me very wet.

NICK: *(Coughs.)* Oh.

AMIE: The chef's assistant was able to help with that. Now, I am ready.

NICK: You know, uhhh . . . I believe I would actually like something from the bar before . . . before I order.

AMIE: Certainly, sir. What would you like?

NICK: *(Eyes slipping down to Amie's crotch, back up quickly.)* Uhh, three fingers of Glenlivet, straight up.

(He holds up three fingers, pressed together; she looks at the fingers, he looks at her crotch then his fingers, quickly pulls his hand down.)

NICK: I mean, you know, just . . . uhhh . . . that much.

(He holds his thumb and index finger about two inches apart. Amie looks at it, then him; he again realizes the potential significance, withdraws his hand).

NICK: Make it a large.

AMIE: Gladly. Is there anything else you desire, sir?

NICK: *(Squeaky voice.)* No, no . . . just the scotch . . . a lot of . . . scotch.

AMIE: Are you OK, sir? Your voice.

NICK: *(Trying to clear his throat, forcing out a normal voice.)* Ha! No . . . no . . . long day at work, I guess.

AMIE: With your boyfriend?

NICK: Yes . . . no . . . my boss, yes, my boss . . . Ed.

AMIE: Yes, your boyfriend boss.

NICK: No, see, he is not my boyfriend . . . not my boyfriend . . .

AMIE: Ohhh . . . of course, I do not mean . . . I mean only he is a boy, and he is your friend . . .

NICK: Oh, yeah . . . I guess that's . . . uhh . . .

AMIE: Like I have many girlfriends . . . but I do not date girls . . .

NICK: Yes, yes, like that, I mean, with Ed and me . . . we are boyfriends in that way . . .

AMIE: I wish I had boyfriends . . .

NICK: Uhhh . . . surely you must . . . working here in . . . *(Indicating her state of undress, then catching himself.)* such a nice restaurant.

AMIE: Sad, but no . . . many of the men I service are gay . . . with their boyfriends . . .

NICK: *(Reacting way too loudly and quickly.)* Not me! Nope, not me!

AMIE: Of course.

NICK: *(Way too eager.)* No! No! I like girls! I really, really like girls!

(He eagerly moves about in his seat, but does so in such a jerking manner as to tip the chair over backward, slamming his head onto the hard floor, grabs the back of his head.)

NICK: Oww!

AMIE: *(Coming to his side, kneeling by his head.)* Sir! Sir! Please let me help you.

NICK: I'm all right! I'm OK!

(Embarrassedly tries to roll out of the chair, Amie holds him there.)

AMIE: Please stay, sir.

(She grabs one of the linen napkins from the table, leans forward, which effectively freezes Nick completely as her breasts hang very close to his face. She tends to the back of his head with the napkin.)

AMIE: Oh, sir, you are bleeding. There is a towel in the kitchen. *(She gets up and exits.)*

NICK: *(Rolling out of the chair now, to Amie as she exits)* I'm OK . . . OK, really . . . I think I'll just clean up . . .

(Starts to exit, almost running over Ed in the process, who is fanning his crotch a few more times.)

ED: Whoa . . . everything all right, buddy?

NICK: *(Continuing off without stopping.)* Yes. Bathroom. *(Exits.)*

ED: *(Sitting down.)* Popular place.

(Amie reenters, carrying a towel.)

AMIE: Where did he go?

ED: Bathroom. Is everything OK?

AMIE: Yes, sir. I tried to help him, but as soon as I touched his head, it spurted all over my hand.

ED: Ohh . . .

AMIE: I went to get the towel to help him, but he has come and gone again.

ED: Again?

AMIE: Well, perhaps I will help him with his head later.

ED: Head?

AMIE: I was trying to help with my hands, but I am always blowing such things.

ED: Always?

AMIE: I hope he will forgive me.

ED: Ummmm . . . I wouldn't worry about that.

AMIE: My boss tells me it's most important to make sure customers respect me, then they will respect my service and the restaurant.

ED: I'm sure Nick will respect you just the same.

AMIE: I hope so. Would you like anything to drink, something from the bar, before you order, sir?

ED: Just a milk. *(Panic.)* Whiskey! Whiskey! A whiskey. Make it a quadruple.

AMIE: What brand, sir?

ED: Who's available? *(Panic.)* What! What! What's available!

AMIE: *(At his side, opening his menu and pointing out the whiskey selection, leaning over Ed's shoulder, her breast touching his shoulder, Ed is only able to focus on this point of contact.)* Well, we have this selection here. I would recommend the Jameson, sir, authentic Irish whiskey, very distinctive flavor.

ED: *(Trying to focus.)* That sounds very nipple.

AMIE: *(Standing up.)* Excuse me, sir?

ED: Breasts?

AMIE: Sir?

ED: Yes! Yes! I said yes! I just said . . . yes . . . I . . .

AMIE: The Jameson, sir? On the rocks?

ED: *(Shifting uncomfortably in his seat.)* Straight up . . . straight.

AMIE: Right away, sir. *(She exits.)*

 (Ed stands up carefully, slightly hunched over, hiding his erection, he walks toward the bathroom, sees Nick coming toward him, does a quick turn so Nick sees his back, pretends to look at something.)

NICK: Hey, Ed.

 (As soon as Nick pulls even with Ed, Ed turns back and continues walking to the bathroom.)

ED: Nick.

 (Nick sits down, still checking the back of his head. Amie enters with the two drinks.)

AMIE: Hello, sir, how was the head?

NICK: Fine, fine . . .

AMIE: Did it leak more in the bathroom.

NICK: No, no, not really, just a small bump, a cut . . . I'll be fine.

AMIE: That is good news, sir.

NICK: Was something wrong with Ed?

AMIE: I don't know, sir. He said he wanted it straight up; so I left, and now he is gone.

NICK: *(As she sets his drink down.)* That's a lot of scotch.

AMIE: You asked for a large, sir.

NICK: Yes, so I did.

AMIE: *(She sets Ed's drink down.)* He has ordered a quadruple. That is a very rare request as well.

NICK: I'm sure.

AMIE: Would you like to order a first course now, sir?

NICK: Ummm . . . I think I will wait until my friend returns.

AMIE: Certainly, sir. *(She exits.)*

(Nick watches after her, looks around, surreptitiously walks toward where Amie exited, peaks around the corner, looks for a few seconds. Ed reenters, stops.)

ED: Nick?

NICK: *(Jumping back.)* Ed. Hi . . . yes . . . *(Walking back to the table.)* just checking out the menu. Lots of great food!

(Nick sits down, Ed also with a suspicious look toward Amie's exit.)

ED: Yes. Tons of great fare, all first class.

NICK: You've never eaten here before, though?

ED: No, it comes very highly recommended, thought it'd be a great reward for you.

NICK: Right.

ED: *(Confessionally.)* And . . . you can't really argue with the service, huh?

NICK: *(A sigh of relief.)* No kidding? What is up with our waitress?

ED: No idea.

NICK: Unbelievable.

ED: I had heard that the service was amazing, but this?

NICK: It's almost . . . awkward . . .

ED: She sounds French, perhaps it's a cultural thing?

NICK: Well, then I'm now a huge fan of French cuisine.

ED: And pretty much anything else of French origin.

NICK: I believe I will be back here frequently.

ED: I'm right with you.

NICK: She said we are supposed to be picking out our first course now.

ED: Well, I know one thing that I'd like right away!

NICK: I'd save it for dessert.

(They are laughing as Amie reenters, fully clothed in formal waitress style.)

AMIE: Bonjour, gentlemen.

(Ed and Nick are shocked, speechless.)

AMIE: Have you decided upon a first course?

ED: Uhhh . . .

NICK: Well . . .

ED: We haven't been . . . ummm . . .

(A lightbulb flashes on for Nick.)

NICK: Let me see, just checkin' the menu . . . *(Instead of picking up his own menu, he reaches across the table and picks up Ed's and very obviously knocks the whiskey into Ed's lap with the menu.)* Whoops!

ED: *(Jumping back, standing up.)* Hey! What? Crap . . .

AMIE: Oh, sir, let me help you, there is a towel in the kitchen! *(She exits.)*

NICK: Sorry! Sorry, Ed! Better go clean that up in the bathroom . . .

(Ed fans his crotch again)

ED: I can't believe this . . . aggghhh . . . *(Ed stomps off toward bathroom.)*

NICK: *(Calling after him.)* Use the air dryer. Sorry, man! *(Sits back. To himself, quietly, head tilted up, eyes closed.)* Please work, please work, please work, please, please, please, please, please . . . .

(Nick continues like this until Amie reenters, totally nude again, carrying a towel.)

NICK: *(Muttering triumphantly to himself.)* Yes!

AMIE: Ohh . . . where has he gone?

NICK: *(A big smile crossing his face.)* I think he's getting a blow job in the bathroom.

AMIE: But I could have got it off with this towel.

(Nick now "accidentally" dumps his own drink in his lap.)

AMIE: Oh, sir!

NICK: *(Looking at Amie.)* Damn.

(She moves toward his lap with the towel. Nick smiles.)

(Lights out.)

END OF PLAY

Poor Shem

GREGORY HISCHAK

Poor Shem was originally produced at the Stanford Calderwood
Pavilion, Boston Center for the Arts, May 11 2008, as part of
the Boston Theater Marathon. Directed by Darren Evans.
Cast: Kendel — Craig Houk; Kaitlin — Crystal Lisbon;
Kyle — Nathaniel Gundy.

CHARACTERS

> KENDEL: Thirty-five to fifty-five, a dominant male.

> KAITLIN: Twenty-five to fifty-five, a woman of easily diluted compassion.

> KYLE: Thirty to forty, a less dominant male, probably younger than Kendel.

SETTING

> The setting is an office copying room.

TIME

> The present.

NOTE: Tabbed type in the script indicates where an overlap, or stepping on, of the previous line of dialogue begins.

• • •

Machinery sounds: these are performed by the characters.

KENDEL: Shicka shicka shicka shicka . . . *(Continue as Kaitlin joins in.)*

KAITLIN: Fwoosha ha fwoosha ha fwoosha ha fwoosha ha . . . *(Continue as Kyle joins in.)*

KYLE: Kahlakala kahlakala kahlakala kahlakala kahlakala kahlakala kahlakala klahk.

> *(All stop.)*

KAITLIN: Of all the things you give in your life, none is more precious than your labor.

KYLE: The job you are paid to do.

KENDEL: The job you dedicate your best, most productive years to.

> *(Beat.)*

KENDEL: Shicka shicka shicka shicka . . . *(Continue as Kaitlin joins in.)*

KAITLIN: Fwoosha ha fwoosha ha fwoosha ha fwoosha ha . . . *(Continue as Kyle joins in.)*

KYLE: Kahlakala kahlakala kahlakala kahlakala kahlakala kahlakala kahlakala klahk.

> *(Abrupt, pained, all stop.)*

KAITLIN: Jesus.

KYLE: Don't that beat —

KENDEL: Shit.

KAITLIN: For the love of —

KYLE: I'll be damned.

KAITLIN: Jammed.

KENDEL: Jammed?

KYLE: What happened?

KAITLIN: Jammed.

KYLE: Who jammed it?

KAITLIN: *Nobody* jammed it.

KYLE: It just jammed?

KENDEL: Yes, jammed.

KAITLIN: It *just* jammed.

KENDEL: Christ.

KAITLIN: Christ.

KYLE: There's an eight and a half by eleven stuck in the bypass tray.
    (Thoughtful beat.)

KENDEL: An eight and a half by eleven stuck in the bypass tray?

KYLE: It says so right here . . .

KAITLIN: Try hitting Print again.

KYLE: Don't hit Print.

KENDEL: There's an eight and a half by eleven stuck in the
    bypass tray.

KAITLIN: Push the Green Button.

KYLE: Don't push the Green Button, you'll kill us all.

KENDEL: Let's not panic, people.

KAITLIN: Christ.

KYLE: What do we do?

KENDEL: Open the front panel.

KYLE: What?

KAITLIN: Right. Open the front of the copier.

KYLE: I'm not opening the front of the copier.

KAITLIN: Do I look like I'm dressed to open copiers?

KENDEL: It's not my job to open the front of the copier to fix every
    goddamned paper jam . . . Jesus.
    (Kyle has opened the copier.)

KAITLIN: For the love of . . .

KENDEL: I'll be damned.
    (Thoughtful beat.)

KYLE: That's a jam.

KENDEL: That is *one hell* of a jam.

KAITLIN: What is that?

KENDEL: *One hell* of a jam.

KAITLIN: No, that.

KYLE: What?

KAITLIN: That.

KYLE: You mean right *there?*

KAITLIN: No, *that* right there.

KENDEL: There?

KYLE: There?

KAITLIN: Yeah, right *there.*

KENDEL: What is that?

KYLE: *That?*

KAITLIN: Yes, *that.*

KYLE: That's my abutments and drainage proposal.

KAITLIN: No. What's that wrapped around it?

KYLE: *There?*

KAITLIN: THERE.

KENDEL: That's a tie.

> *(Thoughtful beat.)*

KAITLIN: It's a necktie

KENDEL: Yup, that's a necktie all right.

KYLE: It's a yellow necktie with . . . a . . .

KAITLIN: So, what's *that* then?

KYLE: You mean right —

KAITLIN: There.

KENDEL: Inside the necktie?

KAITLIN: Right there inside the necktie.

KYLE: That would be . . .

> *(Beat.)*

KENDEL: It's a neck.

> *(Beat for examination.)*

KYLE: Yup, that's a neck all right.

KAITLIN: It's a neck.

KYLE: That's a neck in that tie.

KENDEL: Yup.

> *(Beat.)*

KAITLIN: So, it stands to reason that this . . . this neck is attached
. . . to something?

KENDEL: Absolutely.

KYLE: No way around it.

KENDEL: Necks don't just happen.

KAITLIN: So, what's that attached —

KENDEL: to the neck — ?

KYLE: *That* neck?

KAITLIN: Of course *that* neck.

KENDEL: Do you see another neck in there — ?

KYLE: It's Shem.

(Thoughtful beat.)

KENDEL: What?

KYLE: Shem.

KAITLIN: That's Shem all right.

KENDEL: *(Addressing Shem.)* Shem?

KYLE: *(Addressing Shem.)* Shem?

(Thoughtful beat.)

KAITLIN: Jesus.

KYLE: Don't that beat —

KENDEL: Shit.

KYLE: It's Shem, all right.

KAITLIN: *(Addressing Shem.)* Shem?

KENDEL: Shem's in the copier.

KYLE: That's Shem's tie.

KENDEL: How do you know that's Shem's tie?

KYLE: I bought Shem that tie.

KENDEL: You *bought* him that tie?

KAITLIN: That's Shem's tie all right. Poor Shem.

KENDEL: What do you mean you bought him that tie?

KYLE: It was a present.

KENDEL: A present?

KAITLIN: How thoughtful. Birthday?

KYLE: Secret Santa.

KENDEL: Poor Shem.

KAITLIN: Poor Shem.

KYLE: Poor Shem. *(Addressing Shem.)* Shem?

(Thoughtful beat.)

KAITLIN: He's dead isn't he?

KENDEL: Very much so.

KAITLIN: Shem is dead.

KYLE: Crushed to death in the eight and a half by eleven bypass tray.

KAITLIN: Asphyxiated.

KENDEL: Decapitated.

KYLE: Mangled.

KAITLIN: Electrocuted.

KENDEL: Collated.

KAITLIN: Poor Shem.

KYLE: Poor Shem.

    (Respectful beat.)

KAITLIN: How old was he?

KYLE: Thirty-four.

KAITLIN: *Only* thirty-four.

KYLE: His whole life ahead of him.

KENDEL: Apparently not.

KYLE: We should get him out.

KAITLIN: It's the right thing to do.

KYLE: He'd have done it for any one of us.

KENDEL: How do you know that?

KYLE: He was that kind of man.

KENDEL: *What* kind of man?

KAITLIN: Did you say birthday?

KYLE: Secret Santa.

KAITLIN: It's very nice.

KENDEL: Yes, nice tie, Kyle.

KYLE: Thank you.

KAITLIN: Stylish.

    (Beat.)

KENDEL: So, why is it — ?

KYLE: What?

KENDEL: Why is it — we don't have interns for cleaning up messes like this?

KYLE: An intern is an excellent idea.

KAITLIN: On-the-job training.

KYLE: It develops those people skills.

KENDEL: Priceless skills for later . . . in life.

KAITLIN: in life — poor Shem.

KYLE: Struck down in his prime.

KAITLIN: You just never know.

KENDEL: Know what?

KAITLIN: Life.

KENDEL: Oh, that.

KAITLIN: Blink.

KYLE: That's right, blink.

KENDEL: Blink?

KAITLIN: It's that quick.

KENDEL: Look at the time.

KYLE: How did it get to be lunchtime?

KAITLIN: Poor Shem.

KENDEL: It's . . . *really* not my job . . . I mean — scrapping Shem from the copier.

KAITLIN: Do I look like I'm dressed for —

KYLE: Drainage and abutments, that's my job. Poor Shem.

KAITLIN: Poor ol' Shem. We should call his wife.

KENDEL: We should call the copier repairman.

KYLE: Morrie?

KENDEL: Morrie.

KAITLIN: Yes, we should call Morrie.

KENDEL: Morrie will know what to do.

KYLE: Morrie knows his copiers.

KAITLIN: Somebody should call Shem's wife. She'd want to know.

KENDEL: It's not my job to tell people that their husbands were sucked into photocopiers.

KAITLIN: She'd want to know.

KENDEL: It's the right thing to do.

KYLE: Poor Shem.

KENDEL: Poor Shem.

KAITLIN: Poor ol' Shem.

(Longer thoughtful beat.)

KENDEL: Did Shem *have* a wife?

KYLE: No. I mean, I don't *think* so . . .

KENDEL: No wife?

KAITLIN: With a tie like that — and no wife?

KENDEL: Hard to believe, isn't it?

KYLE: It is.

(Beat.)

KENDEL: So then . . .

KYLE: Well . . .

KAITLIN: There you are.

KENDEL: Yup.

KYLE: Poor Shem.

KAITLIN: Poor Shem.

KENDEL: Poor Shem — you know . . . maybe . . .

KYLE: Maybe — ?

KAITLIN: Maybe . . .what?

KENDEL: Maybe the eight and a half by fourteen tray is working?

KAITLIN: *(Mild outrage.)* What?

KENDEL: I mean Shem is stuck in the eight and a half by eleven bypass tray —

KYLE: Tragically mutilated in an eight and a half by eleven bypass tray.

KAITLIN: *(Mild outrage.)* A coworker is dead here.

KENDEL: Yes, poor Shem.

KYLE: Poor ol' Shem — you've got a point, though.

KENDEL: That's right

KYLE: The eight and a half by fourteen tray might be working.

KAITLIN: A *coworker* is dead here.

KYLE: We should call Morrie.

KENDEL: Hit the eight and a half by fourteen, people.

KAITLIN: Maybe we should call a priest.

KYLE: No, we should call Morrie.

KAITLIN: Morrie is not ordained.

KYLE: Morrie knows his copiers.

KENDEL: No, hit the Reset first.

KAITLIN: We should call a priest.

KENDEL: Hit the Reset first.

KYLE: Maybe we should call Morrie *and* a priest.

KAITLIN: A coworker is dead.

KYLE: I know. Do I hit Reset or call a priest? *(Beat.)* Do I hit Reset or call a priest?

> *(Thoughtful beat for moral dilemma.)*

KYLE: Reset, or a priest?

> *(Thoughtful beat for moral dilemma.)*

KYLE: Reset or a priest, Kaitlin?

> *(Thoughtful beat for moral dilemma.)*

KYLE: Kendel, Reset or a priest?

> *(Longer thoughtful beat for moral dilemma.)*

KENDEL: Reset.

KYLE: Reset?

KAITLIN: Reset.

KENDEL: Close the front panel, Kyle.

KYLE: You close the panel, Kaitlin.

KAITLIN: Do I look like I'm dressed for closing the front panel?

KENDEL: Close the front panel, Kyle.

KYLE: I'm closing the front panel then.

KAITLIN: OK. Hit eight and a half by fourteen, Kyle.

KENDEL: No, hit the Reset first.

KAITLIN: Hit Print.

KENDEL: *Don't hit Print.* You waste your time hitting Print until the copier is warmed up.

KAITLIN: A coworker is dead.

KYLE: He had his whole life ahead of him.

KENDEL: Tragically mutilated in an eight and a half by eleven bypass tray.

KAITLIN: Of all the things you could give in your life, none is more precious than your labor.

KYLE: Your labor —

KENDEL: Hit Reset again.

KYLE: — is the most precious. The job you are paid to do; the job you dedicate the best, most productive years of your life to. Nothing is more precious than that.

KENDEL: *I've* always believed that.

KAITLIN: I've *always* believed that.

KYLE: *Nothing* is more precious than that.

(Thoughtful beat.)

KENDEL: So, we'll wait for the Green Button to light up.

KAITLIN: And when it lights up —

KYLE: — we'll hit Print.

KENDEL: Wait for the Green.

KYLE: I'm waiting for the Green.

KENDEL: It's warming up . . . it's warming . . .

KAITLIN: Let it warm up.

KYLE: I'm *letting* it warm up, already.

KENDEL: Wait for the Green.

KAITLIN: And when it turns Green.

KYLE: We'll hit Print.

KENDEL: Almost lunchtime.

KYLE: I'm starved.

KAITLIN: Wait for it.

KYLE: I'm waiting.

KENDEL: Wait for it.

KYLE: I'm waiting.

KENDEL: Wait for the Green.

KAITLIN: Of all the things you could give . . .

KYLE: Nothing is more precious . . .

KENDEL: I've always believed that.

KYLE: I've always believed that.

> *(Beat.)*

KENDEL: Shicka shicka shicka shicka . . . *(Continue as Kaitlin joins in.)*

KAITLIN: Fwoosha ha fwoosha ha fwoosha ha fwoosha ha . . .*(Continue as Kyle joins in.)*

KYLE: Kahlakala kahlakala kahlakala kahlakala kahlakala kahlakala kahlakala klahk.

> *(All stop.)*

KENDEL: Poor Shem.

KYLE: Poor Shem.

KAITLIN: Poor ol' Shem.

> *(To black.)*

END OF PLAY

Transpiration

Vincent Delaney

Transpiration was originally produced at Seattle University,
February 2008, as part of the SITE Specific Festival.
Directed by Vincent Delaney. Cast: Engelman — Erin Kraft;
Hake — Ray Tagavilla; Beatty — James Stark.

ENGELMAN: Mid- to late twenties, female, scientist.

HAKE: Mid- to late twenties, male, scientist.

BEATTY: Fifties, male, scientist.

SETTING

A garden lit by floodlights. A lush space, dense but well tended. The floods create sharp shadows where the lights don't penetrate. Behind this bright space is an impenetrable darkness. The effect is slightly creepy. Center stage is a simple white bench.

TIME

Evening, eleven years from today.

• • •

Engelman enters in full hazmat bodysuit, including hood. She surveys the garden, sees a plant specimen, collects it carefully, using tweezers. Hake enters, also full suit. He pulls out a camera, motions Engelman to pose. She's bashful. He insists. She relents, holds up the specimen. Hake takes her picture. Shows her the result. She doesn't like it. He tries to do it again. She resists. Finally, he convinces her to pose with him, side by side. He takes the picture, camera outstretched in one hand. They admire the result. She moves away, bashful. He sees a flower. Makes sure she isn't looking. Lifts his hood, smells it. It's glorious. He plucks the flower, tucks it into his suit. He puts his hood back on. She's watching him. He sees her. Their voices are muffled.

HAKE: Hi.

ENGELMAN: What was that?

HAKE: Sorry?

ENGELMAN: What did you do?

HAKE: Huh?

ENGELMAN: I said, what did you —

HAKE: I can't — what?

ENGELMAN: You heard me.

HAKE: Say that again?

ENGELMAN: You know exactly what —

HAKE: Sorry, can't hear.

(She pulls off her hood.

ENGELMAN: You removed something.

HAKE: Whoah. Engelman?

ENGELMAN: What was it?

HAKE: Are you sure you want to do that?

ENGELMAN: Show me.

HAKE: You're breathing all over everything.

ENGELMAN: What did you take?

HAKE: Random sample.

ENGELMAN: Show me what you took. Now.

(He pulls out the flower. She's furious.)

ENGELMAN: You can't just —

HAKE: I know —

ENGELMAN: Everything is monitored, we can't just —

HAKE: I won't do it again —

ENGELMAN: What were you thinking?

HAKE: It's pretty.

ENGELMAN: What? *(He pulls off his hood.)*

HAKE: I just think it's pretty. *(He offers her the flower.)* You like purple. Don't you?

ENGELMAN: I love purple.

(She takes the flower.)

HAKE: I think sniffing is allowed.

(She sniffs. He pulls out a spray bottle, begins spraying the grass.)

HAKE: I'm really steamed about San Francisco. Everyone knows they're idiots, but you'd think they'd prefer not to flaunt it. They get the gas exchange right, no pathogens, all the UV shielding, and they forget the water table. Shriveled roots and dead stems. Isn't that just like Stanford? Overeducated jerks. *(He kneels down.)* Do you know what this is? Crabgrass. I'm serious, it's a weed. It's replicating on its own. I feel like a hero. We're good, you know that? Are we good?

ENGELMAN: We're good.

HAKE: Sure we're violating containment, but I'm mainly breathing through my nose. Plus I feel great, which improves my job performance. I actually feel better breathing this stuff. You should try it.

(She doesn't respond.)

HAKE: I'll put my hood back on.

ENGELMAN: It's too late.

HAKE: You know people used to just go out in the woods and breathe. Isn't that shocking? Most of the time the botany survived just fine. In some cases it thrived. You want to take a break? Let's take a break. *(Beat.)* I'm sorry.

ENGELMAN: It's just —

HAKE: I know.

ENGELMAN: There are protocols —

HAKE: I'm sorry.

ENGELMAN: We have to be careful.

HAKE: We're not San Francisco, we're not Cleveland, we're smart. We know how to fertilize, we know how to water.

ENGELMAN: I've made so many errors.

HAKE: No.

ENGELMAN: With the reduced climates —

HAKE: Not this one.

ENGELMAN: And all the perennials dying off —

HAKE: They were weak.

ENGELMAN: And the ribosomal vectors are all wrong —

HAKE: I know —

ENGELMAN: I've got RNA strings that are just scary, I don't know what they do —

HAKE: Silly RNA —

ENGELMAN: And I keep getting these, these large flowering things, even though we eliminated seed-based migration. I mean, what are they?

HAKE: Flowers.

ENGELMAN: We eliminated flowers. Flowers are gone. Plus I think I'm on probation.

HAKE: No.

ENGELMAN: I think that's why they still have me doing field work.

HAKE: You're a gifted botanist.

ENGELMAN: Anyone can take samples.

HAKE: You're senior team leader, they trust you, you have the eye.

ENGELMAN: Probation.

HAKE: What about me, I'm not on probation. Why keep me on, if it's just a punishment detail?

ENGELMAN: I asked for you.

(Beat.)

HAKE: We've never made out in the biome.

(Beat. She stares at him.)

HAKE: Joking, hey, come on, Engelman, lighten up.

ENGELMAN: I thought you —

HAKE: No. No.

ENGELMAN: Because that would be —

HAKE: I know, I was just —

ENGELMAN: Really fantastic. *(Beat.)* Remember how we met?

HAKE: The biohazard conference. You were sensational.

ENGELMAN: It was just a paper.

HAKE: The best one. The very best. I knew right then —

ENGELMAN: You did not.

HAKE: I did, I did —

ENGELMAN: From my conference paper? You don't even remember the topic.

HAKE: Opportunistic Pathogens in an Accelerating Thermal Climate.

ENGELMAN: You remembered.

HAKE: It was so well written.

ENGELMAN: You're too good for me.

HAKE: *(Looking out.)* Look at it. Go on, look, really look. You see it?

ENGELMAN: Yes.

HAKE: You don't, you're not even looking.

ENGELMAN: I am, I am —

HAKE: Really look, it's, what's the right word, it's verdant. It's sylvan, it's —

ENGELMAN: Dense.

HAKE: Herbaceous, riotous, sumptuous —

ENGELMAN: Dense.

HAKE: Teeming, ambrosial —

ENGELMAN: Dense. It's dense.

HAKE: Good descriptor.

ENGELMAN: Hake? I'm glad you're here.

HAKE: People used to sit in the woods. In normal clothes, no urban habitats. Just go off and stare at biologies. They'd travel for days to watch various random things grow and decay.

ENGELMAN: I've never understood it.

HAKE: Me neither.

ENGELMAN: Do you think Nature hates us?

HAKE: Who?

ENGELMAN: Nature. For what we did to it.

HAKE: You mean plants?

ENGELMAN: No, Nature, capital N.

HAKE: I don't — what?

ENGELMAN: A, a presence, a force opposed to us, Life, all consuming, rapacious. As the Greeks believed. Mythic. Do you understand me at all?

HAKE: Oh my God. Are you religious?

ENGELMAN: No —

HAKE: Because it's fine, it's good, I've heard of scientists getting religion, not that it has any application to what we're doing, but that's a choice which I can respect, I'm sure you can work with it to some kind of positive result, please tell me you're not religious.

ENGELMAN: That's not what I mean.

HAKE: Whoah. You had me so scared.

ENGELMAN: Sometimes I think it's just waiting for us to leave. The only real problem here is us. And when we vanish, it will reclaim what it owns.

HAKE: I've been naughty. Want to see?

(He pulls the end of a long snaking straw from his suit. It's connected to an inner pouch. He offers it to her.)

ENGELMAN: What is that?

HAKE: Shiraz.

ENGELMAN: Are you insane? That is so not allowed.

HAKE: They won't know. Unless you tell them.

ENGELMAN: That's organic material. You spill any of it, the contamination will be off the chart.

HAKE: Then we'd better not spill. Drink up.

(She drinks. He drinks. A beat.)

HAKE: I think we should apply for sex privileges.

ENGELMAN: Hake.

HAKE: I know, but we're compatible, you know it's true, we have chemistry, don't say we don't have chemistry.

ENGELMAN: We're at work.

HAKE: Yes, we're working, it's evening, romantic, there's a view, I thought this would be the time, I've killed the mood, I've completely killed it. I'm a loser.

ENGELMAN: Hake. I'd love to apply for sex with you. I think we'd be approved, I really do. I just can't. *(Silence.)* I'm sorry.

HAKE: Don't talk to me.

ENGELMAN: I sent the monitor crew home. No one's watching. We could kiss.

HAKE: Too late.

ENGELMAN: I'd really like to kiss you, Hake.

(He gets up, stalks away, upset, kicks at trees.)

ENGELMAN: Please don't do that.

(He kicks some more.)

ENGELMAN: Beatty is still missing.

HAKE: So what.

ENGELMAN: It's been weeks.

HAKE: I thought they found him.

ENGELMAN: The press office put that out. To keep things calm. He's still out here.

HAKE: Out here?

ENGELMAN: They don't know why.

HAKE: Beatty is a hothead. He probably quit and didn't tell anyone.

ENGELMAN: No. He's here.

HAKE: How do you know that? Let me guess, you have a thing with Beatty. Is that what goes on out here, when I'm off shift? You and him? *(Calls out.)* Hey Beatty! You can do better! I mean it, you could do much better! What are you, scared of me? Come on out, let's do this thing, right here and now! Beatty!

ENGELMAN: He won't answer. He can't.

HAKE: I'm going back. This sucks.

ENGELMAN: Please don't! Please stay with me! *(Beat.)* I saw him. There on the grass. It wasn't him any more. I think he saw me. I meant nothing to him, he was — absent. Gone. Beatty wasn't the first. They said Jefferson retired? It's not true. He's here. Klein and Robeson, killed in traffic? Not true. They're here. All of them. I've seen them. They've been taken.

HAKE: Engelman?

ENGELMAN: I'm never going to get another grant. I know it.

HAKE: How could they be out here? They wouldn't do that.

ENGELMAN: Do you ever think it's coming for us?

HAKE: What? What's coming? We are doing fantastic work. Look at the work we've done out here! Look, this is crabgrass, it's coming back! On its own! With no help from us! We are creating a healthy reproductive environment!

(The floodlights click off. It's suddenly dim, shadowy. Hake pulls out a flashlight.)

ENGELMAN: What's happening?

HAKE: *(Calling out.)* Great. Great, thanks a million guys. You're five minutes too late.

ENGELMAN: Who did that?

HAKE: The spirit of Nature, capital N. We're going to be absorbed and join the ranks of the naturally deselected.

ENGELMAN: Do you really think —

HAKE: It was me! I asked the guys to dim them for the shiraz moment. So I could propose. Schmucks.

ENGELMAN: You did the lights?

HAKE: Thanks, guys! Thanks a lot! Good instinct for romance!

ENGELMAN: Oh, Hake.

HAKE: I'll go get the floods back on.

ENGELMAN: It was a nice touch. It really was.

HAKE: Lot of good it did. You know, we should transfer out. You're a fine botanist, but honey, this job is making you morbid. They need good people at Stanford.

ENGELMAN: Don't go.

HAKE: I'll be right back.

ENGELMAN: Please don't.

HAKE: I'm just going to do the lights.

ENGELMAN: Hake. You're a good scientist. I've always believed that.

(He steps into the woods. A silence. She shines her light around. It's very dim. Shadows play everywhere.)

ENGELMAN: *(Whispers.)* Hello? Who's there? Hake? Is that you?

(Suddenly there's a horrible thrashing, gurgling noise from the bush where Hake has vanished. Like he's being completely devoured. The branches and leaves whip back and forth.)

ENGELMAN: Hake? Hake, what is it? What happened? Are you all right?

(Silence.)

ENGELMAN: Hake?

(From the bushes, laughter. Hake emerges, laughing, pleased with himself.)

HAKE: Got you.

ENGELMAN: You bastard. That was cruel.

HAKE: You peed the suit. Didn't you? Fess up.

ENGELMAN: Of course I peed the suit. Asshole.

HAKE: I'm funny when I want to be.

ENGELMAN: You are mean spirited. Jerk!

HAKE: I know you like it. Give me a kiss.

ENGELMAN: No.

HAKE: Oh hell. *(Kisses her.)* Be right back.

(He goes off. She sits, calming down. A pause. Beatty emerges from the deep woods. He wears a shredded HazMat suit. He's filthy, pale skin, red eyes. No expression. His movements and speech are awkward, not quite human.)

ENGELMAN: Beatty? Beatty, is it you? Are you all right?

(Beatty stares out, blank.)

ENGELMAN: We've been worried about you. Your family, you've been gone so long. Where are your clothes? You must be freezing out here like this. You must be chilled.

(She touches him, recoils.)

ENGELMAN: You're not Beatty, are you? Oh my God.

BEATTY: Come.

ENGELMAN: What did you do to him? Tell me what you did to him! What are you?

(Silence. He stares, expressionless, waiting.)

ENGELMAN: I won't. I haven't done anything wrong. I won't go.

BEATTY: Come.

ENGELMAN: I'm sorry! For what we've done. We knew better. We destroyed so much. Habitats gone, destroyed. We've tried to bring it back. We are trying to fix it! You have to forgive us!

(Beatty steps away, waits for her to follow.)

ENGELMAN: I am not a bad person! I've done my best! DO YOU HEAR ME? We're doing our best! PLEASE don't make me!

(Beatty takes a step into the darkness, waits for her.)

ENGELMAN: What will happen to me? Tell me what will happen. Please.

BEATTY: Come.

ENGELMAN: All right. Yes. All right. I will. I will.

(Beatty exits into the darkness. She follows. Hake returns with his flashlight. Shines it around. Sees he's alone.)

END OF PLAY

Reverse Evolution

BRIAN POLAK

Reverse Evolution was first produced at the Alonguin Theatre,
New York City, by At Hand Theatre Company,
May 2008, as part of POP!, their annual one-act festival.
Directed by Tom Berger. Cast: Jay — Michael Littner;
Len — Stephen Hershey; Jess — Rachel Gentile.

CHARACTERS

    LEN: Mid- to late twenties, well-meaning slob.

    JAY: Mid- to late twenties, trying to be better than a well-meaning slob.

    JESS: Jay's girlfriend.

SETTING

    A typically male apartment.

TIME

    The present.

• • •

Evening in an apartment. There is a brown couch, coffee table, and television (implied). On the coffee table there is a laptop computer, several beer cans, and fast-food wrappers. This is the apartment of typical twenty-something-year-old males and is decorated accordingly. Len, dressed as if he tends to sleep in his clothes, is relaxing on the couch watching TV. Jay, dressed as if he is cut from the same mold as Len but trying to change, is in the kitchen. Jay yells from the kitchen.

JAY: Len, jerk, I told you to wash the friggin' pans so I could cook for Jessica tonight.

LEN: What? What did I do?

    (Jay enters holding a dirty frying pan.)

JAY: You didn't wash the pans is what you did you jerk. You're a shitty ass roommate.

LEN: My shitty ass is sorry.

JAY: Whatever . . .

    (Jay returns to the kitchen)

JAY: *(Offstage.)* I'm washing your pans.

LEN: Awesome. I am watching SportsCenter.

    (Jay sticks head through the kitchen doorway.)

JAY: Can you at least pick up your Taco Bell wrappers so Jess doesn't have to sit in your filth?

LEN: Yeah. No problem.

    (Len begins picking up wrappers)

TV: A bomb, believed to be nuclear, was detonated this afternoon at a gas station in Framingham, Massachusetts, a suburb of Boston . . .

LEN: What the crap! Jay, a nuke just went off in Framingham!!

(Jay enters quickly with two yellow rubber dishwashing gloves on his hands.)

JAY: What the crap?

LEN: I said the same thing!

JAY: What the crap?

LEN: Yes, what the crap!

JAY: No, I mean WHAT THE CRAP are you talking about?

LEN: Oh, on the news, they just said it.

JAY: I thought you were watching SportsCenter?

LEN: I know, I was, I can't believe they reported that.

(Len turns up volume by pushing the button on the TV — does not use remote control.)

TV: Multiple sources have reported that a massive explosion occurred at the Exxon station on Route 9 in Framingham. An anonymous source has confirmed with ESPN that the cause of the explosion was a nuclear device. No parties have stepped forward claiming responsibility for the bomb. Due to potential radiation poisoning, it's recommended that people within a one-hundred-mile radius of Framingham close all doors and windows and remain inside. Do not venture outdoors. We repeat do not leave your homes.

JAY: I can't believe it.

LEN: *(Shouting at the TV.)* What the hell's the Knicks score?

JAY: Are you kidding me? How can you give a shit about the Knicks?

LEN: I know. They stink. But I can't help it. I've loved them since I was a kid.

JAY: A NUCLEAR BOMB JUST BLEW UP IN FRAMINGHAM!

LEN: No kiddin'. But the Knicks play in NEW YORK you idiot.

JAY: Oh my God, Jess is out there, on her way here!! The radiation. She could be dead. Oh my God.

LEN: Man, you never even got to nail her.

JAY: You can be real insensitive sometimes.

LEN: Hey, chill. I am just saying, if she had to go it would have been nice to be able to remember her, you know, in the carnal way . . .

(Jay walks over to the window.)

JAY: All I can see out of these windows is brick. We're living in a tomb. This apartment sucks.

LEN: Yeah, well this apartment might save our lives. All that brick. That nuke stuff ain't getting in here.

JAY: Wait a second. This has got to be bullshit. I mean, what's this, the cold

war? Who uses nuclear bombs? And what's there to bomb in Framingham? Change the station. Check CNN.

LEN: I hate CNN. I only watch Fox News.

JAY: Whatever. Just put on the news.

LEN: It ain't working.

JAY: What ain't working?

LEN: The remote.

JAY: Why not?

LEN: I think the batteries are dead.

JAY: So walk over to the TV and change it you lazy piece of crap.

LEN: The button's busted. The only way to change the station is with the remote.

JAY: Oh my God. So we're stuck on SportsCenter? Hand me my laptop.

LEN: Why?

JAY: What's wrong with you . . . why . . . just hand it to me!

LEN: Dang. You don't have to yell at me. A bomb just went off you know.
You're gonna have to start being nice to me.

(Len hands Jay the laptop.)

JAY: Right.

(Jay attempts to log onto the Internet.)

JAY: The Internet's down! Holy shit. It might be true. I can't log on. It might
be true. The Internet.

LEN: The Internet isn't working.

JAY: I just said that.

LEN: No. It's not working because we stopped paying for it.

JAY: What do you mean we stopped paying for it?

LEN: We used the money to pay the cable bill.

JAY: I gave you enough money to pay both of them.

LEN: No, you didn't.

JAY: YES, I did.

LEN: NO, you didn't. Our cable bill was a bit higher this month.

JAY: And WHY is that?

LEN: I ordered some extra . . . uhh . . . services for us.

JAY: Services?

LEN: Yeah, us. I thought you knew.

JAY: No I didn't know. What were the extra . . . never mind. It doesn't matter.
I don't care.

LEN: Why don't you just call Jess on her cell?

JAY: Why didn't I think of that? Yes. Where's my phone?

(Jay starts looking around the apartment, panicked.)

JAY: Oh my God. My cell phone is in my car. *(Jay slumps down on the couch.)*

LEN: *(At the TV.)* ALL I WANT TO KNOW IS IF THE KNICKS WON! God I hate SportsCenter. All they talk about is hockey and Nascar.

JAY: I am going to die sitting on a crappy leather couch in this bricked chamber of death with an idiot.

LEN: *(Notices under the coffee table.)* Nice! I left my nachos under the coffee table last night! *(Starts munching.)*

JAY: Ugh. *(Jay rises as if to leave.)*

LEN: Where're you going? You can't go outside.

JAY: I am not staying in here to die with you.

LEN: The TV said not to go outside.

JAY: They're sports anchors.

LEN: They're usually very accurate. And what if they're right? You walk out that door and you breathe in all that radiation and DIE an ugly and painful death.

JAY: Dammit. *(Slumps down on couch. Beat.)* I can't believe this is happening. There's a chance she survived, right? I mean there's gotta be.

LEN: Oh yeah. Sure. I am sure she's fine.

JAY: Yeah, like she coulda been on the subway when the bomb went off and is now underground safely away from the radiation.

LEN: Oh, totally. Like those people from *Beneath the Planet of the Apes.* They survived the big one goin' off because they retreated underground.

JAY: Exactly!

LEN: But then again, they ended up losing an outer layer of flesh and worshipping a giant missile as a god.

JAY: Ohhhhhhhhhhhh.

(Long beat.)

LEN: What if we're it?

JAY: What do you mean?

LEN: What if we're the only ones left, like in the world?

JAY: Len, if we were the only people left on the planet, do you think SportsCenter would still be running scores?

LEN: That's the thing, maybe this is on tape delay! Maybe this episode of SportsCenter was taped hours ago! The bomb could have gone off like two hours ago, and we're just finding out now. That's probably why they haven't given the score of the game yet!

JAY: That's idiotic. Len, turn up the volume. Let's see if ESPN'll give us an update.

(Len turns the volume up by pushing the volume button on the TV.)

TV: The Detroit Lions fired offensive coordinator Doug Shoenweiss today after Sunday's third consecutive abysmal shutout. Matt Millen, Detroit Lions General Manager, released a statement explaining . . . .

JAY: Shut it off. This is ridiculous.

LEN: Wait. I wanna hear this.

JAY: Forget the motherfucking sports you jackass!

LEN: Fine. *(Turns volume down.)* You could try and be a little nicer to me.

JAY: I'm sorry. It's just I'm freaking out over this. Why are you so calm and collected anyway? Aren't you scared?

LEN: Hey man, I'm as cool as the other side of the pillow. I'm like Big Papi when the game's on the line. I just don't worry about things out of my control. So a nuclear bomb went off. What am I gonna do about it? What'll happen if I worry? The same things will happen whether I worry or not. So why not just sit back, relax, and let the cards play themselves. All I know and care about right now is that I am alive and doing fine. *(Pause. Looking back at the TV.)* And what the score of the Knicks game is.

JAY: You know, Len, I should give you a little more credit. I never thought I would catch myself saying this, but I could actually learn something from you.

LEN: Yeah, Jay, you could totally benefit from a less stressful lease on life.

JAY: Probably.

(Jay finds a space on the couch next to Len. Long beat.)

LEN: You ever see *Jurassic Park*?

JAY: Yeah, the dinosaur movie. I saw it in the theater when it came out.

LEN: Me too. I love that movie. I've seen it like fifty times.

JAY: Why doesn't that surprise me?

LEN: And you know the reason why the dinosaurs got out of control in that movie?

JAY: They sat on their couches, watched ESPN, and ate Taco Bell twenty-four hours a day?

LEN: No. They learned how to evolve. The scientist who figured out how to take dino DNA knew how to create only males to keep them from breeding. But when faced with extinction, these things evolved and found a way to procreate. It's amazing what creatures can do when their backs are against the wall.

JAY: Dude, you do realize that *Jurassic Park* was not a documentary, right?

LEN: No shit, but come on Jay. Think about it. You can't make that shit up.

It was based on science. And it makes sense to me. I think it can happen. And I am OK with it.

JAY: OK with it?

LEN: Yeah, like if I was in a similar situation, I would be OK with learning how to procreate.

JAY: If you need me to teach you the birds and the bees . . .

LEN: No, I mean if I had to evolve to the point where I could produce children to repopulate the earth, I would be OK with it.

JAY: Dude, are you coming out?

LEN: I'm just saying that I'm OK with doing whatever I have to do to save the planet.

JAY: Well my planet saving stops with recycling beer cans and riding my bike to work. If you want to repopulate the planet, you're on your own. Maybe you can evolve to the point where you can mate with yourself and create a bunch of little you's.

LEN: You say that now. But just wait until you're pushed to the point of extinction. Don't come crying to me when you decide you're ready to make babies.

JAY: I promise I won't.

(Long beat.)

JAY: Let's just say that if it came to that, you know, two dudes having to do something to repopulate the earth. I would be OK with it too. You know . . . errr . . . uhh . . . I ummm, I'd be proud to repopulate the planet with a guy like you.

LEN: Wow. Thanks man. That's like the nicest thing you've ever said to me. *(Len rises, holds arms out inviting a hug.)* Come on Jay . . . c'mere.
(Beat. Jay walks over and they give each other a hug. They look into each other's eyes. Long beat. Jess walks through the door and catches them in an embrace.)

JESS: Hello?!
(Len and Jay break away from each other and yelp.)

LEN: Close the door! The radiation!!
(Len runs over and closes door.)

JAY: Oh my God! I thought you were dead.

JESS: What are you talking about?

JAY: The nuclear bomb that went off in Framingham. We're in the middle of the hot zone. Do you feel sick at all?
(Len starts touching Jess's face.)

JESS: Get your hands off my face you idiot.

LEN: She doesn't seem to be losing her outer layer of flesh.

JESS: What the hell is wrong with you two?

JAY: Didn't you hear the news? A nuke was detonated earlier. Everybody within one hundred miles could be affected.

JESS: You can't be serious. That was a gas station that exploded. Some guy left a cigarette burning at one of the pumps. It was all over the news. Where the hell did you hear about a nuke?

JAY: On SportsCenter.

JESS: What kind of moron gets their news from SportsCenter?

LEN: They're usually very accurate.

JAY: We couldn't change the station.

(Jay slumps onto the couch. Confused. Turns the TV on.)

JESS: And what was with that hug? Is there something I should know?

LEN: Jay and I were fully prepared to evolve and repopulate the planet in the event of a nuclear catastrophe.

JESS: Darwin would be dumbfounded by you two.

(Jay turns volume up on TV.)

TV: In a correction to a story reported earlier, the explosion in Framingham, Massachusetts, was caused when a cigarette butt ignited a gas pump and not a nuclear bomb as earlier reported. We repeat, there was no nuclear bomb detonated. We apologize for any confusion. In NBA news, the New York Knicks were blown out by the Boston Celtics 109 to 79. You might say that the Celtics nuked the Knicks today.

(Len turns off the TV.)

LEN: Friggin' Knicks.

(Black out.)

END OF PLAY

PLAYS FOR
TWO MEN AND
TWO WOMEN

Beautiful Noises

Scott C. Sickles

Beautiful Noises was originally produced by
Pyramid Productions, Pittsburgh, November 1995, as part of
the 1995 No Doze Dozen. Directed by Chris Potocki.
Cast: Rachel Bergman — Kathryn Slyker; Joel Bergman —
Robert S. Kleinedler; Emma Bergman — Claire Fraley; Arliss
Windsor — John Highberger. *Beautiful Noises* was most
recently produced by Mind the Gap Theatre, New York City,
October 2008, as part of BritBits4. Directed by
Paula D'Alessandris. Cast: Rachel Bergman — Lucy Rayner;
Joel Bergman — Sam Redford; Emma Bergman —
Christine Rendel; Arliss Windsor — Stephen Donovan.

For Paula D'Alessandris, Lissa Brennan, Audrey Castracane, John Highberger, Bobby Kleinedler, Amir Arison, Brian Hutchison, Greg Skura, Sam Turich, Patricia O'Connell, Lori Faiella, and Michael Montel

CHARACTERS

RACHEL BERGMAN: Twenty-one, lonely, whimsical, deceased.
BERGMAN: Twenty-seven, charming, warm and loving, deceased.
EMMA BERGMAN: Fifty-three, austere, angry, contained.
ARLISS WINDSOR: Twenty-eight, high-strung, opinionated.

SETTING

A cemetery.

TIME

A lovely, autumn afternoon.

• • •

At rise: The stage is bare. Darkness. We hear Rachel's voice.

RACHEL: Joel! Joel! Are you there?
JOEL: Rachel?
RACHEL: Yes, it's me!
    (Lights up to reveal Rachel, a vivacious young woman, embracing Joel, a handsome man.)
JOEL: I wondered if I'd find you here. I sort of hoped I wouldn't. You know what I mean.
RACHEL: Oh my God, you're all grown up! How long have I been gone?
JOEL: Eight years.
RACHEL: Eight years? Is that all? Jeez, you look like Dad.
JOEL: Have you seen him?
RACHEL: I'm sure he's in a better place.
JOEL: So, are we . . .
RACHEL: No-no-no-no-no-no-no. Not there.
JOEL: So, are you my guide?
RACHEL: Actually, you're mine.
JOEL: But I just got here.
RACHEL: Can you talk to Mom?

JOEL: I don't think so. I've tried, but she doesn't seem to hear me. They just stand there.

RACHEL: Who's "they"?

JOEL: Mom and Arliss. Arliss is my significant other. He's standing right next to her. Can't you see them?

RACHEL: They won't let me. It's my penance. I left you and Mom behind without any closure, so they don't allow me any. I don't mean it to sound like a conspiracy, but sometimes it feels like it is.

JOEL: Do "they" talk to you?

RACHEL: You'll find while you're here you'll get sudden, clear notions that wouldn't have otherwise occurred to you. Those are messages from them.

JOEL: God?

RACHEL: Whoever.

JOEL: With an attitude like that —

RACHEL: How does Mom look?

(Lights up on Emma in black and Arliss, a mournful man wearing black suit, overcoat, and shoes with a white shirt and a tie, standing apart at the edge of Joel's grave.)

JOEL: Sad. She's looked sad for a long time.

RACHEL: That's my fault.

JOEL: Funny, she thinks it's hers.

RACHEL: I didn't run away because of Mom.

JOEL: It's not like it matters now.

RACHEL: Don't say that, Joel!

JOEL: Why did you run away?

RACHEL: No reason. I just did it.

JOEL: Why does she feel so guilty? You had another fight, didn't you? Right before you left?

RACHEL: But, that's not why I left. I just . . . I needed to get away.

JOEL: This is just like you.

RACHEL: I was going to come back, Joel.

JOEL: Hurting other people on a stupid whim.

RACHEL: It's not like I planned to die. *(Pause)* I wanted to see the ocean. I stood on the Atlantic shore at three in the morning watching lights reflect on water. I could taste the salt in the air; feel the moisture in my joints. I kept cracking my knuckles; it would have driven you crazy.

JOEL: Was it worth it?

RACHEL: I thought so at first. The scent was so exhilarating, I wanted to stand there forever. I closed my eyes and listened to the ocean. Putting a shell to your ear is nothing compared to this. The waves . . . the birds . . . the boats at night . . . All those beautiful noises bombarding me at once. I had to go swimming. So, I did. And then I drowned.

JOEL: Oh.

RACHEL: So, I guess the answer is: no, it wasn't worth it.

JOEL: I'm sorry.

RACHEL: Every moment since has been exactly like the last time I went under. Joel, you've got to help me. If I can't make Mom realize it wasn't her fault, I'm going to spend the rest of eternity in darkness.

JOEL: How?

RACHEL: We'll think of something. Tell me: What does your Arliss look like?

JOEL: He's lovely.

RACHEL: And what is it you love about him? What do you cling to?

JOEL: His gasp. Whenever Arliss cries — at the movies or after we've had another argument — he gasps. Like this: *(Imitates Arliss's gasp, his eyes closed.)* My heart buckles every time I hear it.

RACHEL: What does Mom think of Arliss?

EMMA: Would you mind if I have a moment alone with my son?

JOEL: That's my problem.

ARLISS: Mrs. Bergman.

RACHEL: They don't get along?

ARLISS: In five minutes, I will be on a plane back to Washington and out of your life forever. You can have your moment then.

JOEL: An understatement.

(Emma crosses away from Arliss.)

JOEL: Oh, Rachel, how am I going to do this? Before I died, I promised myself —

RACHEL: — You swore you'd make peace between them, right? Big mistake. They take oaths very seriously here.

JOEL: She thinks anyone who doesn't love Barbra Streisand is an anti-Semite. He thinks anyone who doesn't love Barbra Streisand is a homophobe. I thought they'd love each other.

ARLISS AND RACHEL: Joel.

JOEL: *(To Rachel.)* Hang on.

ARLISS: Here goes. I miss you. What I've discovered I miss the most is how you'd sing in your sleep. How you'd mumble all those Cole Porter tunes.

JOEL: *(To Arliss.)* I never believed you until you taped me.

RACHEL: What? Your sleep-singing?

ARLISS: "Ev'ry Time We Say Goodbye."

JOEL: "All of You."

ARLISS: "My Funny Valentine."

JOEL: Arliss, shame on you. That's not Cole Porter.

ARLISS: Oh, Joel.

JOEL: That's Rodgers and Hart.

ARLISS: I'm going to miss holding you and — wait . . . "My Funny Valentine"
isn't Cole Porter.

JOEL: No, it's —

JOEL AND ARLISS: Rodgers and Hart.

RACHEL: Joel.

ARLISS: That's it.

RACHEL: Can Arliss hear you?

JOEL: I'm not sure.

EMMA: He always did that. Even as a boy.

ARLISS: Excuse me?

EMMA: Joel sang in his sleep. When he was little, it was campfire songs. As he
got older, it was Sondheim and Streisand. That's when his father and I
knew.

ARLISS: I'll bet that burned you up.

EMMA: Why do you say that?

ARLISS: It's obvious you don't like homosexuals.

EMMA: Are you trying to tell me I don't love the son I just buried.

ARLISS: I'm saying you didn't approve of who he was. Why else would you be
so hateful toward me?

EMMA: I don't want to get into this. Besides, it doesn't matter anymore.

ARLISS: I never mattered to you. Because I'm gay.

EMMA: Who do you think you're talking to? André's mother? I loved Joel. I
liked most of his boyfriends. In fact, I've never had a problem with gay
people, Arliss. I just never liked you.

ARLISS: What did I ever do to you? Besides treat you with courtesy and respect?

EMMA: You took Joel away from me. You knew what losing my daughter did
to me and you took him anyway!

ARLISS: I didn't "take" him. He left on his own.

JOEL: Arliss.

ARLISS: Maybe he needed to get away from you before you smothered him.

JOEL: That's not true.

EMMA: So you blame me for this.

JOEL: He doesn't, Mom. He's just angry.

RACHEL: She can't hear you, Joel.

EMMA: If I weren't such a smothering bitch, he wouldn't have moved to Washington with you.

RACHEL: It's not your voice she's listening for.

EMMA: Then, he wouldn't have to drive all this way to see me. And he wouldn't have been in that car when the truck slammed into it.

RACHEL: It's mine.

EMMA: If I weren't such a horrible person, Rachel wouldn't have run away and got herself killed.

RACHEL: Mom! Mom, I'm here!

ARLISS: You don't know she's dead.

EMMA: Mothers feel it when their children stop living.

RACHEL: Mom, it's not your fault.

EMMA: I felt it when Joel died. I had the same feeling three days after Rachel ran away.

RACHEL: I can't tell, Joel. Can she hear me?

EMMA: You're telling me I killed my children.

JOEL: She can't hear either of us.

EMMA: You go to hell.

(Arliss begins to exit. Joel follows him.)

JOEL: Don't go! Not until you tell her the truth. Arliss! If you love me, you will turn around and tell her the truth!

(Arliss stops and turns back to Emma.)

ARLISS: Mrs. Bergman. I didn't mean —

EMMA: Yes. You did.

RACHEL: Joel, if Arliss can hear you . . .

ARLISS: Joel didn't leave to get away from you.

RACHEL: . . . maybe, you can tell him . . .

JOEL: Rachel didn't either, Arliss.

EMMA: I'm glad at least one of my children didn't.

JOEL: Arliss.

ARLISS: Rachel didn't leave because of you either.

EMMA: And how the hell would you know that?

RACHEL: Tell her about the kitchen music.

ARLISS: It was something Joel said . . .

JOEL: It was the kitchen music. What's kitchen music?

EMMA: You never even knew Rachel!

RACHEL: When she'd bake, she'd make up songs while she mixed things.

EMMA: Who the hell are you to tell me how my dead daughter felt about anything —

ARLISS: Kitchen music.

EMMA: *(Beat.)* What did you say?

JOEL: Arliss. When she'd bake, she'd make up songs while she mixed things.

RACHEL: To the sound of —

JOEL: To the beat of the mixing noises. She'd sing them to Rachel.

ARLISS: Joel once told me you'd let Rachel watch you work in the kitchen. You'd sing songs to her to the rhythm of the mixing noises. She called it kitchen music.

EMMA: Still. It doesn't change that she left because of me.

JOEL: Arliss, tell her . . . tell her Rachel . . .

ARLISS: Joel told me it's why she could always forgive you. No matter what.

JOEL: Nice, Arliss.

RACHEL: What did he tell her?

JOEL: The truth.

EMMA: Why didn't Joel ever tell me?

ARLISS: He probably thought it was obvious how much Rachel loved you.

RACHEL: Oh, my God. Joel. I can see her.

ARLISS: I'll leave you with your son now.

RACHEL: Mom, I can see you.

ARLISS: Mrs. Bergman.

RACHEL: Mom.

ARLISS AND RACHEL: I'm sorry for —

ARLISS: — what I said.

RACHEL: . . . everything.

EMMA: There's nothing to apologize for.

   (Arliss turns to go.)

RACHEL: Thank you, Arliss.

EMMA: Arliss, wait.

RACHEL: Can you hear me?

EMMA: I can visit anytime. You can't. Why don't you take a few more minutes.

ARLISS: Thank you, Mrs. Bergman.

EMMA: My name is Emma.

RACHEL: I love you, Mom.

   (Emma takes a small stone, kisses and places it on Joel's headstone. As she crosses to exit, Rachel follows part of the way. As Emma exits:)

RACHEL: Good-bye, Mom.

(Joel reaches around Arliss and embraces him from behind, sliding his hands into Arliss' overcoat. Arliss hangs his head and begins to cry.)
(Joel begins whispering/half-singing "Ev'ry Time We Say Goodbye."* On the second line, Arliss softly, almost unconsciously, joins in. As they finish the line together, Arliss, crying, gasps. At this, Joel nuzzles Arliss's neck.)

ARLISS: I'm sorry I won't be able to come back.

JOEL: That's OK. I won't either. I love you.

ARLISS: I love you, too.

RACHEL: Joel. I'm afraid we have to go now.

JOEL: I know. I had a sudden, clear notion that wouldn't have otherwise occurred to me.

(Joel squeezes Arliss one more moment and lets him go. As Joel lets go, Arliss runs his hands up and down his own arms, feeling Joel's presence leave him. Arliss closes his overcoat. Joel crosses to Rachel and she takes his hand.)
(Fade to black.)

END OF PLAY

Cate Blanchett Wants to Be My friend on Facebook

ALEX BROUN

Cate Blanchett Wants to Be My Friend on Facebook was first
presented at the Gene Frankel Theatre, New York City,
July 17, 2008, as part of the 2nd Annual Salute UR Shorts
New Play Festival. Directed by Mariah MacCarthy.
Cast: Cate Blanchett — Mary Greenawalt; Barry — Lino del
Core; Sarah — Lauren Hennessy; Morris — Richard Durstine.

CHARACTERS
  BARRY: Twenties to forties, construction site worker.
  MORRIS: Thirties to fifties, construction site foreman.
  SARAH: Twenties to thirties, construction site office manager.
  CATE BLANCHETT: Thirties, a world-famous actress.

SETTING
  Construction site office in a large city.

TIME
  Morning, working day.

• • •

Barry sits at a desk working on a computer. Morris enters.

MORRIS: Morning Barry.
BARRY: Morris.
MORRIS: You gettin' on to that pouring this morning?
BARRY: First thing. Just checking my Facebook.
MORRIS: Don't be too long.
BARRY: I won't.
  (Morris goes through some folders, looking for something.)
MORRIS: You see that invoice from the cement company?
BARRY: Put it in the folder.
  (Morris continues to look.)
BARRY: You know someone called *(Reading.)* Cate . . . Blatchett?
MORRIS: Who ?
BARRY: Cate Blatchett?
MORRIS: Don't think so. Why?
BARRY: She wants to be my friend on Facebook.
  (Morris stops looking in folder. Thinks. Beat.)
MORRIS: How you spelling it?
BARRY: C-A-T-E
MORRIS: C not K?
BARRY: Yeah C.
MORRIS: And the last name?
BARRY: B-L-A-N-C-H-E-T-T
  (Morris thinks. Beat.)

MORRIS: I think you'll find that's Blanchett.

BARRY: Yeah.

MORRIS: *(Coming over to screen.)* B-L-A-N-C-H-E-T-T. Blanchett.

BARRY: Right. You know her then?

(Beat.)

MORRIS: Can't say I do. *(He goes back to the folder.)* You sure that invoice is in here?

BARRY: Yeah. Says here she won an Academy Award.

MORRIS: What for?

BARRY: *The Aviator.* Best Supporting Actress.

MORRIS: Well, that's obviously bullshit.

BARRY: You reckon?

MORRIS: Course. If you've actually won an Academy Award, you're not going to brag about it on Facebook are you? You're going to be humble about it. Let people work it out for themselves.

BARRY: True.

MORRIS: Probably some wannabe. Just hit ignore.

BARRY: But then she'll know won't she?

MORRIS: No mate. That's the good thing about Facebook. People don't know when you ignore them.

BARRY: But she'll see I'm not in her friend list.

MORRIS: Take her awhile to work that out. How many friends she got?

BARRY: Three.

MORRIS: Maybe not so long then.

BARRY: If I make her my friend then I can bite her with my vampire.

MORRIS: What vampire level you up to?

BARRY: Ice.

MORRIS: Ancient. You sure that invoice is in here?

BARRY: Unless Sarah paid it already.

MORRIS: She in yet?

BARRY: Getting coffee.

MORRIS: Come and get me when she gets back. Just going to go and have a look at that copper piping they dug up yesterday. *(Leaving.)* And Baz, really need you to get on to that pouring.

BARRY: On my way.

(Morris exits.)

BARRY: Confirm — ignore — confirm — ignore.

(Sarah enters with coffees.)

SARAH: *(Handing one to Barry.)* Here you go. Skim decaf flat white with one sweetener.

BARRY: Thanks.

SARAH: There's some woman at the front gate for you.

BARRY: Who?

SARAH: Says her name's Kate Blatchett.

BARRY: Cate Blanchett?

SARAH: I'm pretty sure it was Blatchett.

BARRY: What did she look like?

SARAH: Plain. Very pale skin. Wearing a big hat. Not sure why. Not like there's any sun out there.

BARRY: Could be "beautiful in certain lighting conditions"?

SARAH: Guess so. Why?

BARRY: *(Pointing to computer.)* That's what it says here, under "About Me." "Beautiful in certain lighting conditions."

SARAH: Is that her? Good picture.

BARRY: She doesn't look like that?

SARAH: Not at all.

BARRY: She wants to be my friend on Facebook.

SARAH: Yeah? What did you say?

BARRY: Haven't decided yet.

SARAH: What's she doing here?

BARRY: I don't know.

SARAH: Maybe she's stalking you.

BARRY: Yeah, right. Morris wants to know where that invoice is for the cement.

SARAH: Under the folder.

BARRY: Under? I said in.

SARAH: The paid ones are in. The unpaid ones are under. I told him that yonks ago.

BARRY: Sorry. Didn't know.

SARAH: Don't worry. I'll go tell him.

BARRY: Went to check on that copper piping.

SARAH: Later.

BARRY: Hey, what do I do about Cate Blatchett?

SARAH: Wasn't it Blanchett?

(Sarah exits. Barry looks at the screen again.)

BARRY: Confirm — ignore — confirm — ignore? *(Beat.)* Ignore.

(Cate Blanchett enters, wearing dark glasses and a large hat.)

CATE BLANCHETT: Hi, I'm Cate Blanchett.

BARRY: Not Blatchett?

CATE BLANCHETT: No, Blanchett.

BARRY: Nice to meet you.

(Cate Blanchett holds out her hand. Barry shakes it.)

CATE BLANCHETT: Great office.

BARRY: Think so?

CATE BLANCHETT: Very urbane. Functional.

BARRY: It's an office.

CATE BLANCHETT: Still, as offices go . . .

BARRY: What are you doing here?

CATE BLANCHETT: I like it. A man of — Cutting right to —

BARRY: Excuse me.

CATE BLANCHETT: The chase. Action. Getting — to — it.

BARRY: Meaning?

CATE BLANCHETT: I needed to speak with you.

BARRY: Right. Any particular reason?

CATE BLANCHETT: The reasons are many and varied.

BARRY: Right. How did you find me?

CATE BLANCHETT: I have people.

BARRY: People?

CATE BLANCHETT: Who do things for me.

BARRY: What things?

CATE BLANCHETT: Many and varied.

BARRY: Great, but you're not actually allowed on the site.

CATE BLANCHETT: Of course. I'll toodle off just freshly. But first — I'm wondering — why you haven't replied to my friend request?

BARRY: I have replied.

CATE BLANCHETT: Confirm or ignore?

BARRY: *(Beat.)* Confirm.

CATE BLANCHETT: Let me check.

BARRY: *(Blocking computer.)* Can't.

CATE BLANCHETT: Why not?

BARRY: It's a work computer. No personal surfing allowed.

CATE BLANCHETT: *(Looking at computer.)* But I can see your Facebook profile.

BARRY: I was just checking it quickly before the boss came in. But he's here now.

CATE BLANCHETT: Is he?

BARRY: Just checking on some copper piping.

CATE BLANCHETT: Piping?

BARRY: Dug up some copper piping yesterday. Wasn't on the charts. Just gone to check it out. Back in a minute.

(Beat.)

CATE BLANCHETT: So you definitely added me as a friend?

BARRY: Yep.

(Beat.)

CATE BLANCHETT: (Suddenly.) You're lying!

BARRY: No I'm not.

CATE BLANCHETT: Yes. You are!

BARRY: All right. I am. I ignored your request.

CATE BLANCHETT: But why?

BARRY: Does it matter now?

CATE BLANCHETT: Yes, it does.

BARRY: I don't want to rub it in.

CATE BLANCHETT: Please, Barry. If I understand why you ignored me, it will help me to deal with the pain. And help me in obtaining more Confirms in the future.

(Beat.)

BARRY: All right. (Beat.) You sure you want to hear this?

CATE BLANCHETT: Go on Barry. I can take it.

BARRY: Well . . .

CATE BLANCHETT: Say it Barry. Say it.

BARRY: You're an actor.

CATE BLANCHETT: So?

BARRY: Well, it's not really a very honorable profession.

CATE BLANCHETT: Isn't it?

BARRY: No.

(Beat.)

CATE BLANCHETT: I see. Why isn't acting an honorable profession?

BARRY: Well, you're sort of famous —

CATE BLANCHETT: Sort of? I'm —

BARRY: But you don't really do anything. You're like one of those people.

CATE BLANCHETT: Which people?

BARRY: You know like Paris what's-her-name? Famous for being famous.

CATE BLANCHETT: That's not true.

(Beat.)

BARRY: Well, actually it is.

CATE BLANCHETT: But I won an Academy Award.

BARRY: Actually, there's a few questions about that.

CATE BLANCHETT: A Golden Globe.

BARRY: Who hasn't?

CATE BLANCHETT: I won the Volpi Cup at the Venice Film Festival.

BARRY: See, now you're just making that up.

CATE BLANCHETT: I played Galadriel in Lord of the Rings one, two, and three.

BARRY: I'm not sure I'd be owning up to that.

CATE BLANCHETT: Return of the King and Two Towers are two of the top ten grossing movies of all time.

BARRY: Doesn't make them good.

CATE BLANCHETT: Many people have congratulated me on my portrayal of the Elf Queen.

BARRY: Any who weren't members of your immediate family?

CATE BLANCHETT: You didn't like it?

BARRY: Missed the character's core — by some margin.

CATE BLANCHETT: She's ethereal.

BARRY: There's also a steely resolve.

CATE BLANCHETT: Didn't get that?

(Barry shakes his head, sadly.)

CATE BLANCHETT: And your profession is honorable?

BARRY: Now you're just being nasty. And you know it.

CATE BLANCHETT: Sorry.

BARRY: Cheap shot Cate. We build. Houses for people to live in, places of work, community centers, schools, hospitals. We make things that exist in the real world. While you create —

CATE BLANCHETT: Fantasy?

(Barry nods, again sadly.)

CATE BLANCHETT: I entertain.

BARRY: *Bandits? Elizabeth: The Golden Age?* Entertain is not the word I'd use.

CATE BLANCHETT: I provide those little people, out there in the dark, with an escape. From the daily grind.

BARRY: At best, a momentary diversion. At worse — a reminder.

(Beat.)

CATE BLANCHETT: I'm a mother. I've raised three children.

BARRY: There's something to be proud of.

CATE BLANCHETT: Then will you accept my friend request?

BARRY: I would if you'd listed that under your achievements.

CATE BLANCHETT: What does it say?

BARRY: "Actor. Academy Award. Elf Queen."

CATE BLANCHETT: I just forgot to put mother in.

BARRY: Forgot being a mother? I'm not sure I really want to be friends with someone who puts their achievements as an "actor" over their achievements as a "mother."

CATE BLANCHETT: But I don't.

BARRY: Cate . . .

(Barry shakes his head again, sadly.)

CATE BLANCHETT: But I didn't write it. One of my people did.

BARRY: You know what they say about bad builders?

CATE BLANCHETT: No. What do they say?

BARRY: Blame their tools.

(Beat.)

CATE BLANCHETT: You're not going to confirm me as a friend are you?

(Barry shakes his head.)

CATE BLANCHETT: Maybe if you got to know me a bit better.

BARRY: I'm a bit fussy who I accept as a friend.

CATE BLANCHETT: You could come over for dinner? Andrew will cook.

BARRY: I don't think it will work now. We've kind of got off on the wrong foot.

CATE BLANCHETT: What if I make it worth your while? Have you seen *Notes on a Scandal.* I can be pretty hot stuff.

BARRY: You see, now that's just sad.

(Beat.)

CATE BLANCHETT: *(Dropping to her knees, begging.)* Barry, please!

MORRIS: *(Entering.)* Still can't work out where that piping's coming from.

(He sees Cate Blanchett kneeling in front of Barry.)

MORRIS: Everything all right?

BARRY: Good, thanks Morris.

(Beat.)

MORRIS: You getting on to that pouring?

BARRY: Just on my way.

SARAH: *(Entering.)* Morris, the invoice is under not —

(She also sees Cate Blanchett kneeling in front of Barry. Beat.)

SARAH: In.

(Beat. Cate Blanchett stands.)

BARRY: Morris. Sarah. This is Cate Blatchett.

CATE BLANCHETT: Blanchett.

MORRIS: Nice to meet you.

(Sarah gives a little wave.)

CATE BLANCHETT: Morris. Such a nice name. Strong. And Sarah. So . . . pretty.

MORRIS: As Barry knows, we have a rule about visitors on site.

BARRY: I didn't invite her. (Beat, looking at Cate Blanchett.) Well I didn't. (To Morris.) She wants to know why I ignored her friend request on Facebook.

MORRIS: (To Cate Blanchett.) Whatever the reason we've got a busy morning. Cement pour and we found some copper piping where it really shouldn't be. So if you wouldn't mind . . .

(Morris indicates the door.)

CATE BLANCHETT: Of course. Well Barry, see you 'round. Online.

BARRY: No you won't. Remember — "ignore."

CATE BLANCHETT: Maybe you'll change your mind. In a month or two?

BARRY: Not likely.

CATE BLANCHETT: A year? Five years?

MORRIS: (Ushering Cate Blanchett to the door.) Really flat out this morning.

CATE BLANCHETT: (To Morris.) Would you like to be my friend ?

MORRIS: Sorry. Too many already. Can't keep up.

CATE BLANCHETT: (To Sarah.) Sarah?

SARAH: (Shaking head.) Sorry.

BARRY: (To Cate Blanchett.) You're acting desperate now.

CATE BLANCHETT: Big turn off?

(Sarah, Barry, and Morris nod their heads.)

CATE BLANCHETT: (Trying to regain some dignity.) Right, well . . .

MORRIS: Straight down the path and back through the gate.

CATE BLANCHETT: Morris, Sarah, Bazza.

BARRY: It's Barry.

CATE BLANCHETT: Of course. Good-bye.

(Cate Blanchett exits.)

BARRY: Thought she'd never leave.

SARAH: Sad.

BARRY: Very.

(Morris looks at Barry.)

BARRY: What? I didn't invite her.

(Morris moves to the folder.)

MORRIS: Have a word to Neil at the gate. No visitors. And pouring — now.

BARRY: On it.

MORRIS: That'd be good.

(Barry exits.)

MORRIS: Facebook. More trouble than it's worth really. *(To Sarah.)* Now, where's that invoice?

(Sarah and Morris look through the folder as the lights fade.)

END OF PLAY

Letters from Quebec to Providence in the Rain

DON NIGRO

CHARACTERS

> PETRUS: Late twenties.
> VANESSA: Late twenties.
> JONATHAN: Early twenties.
> MARIANNE: Early twenties.

SETTING

> An old house in Quebec, and another old house in Providence. Both are present onstage at once. Some furniture, which is part of both houses. Time and space interpenetrate. There's a desk and chair down right, a bed right, an old-fashioned clawfoot bathtub up center, a sofa left, and a chair and small round table down left.

TIME

> The present, and the not too distant past.

• • •

> *Sound of whippoorwills in the darkness. Lights up on Petrus at the desk down right and, in dimmer light for the moment, Jonathan sitting in his chair down left and Marianne in the bathtub up center.*

PETRUS: *(Taking some letters out of an old book.)* This is very odd.

VANESSA: *(Coming into the light, in bathrobe, barefoot.)* This is Quebec. Everything is odd here. Not very odd. Just a little bit odd. Just a bit off center, as if one were living in two places at the same time. Everything has two reflections here.

PETRUS: I've found some letters in this old book.

VANESSA: Whose book is it? Yours or mine?

PETRUS: I don't know whose book it is. Well, it's mine now. I bought it this morning, on impulse, from a girl selling books by the river. When I got home, I opened it up, and these letters fell out.

VANESSA: You didn't open the book before you bought it?

PETRUS: It was raining. I was rushing to get home.

VANESSA: You were rushing to get home, so you stopped to buy an old book?

PETRUS: I had a sudden impulse. She looked so lonely, there in the rain.

VANESSA: She was selling books in the rain?

PETRUS: It's Drago's *Occult Notebooks*. I've been looking for this book for many, many years. I thought I'd never find a copy.

VANESSA: Who is Drago?

PETRUS: N. J. Drago. A Romanian writer. Rather obscure and difficult, but brilliant. It's quite a rare book. I got it for practically nothing.

VANESSA: So you stole from the poor girl?

PETRUS: I didn't steal from her. I paid what she asked for it.

VANESSA: But you knew it was worth more. The creature is half mad, selling books in the rain, and you're drawn to her on impulse, no doubt because of her melancholy beauty, and then you cheat her out of a rare book.

PETRUS: You're missing the point here.

VANESSA: No I'm not. I have always very much appreciated the romance of found objects. At least, I seem to remember that I have. Everything is still a little blurry in my head. Found objects can seem to radiate a powerful numinosity. Now there's a word I didn't know I knew. Numinosity. Is that a word? A sense that objects or events or even certain persons or places possess tremendous significance, that one has stumbled upon them for some purpose unknown to one, that one is suddenly able to perceive the vague outline of a pattern in what would appear to be entirely random events. It appears I may be more intelligent than I'd realized. Or possibly just demented.

PETRUS: What's really interesting here is the letters.

VANESSA: You found some letters in an old book. One's likely to stumble upon anything in the pages of an old book. Flowers. Note cards. Fragments of human skin.

PETRUS: They're written to someone named Vanessa.

VANESSA: And that is interesting because — ?

PETRUS: Because your name is Vanessa.

VANESSA: And?

PETRUS: Doesn't that seem an odd coincidence to you?

VANESSA: I have no doubt there are a number of persons in Quebec named Vanessa. This is still Quebec, isn't it? Sometimes I wake up from a dream and I seem to be in an entirely different place. I suppose it's the medication.

PETRUS: I'm sure there are other persons named Vanessa in Quebec. But they're not living in my house, are they?

VANESSA: Not that I know of. Who are the letters from?

PETRUS: They're from somebody named Jonathan. And they were mailed from Quebec to Providence.

VANESSA: So this is Providence?

PETRUS: No. This is Quebec.

VANESSA: If they were mailed to Providence, then how did they get back to Quebec?

PETRUS: Clearly, in this book.

(Lights up on Jonathan, sitting at the table down left, speaking as a letter but not writing.)

JONATHAN: Dearest Vanessa. I got the key to Rum House from a horrible old woman with a face like a salamander and moved in three days ago. The plaster is flaking off the walls, and there's something scuttling in the cupboards, but I feel surprisingly at home in Quebec, as if I'd lived here in a previous life.

VANESSA: I had a brother named Jonathan.

PETRUS: A brother? Did you?

JONATHAN: It rains here every evening, and in the morning there is fog, and always the song of the whippoorwills in the cherry trees by the river.

PETRUS: You've never mentioned having a brother.

JONATHAN: I've been exploring the overgrown garden, which is a miasma of tangled vines.

VANESSA: I don't any more. He's dead now.

JONATHAN: I have on more than one occasion had the overwhelming sensation that I am not alone in this house. Last night I could have sworn I heard a young girl talking to herself upstairs in the bath.

(Lights up on Marianne in the tub.)

MARIANNE: Once upon a time, she said, Vanessa and Jonathan lived in Quebec.

PETRUS: What did your brother die of?

MARIANNE: Then Vanessa went to college, to Brown University, in Providence, Rhode Island, to study creative writing, and there she met her roommate, Marianne.

JONATHAN: When I made my way up the creaking steps to the lavatory, I saw that I had apparently left the light on.

VANESSA: He fell down a staircase and broke his neck.

JONATHAN: I opened the creaking door. The water was running. The tub was about to overflow. But nobody was there.

MARIANNE: Marianne was an apothecary's daughter who loved telling herself stories in the bath.

PETRUS: Did your brother write you letters?

MARIANNE: Petrus, you wicked boy, will you close that door? You're letting in goblins.

VANESSA: Yes. As a matter of fact, I believe he did. When I lived in Providence. I went to school there. At Brown. I went to Brown.

MARIANNE: At Christmas break, Vanessa brought her roommate Marianne home to Quebec to meet her brother. Marianne was a very beautiful creative writing major, and when Jonathan met her, he fell hopelessly in love with her, as nearly everybody did.

JONATHAN: The bathroom smelled like the freshly shampooed hair of Marianne.

VANESSA: I might have gone to Princeton or to Harvard, but I was fascinated by Lovecraft. The writer. H. P. Lovecraft. Dark creatures lurking in basements. Unspeakable impossibly ancient gelatinous beings from outer space. Lovecraft lived in Providence. He prowled the streets at night, looking for God knows what. He was terribly lonely. I used to walk the streets at night and think of him.

PETRUS: He mentions a girl named Marianne in these letters.

VANESSA: I knew a girl named Marianne. I brought her home for Christmas break, and my brother fell hopelessly in love with her. But she was used to it. Many people fell in love with her. She had a certain melancholy beauty. It was very annoying. The surest way to make someone not want you is to love them. Don't you find that?

MARIANNE: I used to walk by Lovecraft's house at night, in Providence. *(Sound of whippoorwills.)* He was haunted by the sound of whippoorwills.

JONATHAN: How is Marianne? I haven't seen her in so long. Does she ever speak of me? You never mention her any more in your letters.

MARIANNE: Petrus? Is that you out there on the staircase?

VANESSA: Idea for a story. A man stops at a girl's book stall by the river one morning in the rain, drawn there perhaps by the melancholy beauty of the girl. He opens one of the books and some old letters fall out. He's always been fond of the little mysterious things found in old books. He has always appreciated the romance of found objects. Query to self: What is the book? Lovecraft's *Color Out of Space*? The *Occult Notebooks* of N. J. Drago? How old are the letters? Do they smell like perfume? Sweet or citrus? His name is Petrus Van Hoek. He's an artist.

MARIANNE: After her return to Providence, Jonathan wrote Marianne hundreds of love letters, passionate, desperately tender, beautiful letters. But Marianne never wrote back.

VANESSA: Is there perhaps a photograph in among the letters? A photograph of a girl?

JONATHAN: Dearest Marianne. I am writing to tell you that I've fallen desperately and hopelessly in love with you. It would perhaps be more prudent to pretend this was not the case, but I feel so strongly that all deception in my relations to you are repugnant to me.

MARIANNE: I love a strange city where I do not speak the language. I prefer it that way.

PETRUS: There is a photograph in this letter. Of a very pretty girl.

VANESSA: Does she have a melancholy beauty?

PETRUS: She looks rather familiar.

VANESSA: Yes. That's good. A girl who looks oddly familiar. He's overcome by the eerie sensation that he's known her before, in another life, perhaps. On the back of the photograph it says "From Marianne, With Love."

PETRUS: It does say that, actually.

VANESSA: Of course it does. Does the man who buys the book fall in love with the girl in the photograph?

PETRUS: I don't know. Does he?

MARIANNE: Everybody falls in love with me.

JONATHAN: I wonder if somehow my letters to you have gone astray.

VANESSA: The man is convinced he knows the girl. But he can't quite remember. Perhaps he doesn't want to remember.

MARIANNE: Petrus, is that you?

VANESSA: Perhaps it involves the memory of something terrible that happened. Something he wants to forget. Is the girl in some danger? Is there something about the letter that terrifies him? Is there a lock of hair, perhaps?

PETRUS: Vanessa, look at the photograph. Do you know this girl?

VANESSA: (Examining the photograph.) I'm not certain. It's so difficult to tell what's real. You know I've just got out of that place. Between the drugs I took before I went there, and all the drugs they gave me, and the shock treatments, my memory is like scrambled eggs.

MARIANNE: Oh, Vanessa, I have met the most wonderful young man. His name is Petrus Van Hoek, and he is an artist who studies the anatomy of young women. He has been studying my anatomy in great detail, and he reports that it is magnificent. He says I have a marvelous, melancholy beauty. He is presently taking photographs of me in the bath.

VANESSA: I remember a basement full of embalming bottles. And the cries of the whippoorwills.

JONATHAN: Dearest Vanessa. I have seen her. I have seen her naked in her bath.

VANESSA: There are some things I don't exactly remember, but I seem to remember having once been able to remember. Unless of course I've made them up. But are they my stories, or Marianne's stories? And are they fiction, or are they reminiscence? Madness must be like this.

MARIANNE: Petrus? Would you like to come up and wash my back?

VANESSA: I remember that she had a lover.

PETRUS: Why wouldn't she have a lover? A beautiful girl like that.

VANESSA: Yes, but up until then, you see, it had been just us two. Just Marianne and me. Many were in love with me, and everybody was in love with her, but mostly we two laughed at them. We were very happy, in our little world in Providence. We didn't want to spoil it by letting men in. Men exist to defile beauty. But then she found this artist. Or he found her. Perhaps she was modeling to put herself through school. It's very expensive, you know. But this one, for some reason, she wanted. And I was jealous.

MARIANNE: I've just met a wonderful man. His name is Petrus Van Hoek.

VANESSA: So the roommate finds her in the tub. She is forever taking long baths.

MARIANNE: Is somebody out there?

VANESSA: And the roommate confronts her.

MARIANNE: Petrus? Is that you?

VANESSA: Why do you give yourself to such a person? she says. He doesn't care about you. Not like I do. Why would you want to spoil everything by allowing this person to violate you?

JONATHAN: I don't understand why she won't answer my letters. It's driving me insane.

VANESSA: He's just a man, she says. He doesn't know how to care about you. But I love you.

MARIANNE: And I love you too, dear.

VANESSA: Says Marianne.

MARIANNE: Would you hand me the towel? I have a date with Petrus.

JONATHAN: I can't stand it any more. I must go to Providence to see her, confront her, tell her how much I love her.

VANESSA: Idea for the ending: jealous girl strangles her beloved in the bathtub.

JONATHAN: I knock and knock at the door but nobody answers. The door is unlocked. I walk into the old house. Vanessa? I say. Marianne? There is no answer. I can hear water dripping upstairs. I walk up the creaking staircase. I open the door to the bathroom. I find her lying dead in the tub. Then suddenly there is only darkness.

VANESSA: The murderess is hiding behind the door. She strikes him violently on the head with the bulldog door stop, and only later realizes that it's her brother. He is never quite right in the head after. But then, he was a man, after all. He'd never been all that bright.

JONATHAN: Lying naked there in the water. So beautiful.

VANESSA: Then she begins receiving mysterious letters from Quebec. She knows her brother must be sending them. Sometimes there are three or four letters a day, all about Marianne. She can't take it any more. Finally she goes back to Quebec to convince him to stop writing her these letters. She confronts him on the staircase.

PETRUS: What does she do?

(Sound of whippoorwills.)

VANESSA: She can hear the sound of whippoorwills.

PETRUS: What did you do?

VANESSA: They find her wandering in the streets of Quebec in the rain. Only she insists that it's not Quebec. It's Providence, she says. You may think it's Quebec, but just look in the mirror. My image in the mirror does not speak this language.

PETRUS: Vanessa, what did you do?

VANESSA: She woke up in another place. A quiet place. And every day a man came to see her. He sat with her every day and read to her. Spoke with her. He read to her from a very odd book.

JONATHAN: I go all about the house, calling her name. But nobody is there. The library is full of old books and papers. I wonder if they're my books and papers. I open an old book on the desk. It's the *Occult Notebooks* of N. J. Drago. The name written on the inside front cover is Petrus Van Hoek.

MARIANNE: Petrus? Is that you?

JONATHAN: I open the book to a random page and read: On my antiquarian trip from Oswego and Ticonderoga to Quebec, I was often confused by the cries of whippoorwills.

VANESSA: You're Petrus. You're the one who loved her.

PETRUS: Yes.

VANESSA: But why did you come to see me every day? Why have you brought me here?

PETRUS: I think you know.

VANESSA: I didn't mean to hurt her.

PETRUS: It's time for your bath now.

VANESSA: Yes. My bath.

MARIANNE: A beautiful girl, drowned in her bath.

VANESSA: I must take my bath now.

MARIANNE: Petrus? Is that you? Is somebody on the stairs?

PETRUS: I'll be up soon.

(*The light fades on them and goes out. Sound of whippoorwills in the darkness.*)

END OF PLAY

Snow

ADAM SZYMKOWICZ

Snow was first produced at Little Theatre at Tonic and by Bluebox Productions at Sticky @ Belly, New York City, 2005. Directed by Shira Milikowsky. Cast: Ed — David Marcus; Frankie — Sarah Gliko; Chuck — Robert Hancock; Sara — Cara Greene. *Snow* was recently produced by White Room Theatre, Edinburgh, Scotland, August 2008, as part of Bite Size Plays, the Edinburgh Fringe Festival. Directed by Shirley Jaffe. Cast: Ed — Ross Forder; Frankie — Miranda Christides; Chuck — Alex Beales; Sara — Lisa Bealby.

CHARACTERS

    CHUCK: Twenties to forties.
    ED: Twenties to forties.
    FRANKIE: Twenties to forties.
    SARA: Twenties to forties.

SETTING

    A bar and Sara's apartment; these can be suggested minimally.

TIME

    The present.

• • •

Ed in spot.

ED: I've been careful, always very careful. Before touching a woman I put on rubber gloves. Some women are taken aback sure, when you pull out rubber gloves and dental dams, but what kinds of women are those? — women that know they have diseases. And those are not the type of women I want to know in any case. So when people ask me if I'm upset at being a virgin at my age, I say no way.

    I'm just looking for a clean woman. I am not against kissing — I just want to make sure her mouth is well cleaned first. If she would brush her teeth and then gargle with mouthwash for a minimum of sixty seconds. I, of course, would also brush and mouthwash. I like cleanliness, that's all. We are all dirty. God knows I scrub my hands before putting those rubber gloves on.

(Sara in spot.)

SARA: I've been careful, always very careful. Sure there are people who leave the house more than I do. They take strolls, they cross streets in the midst of traffic. They get on airplanes and fly halfway across the world. And I say good for them. If they want to risk their lives daily, let 'em. But don't ask me to. I'm fine how I am. It is true I have not left my apartment in three years. Everyone delivers in New York. Everyone. My mother says I would meet more people if I left my apartment — but I have my college friends I still call and e-mail and of course there is a large online community waiting to hear my every word. Anyway, people die when they take risks. I've seen it happen.

(Frankie and Chuck in a bar, looking out the window)

FRANKIE: It's nice to just sit here and watch the snow.

CHUCK: Yeah.

FRANKIE: It's very beautiful. Calming in a way, if you're not watching the people try to get rid of it.

CHUCK: Uh-huh.

FRANKIE: There's something institutional about snow, don't you agree?

CHUCK: I hadn't noticed.

FRANKIE: It's definitely the most institutional precipitation. Take for example how afraid of it people are.

CHUCK: People aren't afraid of snow.

FRANKIE: They would lock it up and put it on tranquilizers if they could. Instead, what do we do? We salt it. We melt it, push it away. Get that away from me. Not that — not snow! Put it on a truck! Get it the hell out of here! It's not melting fast enough. Destroy it! Destroy it before it destroys us! We live in a very Puritanical society still.

CHUCK: I guess so.

FRANKIE: What's wrong?

CHUCK: Nothing. It's just . . . That woman I deliver to — the one who never leaves her apartment. Something she said today really depressed me.

FRANKIE: What?

CHUCK: I don't even know why really. It was so small.

FRANKIE: What'd she say?

CHUCK: She said —

SARA: I don't know, Chuck. I hope you're doing what you like. Most of us never have the chance to be what we want to be.

CHUCK: And it just made me realize. I don't really even want to be inside this body. There are so many people I would rather be.

FRANKIE: Like me?

CHUCK: Absolutely, I'd like to be you. I'd like to be inside you, and I don't just mean have sex with you which is something I also want, as I'm sure you know, but I want to know what it feels like inside you. Like if I touch this and you touch this I know what it feels like when I touch it, but I have no idea what you feel when you touch it. That's minor. But for example, what do you dream? You can tell me about them and try to describe them, but I'll never really know what you see. And that's just the start of the problem because really what I want is to be everybody.

FRANKIE: Everybody?

CHUCK: Well, especially attractive women.

FRANKIE: I'm not going to have sex with you, Chuck.

CHUCK: I know.

FRANKIE: Chuck, look at me. You and I will never have sex.

CHUCK: Never?

FRANKIE: Never.

CHUCK: Are you sure?

FRANKIE: Positive.

CHUCK: I think I should go.

FRANKIE: Because I won't have sex with you?

CHUCK: I'm feeling kind of vulnerable right now.

FRANKIE: I'm sorry.

CHUCK: It's OK. I should go.

FRANKIE: You going to at least finish your drink?

(Chuck downs the rest of his drink.)

FRANKIE: See you soon.

CHUCK: Yeah, whatever.

FRANKIE: Shit!

(Frankie sits there quietly for a few moments. Ed walks in.)

FRANKIE: Ed. Hey, Ed. Over here!

ED: Oh hey, Frankie.

FRANKIE: How's it going?

ED: Good. Good.

FRANKIE: That's really good.

ED: Yeah. Yeah.

FRANKIE: I just had a fight with my friend Chuck.

ED: Sorry to hear that.

FRANKIE: I told him I wouldn't have sex with him.

ED: Oh.

FRANKIE: It's not that I don't find him attractive. I mean you know Chuck.

ED: Sure.

FRANKIE: And it's not that I'm not in the mood. Or I was but then I was trying to tell him something about the snow and he just blew me off. Anyway, every time I have sex with someone I'm friends with, we don't end
up being friends after that.

ED: Right.

FRANKIE: You know what I'm saying?

ED: I do.

FRANKIE: The real problem is, however, I have a nagging feeling I am incapable of love. There was a time when it was ever possible. I thought every

day today I will fall in love. But that never happened. Occasionally I fell into like but never love. I must be broken. What's wrong with me?

ED: Nothing.

FRANKIE: I would probably be fine if I just never believed in it. Why did I have to be born such a fucking romantic?

ED: Dunno.

FRANKIE: Why can't sex be enough? Why am I searching for this thing that if I find it, I'm not even sure I'll recognize it anyway? I guess I believe there's something more out there — that one person I'll find one day. So there's no point in having sex with Chuck. He's not the one.

ED: Yeah.

FRANKIE: How's your sex life, Ed?

ED: It's slow, to be honest, Frankie. It's slow. In fact not moving at all. You could say noexistent, honestly. Having never moved anywhere. Stalled in the driveway.

FRANKIE: Snowed in.

ED: You could say that. I feel like I'm missing everything.

FRANKIE: You're not.

ED: But I am.

FRANKIE: You'll find that special someone.

ED: I think I already did but I messed it up.

FRANKIE: I'm sure you didn't mess it up.

ED: I asked her to douche.

FRANKIE: Oh.

ED: Things kind of went downhill from there. And I'm not saying she was a perfect person. She never left her apartment and she wasn't always cognizant of cleanliness to the degree I would like. But I think we understood each other for a time. I remember she said once —

SARA: There are many things I do not understand although I am an intelligent person. There are things beyond my grasp — things that screech or howl out numbers. There are darknesses I cannot comprehend. There is death somewhere and somewhere black holes and tears in our unconscious.

Somehow the brain works but how I couldn't tell you. One day my heart will stop and so will yours but at this moment we sit beside each other with our beating hearts and our pleasant faces.

We are afraid, you and I. We are terrified people. Many people aren't as terrified as we are. They slip through life without concerns or wants. They don't worry about what they know but instead they purchase things and eat up every new TV program. These people are happy and perhaps we should be more like them. But we are not and no one can control the weather.

Try as we might we are only these creatures with two legs, maybe a soul, some of us a God, all of us hearts beating until they don't. And I will stay here with you because it is what I want. I think it is what you want too. And we will work towards some design perhaps or maybe just screw but either way I will be happy for more than a few moments and maybe someday when we are old, we will sit holding hands looking out the window at the snow falling.

FRANKIE: She sounds great.

ED: She is. Sometimes. I mean we had problems. I dunno. I haven't seen her in a while. Maybe I should go on some kind of drug.

FRANKIE: Can you go back and apologize?

ED: I don't know.

(Chuck reenters.)

CHUCK: I'm sorry I left like that. I'm a mother fucker. Oh, hey Ed.

ED: Hey.

FRANKIE: I'm sorry too.

CHUCK: But are you really sure we will never have sex?

FRANKIE: I don't know. I guess anything can happen, but mostly I'm sure.

CHUCK: Yeah, I mean I guess I knew that. It's a shame, though.

FRANKIE: Be that as it may . . . .

ED: Maybe I should call her up. Say something to her. What would I say? I'm really messed up.

CHUCK: What's going on?

ED: Nothing.

FRANKIE: You should go find her.

ED: I don't have to find her. I know where she is.

FRANKIE: You should go there.

ED: Uh-huh.

FRANKIE: Right now.

ED: I know.

FRANKIE: You owe it to yourself and to her too.

ED: I know.

FRANKIE: Did you love her?

ED: I did.

CHUCK: You gotta go to her then.

ED: I know.

CHUCK: Before it's too late.

ED: I know.

CHUCK: Before she finds someone else.

ED: I should go.

FRANKIE: Are you going to go?

ED: I don't think so. No, I don't think so.

    (Pause.)

FRANKIE: Look at the snow. It's very beautiful, don't you think?

ED: Yeah.

CHUCK: It is.

    (Sara in her apartment also looks out at the snow.)

END OF PLAY

Stick and Move

GREG LAM

Stick and Move was first performed at the Stanford Calderwood Pavilion, Boston Center for the Arts, May 11, 2008, as part of the Boston Theater Marathon. Directed by Sarah Farbo. Cast: Anthony — Josh Rilla; Haley — Kristen Bush; Doris — Pardis Parsa; Sully — Sebastian Hofferberth

CHARACTERS

    ANTHONY: Twenty-six and rugged looking.
    HALEY: Twenty-four and impeccably dressed.
    SULLY: Fiftyish. Weathered features. He's been through a lot of battles.
        Wears a sweatsuit.
    DORIS: Fiftyish. The same as Sully.

SETTING

    An elegant café, suitable for a first date.

TIME

    The present.

• • •

At rise: A nice-looking couple eating at a nice restaurant. Anthony is dressed in an ill-fitting jacket/tie combo. Haley is in an impeccable dress. The couple is quiet as they pick over their nearly eaten entrees.

ANTHONY: I really like this chicken. It's really good.

HALEY: Yeah, so's my pasta.

ANTHONY: It goes good with the wine.

HALEY: I don't know much about wine.

ANTHONY: Me neither. But this is good.
    (Pause.)

ANTHONY: I really like Italian food.

HALEY: Do you cook at all?

ANTHONY: No. But I really like Italian food.
    (Pause.)

HALEY: Do you ever do stuff like rock climbing or anything?

ANTHONY: No. You?

HALEY: A little bit. It's a good time.

ANTHONY: Do you want to try any of my chicken?

HALEY: I'm a vegetarian.

ANTHONY: Oh.
    (A bell rings three times. Anthony abruptly rises from his seat and moves downstage. Sully in a sweatshirt jumps onto the stage with a stool in hand, a towel, a spray bottle, and a bucket. Sully sets down the stool and drapes the towel over Anthony's shoulders. Sully checks on Anthony's condition.)

SULLY: Anthony! How you feelin', T? She tagged you pretty hard at the end there. How you feelin'?

ANTHONY: I'm good, Sully.

SULLY: Yeah, you're so good you just walked into that last one. You didn't notice she was a vegetarian? She ordered the only vegetarian dish on the menu for God's sake.

ANTHONY: She caught me by surprise. She's wily.

(Sully towels off Anthony.)

SULLY: Now listen to me, T. You've got to be more active this round. You can't come at her straight. She'll brush that right off, you understand? Stick and move, stick and move. Use the verbal jabs to keep her at bay, but look for an opening. Use an angle that she's not expecting. If you find something that connects, then go in for a combination, but keep your guard up. Open.

(Anthony opens his mouth. Sully sprays water in with a water bottle.)

SULLY: You have to set the pace for this round. Do not let her dictate the pace, you understand? Anthony nods. Now spit.

(Anthony spits into the bucket that Sully holds.)

SULLY: Now go get 'er.

(The bell rings, and Anthony hops off the stool. Sully gathers his things and hops off the stage, watching the scene from below. Anthony approaches the table warily, like a boxer in a bout, bouncing on the balls of his feet and bobbing his head. Eventually he sits down at the table. Sully paces his area, watching the scene, shouting advice, and reacting to things as they come.)

ANTHONY: So . . .

HALEY: So.

ANTHONY: How about dessert? You look like a girl that really likes her desserts.

SULLY: Oh, jeez! Anthony!

HALEY: You think so?

ANTHONY: I mean not that you're fat or anything. Just that —

HALEY: Just what?

ANTHONY: Just that you seem like a sweets girl.

HALEY: Right.

ANTHONY: I mean the desserts here are really supposed to be great. I mean, nothing but the best, y'know? You like tiramisu?

HALEY: Well, if you say it's that good, then I suppose.

SULLY: Be active, Anthony. Be active!

ANTHONY: Hey, Haley. I don't want to read into things too much, on a first date and all. But I know I'm being a little weird and all. It's just that I think you kind of have an effect on me. Y'know?

HALEY: Really?

ANTHONY: Yeah. I just don't want to screw anything up.

HALEY: You're not screwing anything up, Anthony.

(The bell rings three times. Sully sets up a stool for Anthony in the background. Meanwhile, Doris in a sweatsuit brings her own stool for Haley to flop down on. She too has the bucket, towel, and water bottle. Doris checks on Haley's condition.)

DORIS: Come on girl. You were doing good there for a while. Keep your focus.

HALEY: Sorry, Doris. He surprised me there.

DORIS: Surprise, sur-shmise. The guy hasn't been able to string three syllables together, and you walk right into his sensitive guy act. You should have seen that bullshit coming from a mile away. Instead, it caught you right under the chin.

HALEY: Is it bad?

DORIS: You're still ahead on points, Haley, but you've got to come on strong this round. This guy has thrown everything he's got at you. He's clutching and grabbing instead of engaging. It's up to you to get under his defenses and hit him where it hurts, got it?

(Haley nods. Doris wipes off Haley's head with a towel.)

DORIS: He's been on the defensive the entire night, Haley. All he wants to do is survive the night. He's not going to give you anything unless you take it from him, understand?

(Haley nods.)

DORIS: Open up.

(Haley opens her mouth. Doris squirts water into her mouth with a water bottle.)

DORIS: Now's the time to make your move. Back this sucker up against the ropes and bombs away, OK? Now, spit.

(Haley spits.)

SULLY: This is the time to make your move, kid. You have to bring it.

DORIS: Don't hold back. Give him everything you've got.

(Doris and Sully take away their stuff and hop to below the stage. Haley and Anthony take their seats again.)

ANTHONY: So . . .

HALEY: So.

(Pause.)

SULLY: C'mon! Don't just sit there!

DORIS: Use the heavy ammo, Haley!

HALEY: So, Anthony. My friend Kate is getting married next month.

ANTHONY: Yeah? Really?

SULLY: Cover up, T!

HALEY: Yeah. She's doing it on the beach. Isn't that so romantic?

ANTHONY: Yeah. Right. Romantic.

(Anthony becomes visibly nervous.)

HALEY: Anyhow, I was wondering if you'd be interested in going to the wedding with me.

DORIS: Oh! That got 'im good!

ANTHONY: Yeah, well. Wow. That's really —

SULLY: Counterpunch, Anthony! Counterpunch!

ANTHONY: Y'know, I haven't been to a wedding since my ex-girlfriend's wedding last year.

SULLY: That's my boy!

HALEY: You went to your ex-girlfriend's wedding?

DORIS: Careful!

ANTHONY: Yeah, she's still a pal. We talk on the phone now and then. I was actually her best man.

HALEY: Really?

ANTHONY: Yeah. It's kind of a thing. I like to keep in touch with my ex-girlfriends. I hope that's not a problem.

(Pause. All eyes are on Haley, who now seems visibly shaken.)

HALEY: I think that it's wonderful that you can be so mature as to be in such close contact with one of your former girlfriends.

(The bell rings. Haley and Anthony go to their respective corners. They are both wobbly. Doris and Sully are waiting for them.)

SULLY: There ya go, T! That's a way to tag her!

DORIS: C'mon Haley. You had him on the ropes.

HALEY: He cut me, Doris! He cut me!

DORIS: Shake it off. You're still in this one! You hear me?

SULLY: Beautiful shot, kid! Way to come back!

DORIS: Listen to me, Haley. It's the final round. Last chance to make an impression.

SULLY: Don't get cocky, T! This is it!

DORIS: You need to go for the throat, kid.

SULLY: Keep your eyes on the prize.

HALEY: I can't do this anymore, Doris! Throw in the towel.

ANTHONY: Sully, I'm punched out. It's rough out there.

DORIS: C'mon, girl. This is what you've been training for all this time. All those hours in the gym. This is what it's been for.

SULLY: This is your moment, T. This is your time.

DORIS: It's now or never!

SULLY: It's put up or shut up!

DORIS AND SULLY: It's do or die time! You understand?

(Haley and Anthony nod.)

DORIS AND SULLY: Now spit!

(They spit. The bell rings. Haley and Anthony stumble back to their seats. A long pause as they stare at one another wearily.)

DORIS: C'mon. Don't leave anything on the table!

(Haley glares at Doris, then turns back to Anthony. Her tone is different, more direct.)

HALEY: Listen, Anthony. Let me ask you something. It might sound weird, but do you ever think sometimes that sometimes we just say things because we're supposed to say them?

DORIS: Haley!

HALEY: *(To Doris.)* Quiet. *(To Anthony.)* I mean, do you ever think about all those rules and cautions and things that keep you from connecting from people?

DORIS: What are you doing, Haley?

HALEY: Do you ever think that there's some voice screaming in your ear about how your supposed to act? And that's the only thing that's keeping you from saying what you really feel?

(Pause.)

SULLY: Anthony!

ANTHONY: *(To Sully.)* Ssh! *(To Haley.)* Sometimes, I think that, like, there's this short, you know, fat guy . . . smoking a cigar or something. And he yells all this . . . And it's really weird, if I think about it. I mean, if I think about it too much —

HALEY: I know just what you mean.

ANTHONY: Is . . . Is your voice named "Sully" by any chance?

(Pause. Haley laughs.)

ANTHONY: Do you just want to call our date over and then walk and talk for a bit?

HALEY: Only if it coincides with getting ice cream.

ANTHONY: I'll pick up the check.

HALEY: Please. I already took care of it.

ANTHONY: You're my kind of girl, you know that?
>   *(The bell rings and Haley and Anthony walk off the stage together. Sully and
>   Doris watch them go.)*
SULLY: Doris.
DORIS: Sully.
SULLY: That was a tough one.
DORIS: They all are.
SULLY: So who won?
DORIS: I don't have a clue, Sully. So what are you doing after this?

END OF PLAY

Theft

JERROD BOGARD

Theft was originally performed at the Players Loft, New York City, June 5–8, 2008, by Shortened Attention Span. Directed by Jerrod Bogard. Cast: Shellback — Bridget Handler; Jonathan Featherstone — Howard Mears; Henry — Joshua Karlin; Carey — Erin Singleton.

CHARACTERS

> JONATHAN FEATHERSTONE: Forty-two, psychiatrist with a successful practice; he's comfortable and doesn't want to make any waves in his life.
> SHELLBACK: Thirty-five, police officer; she's professional and courteous but has seen too many cases like his to be incredibly empathetic.
> HENRY: Sixty-five, Jonathan's father; kind smile, steady presence.
> CAREY: Twenty-four, Jonathan's ex-girlfriend; bright-eyed girl next door.

SETTING

> A New York City police department.

TIME

> Night, the present.

SYNOPSIS: When Dr. Featherstone reports a mugging to the police he's ushered into a room wherein lies everything that's ever been stolen from him.

• • •

> *Lights up in the front lobby of a police station. At center is a high desk/window and behind it is Officer Shellback. Jonathan enters in a rush.)*

JONATHAN: *(Approaching the desk.)* Hi. Hello. Hi. Is this —
SHELLBACK: How can I help you?
JONATHAN: I need to make a report. Is this were I make a report?
SHELLBACK: What type of report are you —
JONATHAN: A-a-a-a mugging? A theft? I was —
SHELLBACK: Are you the victim, sir?
JONATHAN: Yes. Yes. Is this where I —
SHELLBACK: Yes it is. One moment. *(She finds some papers.)*
JONATHAN: I'm — My office is in the neighbor — My name is Jonathan Feather —
SHELLBACK: Sir, did you get a look at your assailant?
JONATHAN: Featherstone. My — the assail — Did I get a look at the —
SHELLBACK: Did you see the person who robbed you?
JONATHAN: Yes.
SHELLBACK: Sex?
JONATHAN: No, he only robbed me, thank God.
SHELLBACK: *(Beat.)* Male.

JONATHAN: Right, yes. Male. I'm a little frazzled.

SHELLBACK: Race?

JONATHAN: Yes — or rather, uhm, African American.

SHELLBACK: Right and —

JONATHAN: Or did I just imagine he was black? Oh God. Does it really matter? Do you have some — some water or — or — or —

SHELLBACK: When did this happen, Mr. Featherstone?

JONATHAN: Dawn. I think I was knocked out. The guy is surely gone by now, but I thought I should come and fill out a repo —

SHELLBACK: Where was this? Where did the robbery happen?

JONATHAN: Just outside the park on — uhm, 67th. The west side.

SHELLBACK: Most likely lives in the park. A lot of them do. Height? . . . The assailant's.

JONATHAN: Uhm . . . five eleven?

SHELLBACK: Build?

JONATHAN: Medium?

SHELLBACK: Eyes brown, hair black? . . . Skin tone?

JONATHAN: Uhm . . . I don't —

SHELLBACK: Dark, light?

JONATHAN: Medium?

SHELLBACK: Tattoos or scars or easily identifiable marks?

JONATHAN: No.

SHELLBACK: What was he wearing?

JONATHAN: Some . . . I don't know.

SHELLBACK: Hooded sweatshirt? Jeans?

JONATHAN: Yeah, yes.

SHELLBACK: And Mr. Featherstone, what was stolen?

JONATHAN: I've had my office on 59th Street for fifteen years and I jog, ya know, I'm a jogger.

SHELLBACK: What did he take, Mr. Featherstone? . . . Do you know?

JONATHAN: Every morning pretty much I run up — up through the park and down Park West but I wasn't — This is just — I'm a psychiatrist. My job's to help people.

SHELLBACK: Yeah, it's never easy. Only one more question. Did you do everything in your power to prevent the incident?

JONATHAN: I — well, I . . . I don't know if I fully understand the —

SHELLBACK: Did you do everything in your power to prevent this from happening?

JONATHAN: I believe so, I — I didn't fight the guy if that's what you mean.

SHELLBACK: Did you run?

JONATHAN: Run? I was running when he —

SHELLBACK: Did you cry out?

JONATHAN: Yes — I mean — no. Not as — I was so startled I think. It happened so —

SHELLBACK: And you came here as soon as —

JONATHAN: First thing. Yes, after — I don't know how long I was out. What time is it?

SHELLBACK: It's the economy.

JONATHAN: What is? What's the economy?

SHELLBACK: Economy goes down, crime goes up. People shouldn't go jogging around as though they're unaffected by the economy.

JONATHAN: Well I wouldn't say I'm not affect — That's fine. Is there something I need to sign or something I need to —

SHELLBACK: We'll file this right away.

JONATHAN: OK, but shouldn't I — I mean aren't there —

SHELLBACK: When these things happen, sir, it can take a little while for the gravity of the situation to become clear.

JONATHAN: All right. Yes. I can see that.

SHELLBACK: So what I suggest is —

(The desk phone rings. She picks up.)

SHELLBACK: Seventh Precinct . . . Sir? . . . No, not ye . . . Yes, sir. *(She hangs up the phone.)* Follow me? This way.

(Shell shows Jonathan around the desk. They travel a half circle upstage to the other side of the desk. They continue the circle downstage while rotating the desk 180 degrees. It becomes a filing cabinet.)

JONATHAN: The scariest part of this wasn't even the guy. I mean I'm really — I'm almost embarrassed.

SHELLBACK: No reason to be. Eventually this happens to everyone. No one is immune. Not in this town.

JONATHAN: When it was happening — my only thought was, "who's going to feed Misty?"

SHELLBACK: Your cat.

JONATHAN: Foolish.

SHELLBACK: Pretty common.

JONATHAN: Do you hear that a lot?

(They've circled downstage and approach the filing cabinet from the front.)

SHELLBACK: From people without families. I think it's fairly common. Sure . . . Here.

JONATHAN: What's this?

SHELLBACK: *(Searching the drawer labels.)* Your file.

JONATHAN: You already have me on file?

(She pulls the filing cabinet. It swings round again, this time 90 degrees like a door.)

SHELLBACK: After you. *(He is apprehensive. Pause.)* Come on.

(He follows her upstage through the "doorway." Lights up in the upstage area. Long tables on three sides are covered with a myriad of items- neatly displayed like a garage sale. We see: a sports jersey, a bicycle, a baby blanket, a baseball card, a nice hat, books, toys, CDs, audio tapes, stacks of money in varying amounts from change to several thousand dollars in cash, and much more. Tons of random stuff. Seated at the upstage side of the center table is Henry. Seated at the stage left table is Carey. They are both neatly groomed, quiet and still. We do not notice them until Jonathan notices them. One empty chair sits at the far stage left side of the stage left table.)

JONATHAN: What is this? Like a — is this an evidence closet?

SHELLBACK: This is your file.

JONATHAN: In this mess?

SHELLBACK: This is everything that's ever been stolen from you in your entire life. All this belongs to you, though it's been taken away.

JONATHAN: *(Looking around in awe.)* My file.

SHELLBACK: I hope it is anyway. Do you recognize this stuff?

(Jonathan goes to the stage right table. He picks up a baseball card.)

JONATHAN: *(Looking at the card.)* Topps 1967 Willie Mays, outfield. We had a fort. In the ravine and I left for a minute to go number two behind a tree. Brian Chayhill. I took him to the matt. He looked me in the eye and said he didn't have it. How is this — Is all this in chronological order?

SHELLBACK: Supposed to be.

(He goes to the far stage right — the first object. He picks up a pacifier and then sets it down. He picks up a small, blue blanket with silk trim. He lifts it to his cheek to feel its softness.)

JONATHAN: *(Whisper.)* Banky. *(Louder.)* The silk. Same as my mother's night-gown. I'd rub the silk and suck my thumb. Couldn't sleep without it. Funny. The first bar — first iron bar in my prison of memory.

SHELLBACK: Don't misunderstand, sir. You're not in jail here.

JONATHAN: The prison of memory is the — it's how we keep ourselves from living freely in the present moment. By constantly comparing everything to what we remember.

SHELLBACK: I had a dog one time tipped over a pot of hot grease from the stove. Could never get him to eat bacon after that. Like that, you mean?

JONATHAN: Sorta like that, yeah. Does everybody have a file like this?

SHELLBACK: I don't know what they do across town. But should if ya lived in this precinct.

JONATHAN: *(Holding up a baseball jersey.)* Jasmine Lansing. You bitch. *(To Shell.)* Dog? Would my Caesar be here? *(Calling out.)* Caesar! *(Beat, then to Shell.)* I always wondered.

SHELLBACK: Guess he ran away.

JONATHAN: *(Browsing the items.)* She . . . So this money, all this money . . . *(Pointing to a the largest stack of bills.)* Taxes, right? The war, right? This money is mine? I can take it with me?

SHELLBACK: No, that's not allowed.

JONATHAN: I'll sign a receipt. Everything —

SHELLBACK: Everything stays in the room.

(Jonathan notices Henry sitting at the table.)

JONATHAN: Dad? Oh my God! Dad. It's so good to see you! I — I — *(They hug, cheek to cheek.)* Of course you'd be here. It's so true. Even while you were right in front of us. Even as we were all together, I felt you'd been stolen away.

SHELLBACK: Alzheimer's?

JONATHAN: *(Beat.)* In your life too?

SHELLBACK: No. Thank God.

JONATHAN: Do. It's hard.

SHELLBACK: Someone right there in front of you but like you can't touch them? Or like they can hear you but that you can't speak to them. Nightmare not to be able to just say —

JONATHAN: I love you, Dad.

HENRY: I know.

JONATHAN: I said it and said it. Said it and said it and said it. And it didn't matter. Waited too long. How proud I was he was my dad and how much I — I never told him I didn't — a lot of things. A lot of things. *(To Henry.)* I love you.

HENRY: I knew.

JONATHAN: But I didn't know that he knew. *(Turning away, he sees his bike.)* My bicycle. Damn it, my bicycle. Two seconds — I turn my back. So angry! Only hat like it in the city. Everybody loved this stupid — and I was so angry! Who steals a book of poetry? What good could that have possibly — I stopped writing. So . . . angry. Anger. All anger and helpless. Helpless to possess these objects, keep these things. These things and these people from scattering like falling marbles. And the — the helpless feeling, it becomes anger so easily doesn't it? And the anger — it feeds you. It nourishes you like gruel in this your — your little cell. Your little life. *(Beat, then noticing Carey.)* There she is.

SHELLBACK: There's always one.

(Carey gets up during the following and they do a ritual handshake like silly kids.)

JONATHAN: Carey Carey quite contrary . . .

CAREY: How'd your armpits get so hairy?	JONATHAN: How'd your armpits get so hairy?

JONATHAN: Is it whiskey?

CAREY: Is it rum? . . .

CAREY: If I call it, will it come?	JONATHAN: If I call it, will it come?

JONATHAN: Face in a book, head up my ass, and some horny rich kid plucks her right out of my garden.

(She kisses his cheek, turns with a flip of her beautiful hair, and returns to her seat and her book.)

JONATHAN: I'd kept better watch maybe. Paid more attention perhaps.

SHELLBACK: Did you fight?

JONATHAN: Never for important things.

SHELLBACK: To try and get her back . . . like you did with the baseball card? Did you cry out?

JONATHAN: *(Beat.)* Is this usual? This amount of things in a file — is this common?

SHELLBACK: Some have more, some have less.

JONATHAN: It could have been less.

SHELLBACK: Sure. Could have been a lot less. I've got to get back to my desk.

JONATHAN: Of course.

SHELLBACK: Did you figure out what it was that was taken from you today?

JONATHAN: I should get back to the office. Patients don't know what's happened.

SHELLBACK: Sometimes it happens in the blink of an eye, but sometimes it can take years — so slow you never notice anything is missing.

JONATHAN: What's that?

SHELLBACK: Theft. . . . Good-bye, Mr. Featherstone.

(Shell starts to exit the room/file, and Jonathan goes to follow her. She makes a motion that he is to stay.)

SHELLBACK: Everything that's been taken from you stays here.

JONATHAN: Oh.

SHELLBACK: That's right.

JONATHAN: Oh . . . Oh. I see.

(Shell exits. Sound of a cell door shutting as she closes the door to the file. Jonathan goes to the empty chair at the far end of the stage left table. He sits. Lights fade out.)

END OF PLAY

Yin Yang

Rosanna Yamagiwa Alfaro

Yin Yang was first produced by SlamBoston (Another Country Productions and Company One) at Plaza Theatre, Boston Center for the Arts, April 1, 2008. Directed by Krista D'Agostino. Cast: Molly — Giselle Ty; Richard — Nathaniel Shea; Mol — Chrissy Chanyasulkit; Dick — Chris Lyons.

CHARACTERS

> MOLLY: Asian, wears glasses, no makeup. Her skirt and sweater don't match.
>
> MOLL: A small Asian dog with a bleached ponytail like a spiky fountain on top of her head.
>
> RICHARD: Caucasian, wears a pink shirt and khakis.
>
> DICK: A large Caucasian dog, scruffy, wears T-shirt and cutoffs.

SETTING

> A park bench and a leafy tree.

TIME

> The present.

• • •

Moll enters, pulling Molly after her. They are at opposite ends of a leash. Moll stops to check out the tree.

MOLLY: *(To audience.)* I'm Molly. This is Moll. We're inseparable, head and heart joined at the hip.

MOLL: She's the linguist here. *(To Molly.)* Why are you wearing a sweater? It's ninety degrees in the shade.

MOLLY: It's September, sweater weather.

> *(Moll musses her hair and pulls down her shorts to reveal an ethnocentric tattoo at the base of her spine. She plucks at her halter strap and rubs her back against the tree.)*

MOLLY: You feeling all right? You want some water?

MOLL: I'm hot and itchy, OK? The hairs on my back are standing up. *(She looks offstage.)* And no wonder. Look who's coming. It's Richard traveling on his lonesome without his Dick.

> *(Richard enters, carrying a leash.)*

RICHARD: Well, look who's here. Hi, Molly. Hi, Moll. *(He scratches Moll's back and talks to her.)* Sorry Dick's not here. He saw a couple of squirrels and took off.

MOLLY: I thought I told you I never wanted to see you or Dick again.

RICHARD: And who could blame you after yesterday night's performance? Dick and Moll chasing each other around the sofa, spilling the wine . . .

MOLLY: I can't believe you actually called me "Morry." I mean where and when did you grow up?

RICHARD: I was drunk. We both were. After everything that happened that day . . .

MOLLY: You said, "Morry, forget the flied lice. I want to get rayed."

RICHARD: We'd been talking for hours. I wanted to segue from the dining room to the bedroom. It was a feeble attempt at a joke.

MOLLY: A racist joke.

RICHARD: It wasn't racist. Retrograde maybe, but not racist.

(Moll jumps up on the bench. Richard sits down next to her and scratches her behind the ears.)

MOLL: *(To Molly.)* Richard's clueless, but he doesn't have a mean bone in his body. *(She nuzzles Richard.)* Your shirt smells of Dick.

RICHARD: *(To Moll.)* You're missing him, aren't you? He should be here. After all, this is your bench, your tree.

MOLLY: You're so different when you're drunk. Sober you would never say "flied lice" or "I want to get rayed." You're much too cultivated for that. Instead, you say things like, "You speak English better than I do." You say, "If you wore dark glasses, you'd look just like everyone else."

RICHARD: When you string those things together I feel so . . .

MOLLY: It's worse, actually, than "flied lice."

(She pushes the sleeping Moll off the bench and sits down.)

MOLL: Hey!

(While Richard and Molly talk, Moll sniffs the legs of the bench and stretches out on the grass.)

RICHARD: You can't break up with me, Molly. You don't know how dull work is without you. There's no one to talk to, no one to argue with. I'm surrounded by all those boring run-of-the-mill . . .

MOLLY: Are you saying I'm not run-of-the-mill, not normal?

RICHARD: You're absolutely not normal. I've never met anyone as lovely as you.

MOLLY: On the normal attractiveness scale or on some strange exotic scale you've . . .

RICHARD: I think it has something to do with the way you speak.

MOLLY: So melodic, sweet, and self-effacing?

RICHARD: No one who really knows you would say that.

MOLLY: If you think about it, this is exactly the conversation you'd never have to have with a run-of-the-mill girl. With me there's this thing on your plate you have to eat before you get to your normal everyday problems.

RICHARD: "Solly, but this is vely sirry."

MOLLY: OK, OK. I know I'm being whatever it is I'm being — no one's more aware of it than I am.

RICHARD: I completely understand where you're coming from, but . . .

MOLLY: No one like you could possibly understand.

RICHARD: I realize a little knowledge is a dangerous thing . . .

MOLLY: And a lot of knowledge can send you straight off the cliff. All I'm saying is we shouldn't be putting each other through this. *(Beat.)* For one thing you're too big for me. If we had a child, its nose would be too big for its squinty eyes, its teeth too big for its mouth.

RICHARD: This is ridiculous.

MOLLY: No really. It happened to a Korean friend of mine. She married a Russian, and their kid had these humungous front teeth.

RICHARD: I've never seen a halfie who wasn't gorgeous.

MOLLY: I can't tell you how much I hate this conversation. If I married you, we'd have it all our lives.

RICHARD: Then let's forget about marriage.

(Molly is stunned.)

MOLLY: What? You're saying . . .

RICHARD: Just kidding. Come on. *(He puts his arm around her.)* Look, it was another bad joke. I was just kidding. Haven't I asked you a thousand times to marry me? Haven't we come up with a thousand reasons why we're perfect for each other? I mean you have no Asian friends. I have no white friends.

MOLLY: We don't have any friends period. If we were to die tomorrow no one would notice.

RICHARD: All the more reason to stick together. Every human being needs company.

MOLLY: Look, only a loser would want to marry me, and I hate you for it, OK? *(Beat.)* You have to be sick to want to marry the only person they fired in an office of two hundred very average people.

RICHARD: Twenty, not two hundred.

MOLLY: It makes me so mad. I thought I was doing everything right. I bought those dimestore glasses to obscure my almond eyes. I bobbed my hair to lose that "fresh off the boat" look.

RICHARD: They were idiots.

MOLLY: Were they? I didn't tell you the whole story last night. They said the bottom line was I spent all my time talking to you at the water cooler.

RICHARD: They said that?

MOLLY: I said, "So why don't you fire Richard too?"

RICHARD: That's a joke, right?

MOLLY: I said, "If you think about it, Richard's the one who isn't aggressive enough with clients, who doesn't speak up at meetings. He's the real Asian here."

RICHARD: Very funny.

MOLLY: I said, "Richard's the one who passively sits there, waiting for the spotlight to find him. I, on the other hand, am itching to seize center-stage — if you only took the trouble to look under the surface. But let's face it. Richard's generic, I'm not. You'll never fire Richard. He gets all the breaks even though I'm basically brighter."

RICHARD: That's a stereotype.

MOLLY: Face it, I'm much too bright for you.

RICHARD: I — I don't know what to say . . . If that's the way you feel, then I . . . No one, not even my mother has ever spoken to me like that.

MOLLY: Just kidding. Look, I'm sorry. I'm just kidding.

RICHARD: I'm off. I've got to find Dick. *(To audience.)* Why is it that even when she says these hurtful things, when she hurls abuse at me, I still feel I'm the one to blame, not her? This time, though, she's gone too far. I'm never speaking to her again. Seriously, I'm going home and putting a bullet through my head.

(He exits. Moll jumps up on the bench and sits next to Molly.)

MOLL: Well, you really messed that up.

MOLLY: So what . . . what exactly should I have done? What would you have done that I didn't do?

MOLL: I would have licked his boots, then I would have climbed up on his lap and licked his face. *(Beat.)* What do you think has happened to Dick?

MOLLY: I'm sometimes harsh, I know that. And who am I kidding? I know, believe me, that I'm not a whiz kid anymore. I may still look like a teenager, *(She doesn't.)* but I'm a week away from turning thirty.

(Moll suddenly stands up on the bench, sniffs the air, and peers into the distance.)

MOLLY: Richard's the only one who ever listens to me when I talk, who realizes that I'm great at what I do, not just because I'm an Asian workaholic, but because I'm naturally brilliant. I've done a lot of reassessing lately — about my career choice, my identity, my hopes and dreams, and really I could give it all up for a baby with teeth too big for its mouth.

MOLL: Are you still talking? Just look who's coming! Umm. Umm. I get hungry just looking at him. *(She shouts.)* Over here, Dick! We're over here! *(Moll is beside herself. Molly wraps the leash tightly around her hand. Moll jumps off the bench, pulling Molly after her.)*

MOLL: Richard's hanging on to the leash for dear life. Dick's bounding this way. Just look at him. His tongue is hanging out. His tail's going a hundred miles a minute.

(Dick rushes in, dragging Richard after him. Dick and Moll are each at the end of a short leash, pawing the air, until they simultaneously break free and chase each other around in little circles.)

MOLLY: Moll! Moll!

RICHARD: *(Overlapping.)* Dick! Stop it, Dick!

(Moll pounces on Dick.)

MOLLY: Moll! Don't! Don't do that! You'll hurt yourself! *(Beat.)* I'm feeling dizzy.

(She abruptly sits down on the bench. Richard rushes to her side.)

RICHARD: Are you all right?

MOLLY: It's the heat. It's this prickly sweater.

RICHARD: What should I do?

(Moll has pressed Dick against the tree.)

MOLL: Where were you anyway?

DICK: There were these squirrels.

(Moll sniffs the air.)

MOLL: Do you smell it?

DICK: I smell it, sweetie.

MOLL: It's everywhere — it's in the air, in the bark of this tree.

MOLLY: I'm feeling faint — it's that musty doggy smell of desire.

(Moll and Dick are French kissing.)

MOLL: You likee kissee?

RICHARD: Let me run and see if I can find some help.

MOLLY: No. No. Don't go anywhere. *(She pulls him closer to her.)* We have to talk.

END OF PLAY

PLAY FOR
THREE MEN
AND ONE WOMAN

A Gravedigger's Tale

MARK BORKOWSKI

A Gravedigger's Tale was first performed at The Gene Frankel Theatre, New York City, May 2006. Directed by Mark Borkowski. Cast: Gravedigger — Robert Stevens; Louis — Bruno Iannone; Delores — Michelle Hayes; Valvetto —Ron Moreno.

CHARACTERS
GRAVEDIGGER: Thirties.
LOUIS: Forties/fifties.
DELORES: Early twenties.
VELVETO: Thirties.

SETTING
An old graveyard.

TIME
A cloudy afternoon, the present.

• • •

A gravedigggger stands before a mound of dirt, digging a grave. It is a small plot, no more than three feet long. A child's grave. While digging, he hits rock. He throws down his shovel and takes out his cell phone and dials.

GRAVEDIGGER: *(Into cell phone.* I hit rock . . . Rock — I hit rock! . . . I need somebody over here with a jackhammer! . . . No, I'm not gonna come get it, you send somebody . . . "Who"?, how 'bout the person whose sup- posed to be diggin' this grave? . . . Why am I upset? What d'ya got me diggin'? . . . No, it's not just a grave, it's a three by three! . . . How many times I tell you people "no more kids' graves"? . . . Don't gimme, "I know, I know" — you don't know! The only thing I ask. You can make me dig 'til my hands bleed, work holidays, short my paycheck, I never complain — all's I ask is no more kids' graves — What? . . . Hello? . . . Shit. *(He makes another call.)* It's me . . . the Gravedigger . . . I need some dope . . . A bundle . . . Yeah, I got the money . . . Yeah, all the money . . . Soon as possible . . . Now? Yes, absolutely. She'll find me — who ya sendin'? . . . OK, I'm diggin' a little grave by the East gate . . . Sure, she'll find me, place is empty, can't miss me. *(He hangs up. Blesses himself.)* I'm sorry, kid. It ain't your fault.

LOUIS: Motherfucker!

GRAVEDIGGER: Who is 'at?

(Enter Louis. He is already furious from having just stepped in mud.)

LOUIS: "Who's 'at?" It's the grim fuckin' reaper or your best friend dependin' on what you got to gimme.

GRAVEDIGGER: Hi, Louis.

LOUIS: Don't "hi, Louis" me. Don't act for one second like ya like me. Mud all over my fuckin' shoes. Gimme that rag.

GRAVEDIGGER: What rag?

LOUIS: Hangin' out your back pocket.

(Gravedigger tosses him the rag.)

LOUIS: Who is this? Who ya buryin'?

GRAVEDIGGER: Some . . . kid.

LOUIS: Kid? Shit. Fuck. *(Blesses himself)* 'at's fucked up. Your diggin' a kid's grave?

GRAVEDIGGER: You think I like doin' this? There's diggin' a grave then there's diggin' a grave! I begged 'em, "no more three-by-threes"! 'at's the only thing I asked 'em. Bastards! They know what it does to me! *(Yells off.)* YOU KNOW! YOU KNOW WHAT IT DOES TO ME! *(Back to Louis.)* I'll have nightmares now for the next week. How would you like to wake up with dead children at the foot of your bed?

LOUIS: Some fuckin' life ya got, Gravedigger. Imagine losin' a kid. Shit. Blow my fuckin' head off right then and there. Fuck.

GRAVEDIGGER: Louis, please . . . we try to watch our language here.

LOUIS: Oh do we?

GRAVEDIGGER: Respect.

LOUIS: A degenerate little fuck like you's gonna tell me about respect?

GRAVEDIGGER: You're standing on very sacred ground.

LOUIS: It's dirt!

GRAVEDIGGER: It's not just "dirt." People come here to cry. This "dirt" is fertilized with tears.

LOUIS: "Fertilized with tears"? It's gonna be fertilized with your tears you don't gimme my money. Ya hear me? Gimme my money.

GRAVEDIGGER: Look, Louis . . . I — I —

LOUIS: No, no, no — don't gimme that "look, Louis" bullshit —

GRAVEDIGGER: — I — I —

LOUIS: —"I — I" what?! I don't wanna hear no shit, Gravedigger! You got my money or not?

GRAVEDIGGER: I got . . . some of it.

LOUIS: How much?

GRAVEDIGGER: Hundred bucks . . . or so.

LOUIS: Hundred bucks? You're ten grand deep!

GRAVEDIGGER: I'm sorry.

LOUIS: I'm sorry? Who the fuck you think I am, your mom? I'm sorry?! *(Grabs the shovel and chases Gravedigger.)* I'm sorry I'm gonna have to slam this shovel 'cross your fuckin' head! "I'm sorry." *(Throws the shovel down. Beat.)* I knew this was gonna happen. 'at's why I'm gonna give you an opportunity to make it up to me. 'at's right, in lieu of smashin' your fuckin' head in, I'm gonna make you an offer.

GRAVEDIGGER: An offer?

LOUIS: So's we be even.

GRAVEDIGGER: What kind of offer?

LOUIS: I got a . . . little somethin' I need . . . buried.

GRAVEDIGGER: A "little somethin'"?

LOUIS: That's right. And I want you to . . . bury it.

GRAVEDIGGER: You mean —

LOUIS: Now, let's not get into details. You don't want details dancin' 'round in ya head. You don't wanna know any more then you have to. You don't wanna be an accomplice after the fact.

GRAVEDIGGER: I'd rather pay you.

LOUIS: OK. Pay me.

GRAVEDIGGER: Well, I —

LOUIS: Bullshit! You either pay me now or you go for a fuckin' ride! Your ten large, Gravedigger! And you ain't got shit! I need this favor. Are you re-fusin' me? Gravedigger? *(No response.)* Good. In fact, if it works out, we can make this a regular thing. I mean, what better place to dump shit, if ya know what I mean, then under an existing grave. No corpus delicti, no case.

GRAVEDIGGER: A regular thing?

LOUIS: Perfect for a degenerate gamblin' fuck like you. My right?

GRAVEDIGGER: I was gonna . . . stop.

LOUIS: Stop? Stop what?

GRAVEDIGGER: Gamblin'.

LOUIS: Oh really? When?

GRAVEDIGGER: Ahh —

LOUIS: G'head, say "tomorrow" — say it an' I'll rip your fuckin' lights out! Junkies, gamblers, you all like to jerk off into tomorrow! Well, until (the cum-soaked face of) "tomorrow" comes, you got some insurance. Don't look at me like that.

GRAVEDIGGER: Like what?

LOUIS: Like you don't know what I'm talkin' about. You might be a loser but you ain't stupid.

GRAVEDIGGER: Don't make me do this. 'specially not here. My God, Louis, this is sacred ground.

LOUIS: It's a graveyard! "Sacred ground." This dirt is reserved for the dead. Ain't that the point of a graveyard?

GRAVEDIGGER: Yeah.

LOUIS: So what's the problem? It's appropriate. What's more appropriate then buryin' the dead in a graveyard? It's like stickin' a hand in a glove, it belongs there. Don't look at me like that. We got a deal or what?

GRAVEDIGGER: When do you wanna do this?

LOUIS: Right now.

GRAVEDIGGER: Right now? Are you nuts?

LOUIS: This hole's perfect.

GRAVEDIGGER: No, no, this is — It's a kid's grave.

LOUIS: Shit, that's right. *(Blesses himself.)* Sorry, kid.

GRAVEDIGGER: *(Looks around.)* I have no idea where we can —

LOUIS: Look around, it's a graveyard! Don't play me, Gravedigger, I'll jump this fuckin' hole and cram you into it!

GRAVEDIGGER: OK, OK! It'll have to be tonight.

LOUIS: Time?

GRAVEDIGGER: Ten . . .

LOUIS: Ten?

GRAVEDIGGER: Ish?

LOUIS: Make up your fuckin' mind!

GRAVEDIGGER: Ten!

LOUIS: Ten o'clock, on the dot! *(Beat.)* You made a good decision for once, Gravedigger. I don't mean to risk losin' a good customer but you're one lousy gambler. Shit, when you gimme your bets, I hang up, me an' the guys laugh our asses off. We figured you either stupid or you just got balls. But this decision you made, to me, means you got balls. *(Aside.)* Stupid fuck. *(Beat.)* I always wondered what kind o' person digs graves.

GRAVEDIGGER: It's kind of a . . . calling.

LOUIS: A calling?

GRAVEDIGGER: Sorta.

LOUIS: What, like the priesthood?

GRAVEDIGGER: Kinda.

LOUIS: Well, we all gotta justify what we do, Gravedigger.

(Delores enters.)

DELORES: It's small.

GRAVEDIGGER: I'm sorry?

DELORES: That grave. It's a grave right?

GRAVEDIGGER: 'course it is.

DELORES: 'at's one small person.

GRAVEDIGGER: It's a kid.

DELORES: Aww. Really? Do you know . . . the child?

GRAVEDIGGER: No. Thank God.

DELORES: This is where you work, Gravedigger?

GRAVEDIGGER: No, I just dig graves in my spare time.

LOUIS: Do you know her, Gravedigger?

GRAVEDIGGER: Yeah.

LOUIS: Well, excuse us, li'l lady, but we're kinda having a meeting here.

DELORES: *(Snooty.)* "Excuse me." *(To Gravedigger.)* How much you get paid for doin' this shit?

GRAVEDIGGER: Not enough.

DELORES: Some fuckin' job.

LOUIS: Hey! I said we're having a meeting here.

DELORES: Ya don't have talk to me like that.

GRAVEDIGGER: She's just dropping something off.

LOUIS: OK then drop whateverthefuckitis and get outta here!

DELORES: Screw you!

LOUIS: Who is this broad? This your chick.

DELORES: I'm not his "chick." I was told to meet him here.

GRAVEDIGGER: Louis, I'm sorry, I . . . wasn't expecting you.

LOUIS: Well, ain't that just too fuckin' bad. I'm here! Unfuckin' announced!

DELORES: That's it, I'm outta here.

GRAVEDIGGER: Wait!

DELORES: Fuck this bullshit! Call Velveto.

GRAVEDIGGER: Please!

LOUIS: Velveto?

GRAVEDIGGER: Don't go!

LOUIS: Hold up, lil' lady. You mean, Velveto? Angel Velveto?

DELORES: What's it to ya?

LOUIS: You coppin', Gravedigger? Hah?

GRAVEDIGGER: No, no, no —

LOUIS: Don't lie to me! You ain't got money to pay me but you can cop my dope?!

DELORES: Not your dope —

LOUIS: Velveto works for me!

DELORES: What's he talkin' about, Gravedigger?

LOUIS: How much he coppin'?

DELORES: Is 'is freak forreal?

GRAVEDIGGER: Very much.

DELORES: What's your name?

LOUIS: My name's "ANSWER MY FUCKIN' QUESTION"! NOW!!!

DELORES: A bundle!!!

LOUIS: A bundle? *(Shaking his head, disgusted with Gravedigger.)* A mother-fuckin' bundle o' dope, hah? What, so you can go into a nice semico-matose sleep and forget about payin' me for a few more days?

GRAVEDIGGER: But . . .

LOUIS: But? But what?!

GRAVEDIGGER: I am . . . paying you. So to speak.

LOUIS: *(Remembers their deal.)* Yes. You most certainly are. *(To Delores.)* Give him the bundle.

DELORES: What?

LOUIS: Give — the — Gravedigger — the — bundle.

DELORES: Money.

LOUIS: GIVE HIM THE FUCKIN' BUNDLE!

(She panics and hands the Gravedigger the bundle. Just as the Gravedigger is ready to hand her the cash, Louis snatches it out of his hand.)

LOUIS: Complements. Junkie fuck.

(Louis counts the money. Delores explodes into tears, crying like a helpless little girl.)

GRAVEDIGGER: See, now she's cryin'. You made 'er cry.

LOUIS: Oh gimme a fuckin' break.

GRAVEDIGGER: Don't cry, Delores.

LOUIS: *(Frenzied aside.)* Kid's grave, women cryin', I can't deal with this shit!

GRAVEDIGGER: C'mon.

LOUIS: Yeah, c'mon. Quit the cryin'.

DELORES: He's gonna fuckin' kill me. I don't bring him the money he's gonna —

LOUIS: No, he's not.

DELORES: He's — he's gonna think I did the dope or — or I stole the money. He's —

LOUIS: He's gonna be happy you did Louis the favor!

DELORES: No, no, you don't know him — he's sick — he'll hurt me — he'll —

LOUIS: He'll what? What the fuck is 'at squirmy little worm gonna do?

DELORES: Look.

(She lifts her shirt and reveals her lower back, which is bruised, black and blue.)

LOUIS: He did that to you?

GRAVEDIGGER: Jesus Christ.

LOUIS: *(Grabs her forearm, looks at the tracks.)* Fuck. I don't know what's worse, what he did to you or what you did to you. *(Beat.)* You got a name?

DELORES: Chupa.

GRAVEDIGGER: Delores.

LOUIS: What?

GRAVEDIGGER: Her name —

DELORES: They call me Chupa.

GRAVEDIGGER: It's Delores.

LOUIS: Will you let people introduce themselves! Chupa? Why Chupa? *(To Gravedigger.)* Chupa's spick for "suck," right?

GRAVEDIGGER: Spanish, yes.

LOUIS: Suck?

GRAVEDIGGER: Suck.

LOUIS: Why they call you that? *(Realizes.)* That's fucked up.

GRAVEDIGGER: Her name's Delores.

LOUIS: You could be pretty if ya wanted to be. What d'ya think, Gravedigger? Think she could be pretty?

GRAVEDIGGER: She's . . . beautiful.

DELORES: Thank you, Gravedigger. I ain't gonna be pretty for long I don't give 'em his money.

LOUIS: Listen to me, you tell that punk that Louis said —

GRAVEDIGGER: You can tell him yourself.

LOUIS: What?

GRAVEDIGGER: Here he comes.

(Velveto enters.)

VELVETO: What the fuck, BITCH! *(He sees Louis.)* Louis?!

LOUIS: You gotta fuckin' problem?

VELVETO: Ahhh . . .

LOUIS: Is 'at how you normally burst into a room?

VELVETO: This ain't . . . a room.

LOUIS: Wherever I'm standin', consider it a room! My room! Say it!

VELVETO: Say what?

LOUIS: I just burst into Louis's room!

VELVETO: "I just burst into Louis's room."

LOUIS: And I am very fucking sorry.

VELVETO: "And I am very fuckin' sorry."

LOUIS: Watch your language!

VELVETO: I was — I was just wonderin' what's — what's keepin' 'er?

LOUIS: What's keepin' 'er? I'm keepin' 'er, 'at's what's keepin' 'er. Me. What d'ya think o' that? And guess what else? I just turned Gravedigger onto a bundle of your dope.

VELVETO: Fuck!

LOUIS: On you! You got a problem with that?

VELVETO: Let's go, Chupa!

LOUIS: "Chupa"? Why ya call her that?

VELVETO: Chupa? She's Chupa?

LOUIS: I mean, she must be pretty good she earned a name like that.

VELVETO: Pretty good? Dis bitch spin you to the stars, dawg!

LOUIS: Yeah?

VELVETO: She makes the monster disappear! Tell ya what, I do ya solid, let ya have a taste.

LOUIS: Taste o' what?

VELVETO: Chupa, c'mere. She suck you, dawg.

LOUIS: No, wait a minute. I don't want her to suck me. I want you to suck me.

VELVETO: What?

LOUIS: I want you to suck me.

VELVETO: C'mon, dawg, I don't want no trouble wit' you.

LOUIS: Call me a "dog" again I'll bust ya fuckin' hole! Get on your fuckin' knees!

VELVETO: Hey —

LOUIS: See that car sittin' over there.

VELVETO: Yeah.

LOUIS: You know that big ugly Mick in the front seat?

VELVETO: Yeah.

LOUIS: He's just waitin' to gouge out your fuckin' eyes!

VELVETO: Louis, please, man —

LOUIS: GET ON YOUR FUCKIN' KNEES!

(Velveto drops to his knees)

GRAVEDIGGER: Not here, Louis.

LOUIS: Open ya mouth. C'mon, "Chupa." Whose the little Chupa bitch now?! Open it!

(Louis smacks Velveto's face, his mouth drops open.)

LOUIS: Say "ahhh"!

VELVETO: *(With mouth open.)* Ahhhhhhh!!! Ahhhhhhhhhhh!!!!

LOUIS: Keep it open! Wider!! C'mon, Chupa — Ya wanna make the monster disappear?! Hah?! Ya little bitch! Gimme that rag, Gravedigger!

(Gravedigger tosses him the rag and he stuffs it in Velveto's mouth. He then aims Valveto's face toward Delores.)

LOUIS: See that little lost soul over there? You stay the fuck away from her. Now get the fuck outta here!

(Velveto scurries off. Delores starts to follow him when—)

LOUIS: And you, girlie, hold up . . .

(She stops in her tracks.)

LOUIS: What's her name?

GRAVEDIGGER: Delores.

LOUIS: Delores, wait right over there, will ya, sweetheart?

(Delores waits off to the side)

LOUIS: I'm gonna help the kid out. She's pretty fucked up, right?

GRAVEDIGGER: Say the least.

LOUIS: Take her to one o' those places. Where do you junkie fucks go when you wanna clean up?

GRAVEDIGGER: A detox?

LOUIS: Yeah, one o' them.

GRAVEDIGGER: I need the detox, Lou.

LOUIS: You? No, no, no, I need you fucked up. Your of no use to me if ya clean. Ya liable grow a conscience and 'at be it. *(Checks his watch.)* A'right, I gotta bolt, take care o' business. How 'bout I pick 'er up tonight when I drop off the parcel?

GRAVEDIGGER: You want her to . . . stay with me?

LOUIS: Is 'at a problem?

GRAVEDIGGER: No. Not at all.

LOUIS: Good. You're al right, Gravedigger? I can tell there's a decent person somewhere inside dat slimy bag o' flesh. A "good" kinda person, at heart. Like my mother. That's what's killin' ya. You surround yaself with shit. You sell yourself, like a crack whore, on a daily basis. *(To Delores.)* No offense. *(Back to Gravedigger.)* The compromise, or even the lack of, is what's gonna kill ya. Found dead; on fuckin' life. Other then that, you fuck me tonight, you dirt diggin' degenerate piece o' shit you'll be "M-I-fuckin'-A"! Ya got me? Gravedigger?

GRAVEDIGGER: Ten o'clock.

(Louis exits. Gravedigger sits on the mound of dirt. Delores sits beside him and looks into the grave.)

DELORES: It looks . . .

GRAVEDIGGER: What?

DELORES: Cozy.

GRAVEDIGGER: It's a grave.

DELORES: I just wanna crawl into it. And stay there.

GRAVEDIGGER: No you don't. It's a very lonely place.

(Pause.)

DELORES: Gravedigger?

GRAVEDIGGER: Yeah?

DELORES: You really think I'm beautiful?

GRAVEDIGGER: Yes, I do.

(Pause.)

DELORES: I always wondered what kinda people dig graves.

GRAVEDIGGER: It's a . . . calling.

DELORES: It is?

GRAVEDIGGER: Sorta.

DELORES: Kinda like a priest?

GRAVEDIGGER: Kinda. *(Pause.)* Want a hit o' dope?

DELORES: Sure.

(Lights fade to black)

END OF PLAY

PLAY FOR
FOUR WOMEN

Parkersburg

LAURA JACQMIN

Parkersburg was originally produced Steppenwolf Merle Reskin Garage Theatre, Chicago, May 15–June 15, 2008, as part of the Collaboraction's 8th Annual Sketchbook Festival. Directed by Greg Allen. Cast: 1 — Julie Mann; 2 — Sue Redman; 3 — Tanya McBride; Foreman — Sarah Fornace.

CHARACTERS
    FOREMAN: A woman.
    1: Woman. Realistic. Hard-nosed.
    2: Also a woman. Dreamer.
    3: Yet another woman. Still trying.

SETTING
    A coal mine. Or anywhere, really. As evocative or naturalistic as feels right.

TIME
    The present.

• • •

1, 2, and 3 dig for coal. Each has a pick. Each swings in rhythm. 1, 2, and 3 all swing together: ka-CHUNK. Then 1 swings: ka-CHUNK; then 2: ka-CHUNK; then 3: ka-CHUNK. Foreman enters.

FOREMAN: Find a vein?
1: None today.
FOREMAN: Nobody finds a vein; maybe nobody has a job tomorrow.
1: Is that so?
FOREMAN: That's so.
1: Three of us lose this job, that's whole families'll suffer. Not just three.
FOREMAN: Best look harder, then.
1: Can't make the coal come outta thin air.
2: Can't magic the coal into being.
1: Nice if we could.
2: Real nice if we could.
1: But we can't.
FOREMAN: Somebody better cast a spell. Somebody better dig faster and deeper. Somebody better swing that pick like they've never swung a pick before. Otherwise . . .
1: Fire one of us; not all three. I've found coal, she's found coal. But that one hasn't, not ever.
FOREMAN: No coal? No job. All three. I'm taking the lift up. Get me on the horn when you know which it'll be.
    (Foreman exits. 1, 2 and 3 swing: ka-CHUNK.)

3: Traitor.

1: No sympathy here. I've a live infant; you passed a dead one. Dead ones have no mouth to feed. Must be midnight. Somebody check the bird. My lungs feel thick.

(Ka-CHUNK. 2 looks to the bird.)

2: Bird's alive.

1: It coughing?

2: Can't hear it coughing.

(Ka-CHUNK.)

3: Bird doesn't cough when it's sick. Bird just keels over and dies. That's what happened my last job. We were digging: ka-chunk, ka-chunk. Somebody looks over, sudden. Not even trying to see the bird. And the bird was just flat out. Nobody'd been watching; nobody'd been taking care. Nobody thought we had to, flat mine like that. Surface so close. Fresh air just a few paces away. We cleared the mine fast as we could, but three dropped. Quiet. In the middle of their runs. We took their picks as we stepped over. All of us lost the job. For letting the creature die. The mine was out a bird, plus stuck with paying for burial.

(Ka-CHUNK.)

1: You shouldn't talk so much. Scares away the coal.

3: Can't be scared away. No way no how.

1: Shouldn't talk so much regardless. Jinxes us, talking.

3: Talked at my last job.

1: Three dead plus a bird at your last job. Split up. Take corners. Better chance at rooting a vein.

(1, 2, and 3 go to opposite corners; a triangle sort of shape. Ka-CHUNK.)

2: There's a mine in Parkersburg. Diggers show up at eight, leave at five. Paradise.

3: There's a whole stretch of Appalachians between here and Parkersburg.

2: Train.

3: Train doesn't run through the mountains.

2: Hike, then.

3: Everyone else tried to get over to Parkersburg by hiking? Frozen. Deceased. Bodies et by mountain lions and who-knows-what-else.

2: Hearsay.

3: Cold truth.

1: You're damning us with your talking! Look closer and find a vein.

3: Mine's dry.

2: Hush! Foreman would know if the mine was dry.

3: She wouldn't tell us, maybe. For spite. Or wants us fired for other reasons.

1: Good workers don't get fired.

3: Can't be a good worker if there's no coal to find!

1: There's coal. Has to be. No more talking, now! Dig deeper! Harder! Faster! Root a vein!

(1 digs. 2 digs. 3 digs. 1 digs. 2 digs. 3 digs. 1, 2, and 3 dig: ka-CHUNK. Ka-CHUNK. Ka-CHUNK. Ka-CHUNK. Faster and faster and faster and louder and louder and louder. Then:)

2: I can't!

1: You've got to.

2: I can't take it!

1: Then what do you suggest?

2: Cast a spell. A proper spell. Hold hands.

(1 and 2 hold hands. 3 won't join in, sneers.)

1: Should we say words?

2: In our heads, we say them. Say them now. Repeat them. Over and over.

(1 and 2 have their eyes closed, still holding hands. Inside their heads, they cast a spell. 3, separate, suddenly swings her pick by herself. Ka-CHUNK. Then:)

3: Coal!

1: Liar!

2: Really?

3: I swear it. Dark and thick as my thigh. Look.

(They gather around the vein.)

1: We're saved.

2: It's beautiful. Glowing. It shines black. Bituminous. *(Beat.)* It was my spell did it. My spell saved us. My spell alone.

(3 isn't looking at the vein. 3 is looking off, away, her face falling.)

3: The bird.

1: What about it?

3: Flat out.

(All three look at the bird. Infinitesimal beat.)

2: The bird's dead? What do we do? What do we do?

1: Run.

3: No time to run. Not in a mine like this — not in a mine with a lift. We'll fall in our tracks. It's how it goes.

1: Then just die with the coal?

3: They'll dig it out when they drag for our bodies. Give the money to our families, is the hope.

2: The hope? The hope?

   (2 makes a break for it. She exits. 1 and 3 watch her go.)

1: She's falling.

3: She's down.

   (Beat. 1 and 3 exchange a look. Silence.)

1: Talk a little, please. Fill the time.

3: Parkersburg. The mine. You start at eight, leave at five. There's shafts cutting all the way up, clear to the sky. Fresh air. Clean lungs. Deep breaths. Birds that sing, not keel. Money to feed every mouth, and every mouth full.

1: Paradise.

3: Paradise.

   (1 and 3 look out, suspended. Any second now.)

END OF PLAY

PLAYS FOR
FIVE OR SIX
ACTORS

The Blues Street
Jazz Club Rehearses

WILLIAM BORDEN

The Blues Street Jazz Club Rehearses was produced by Lincoln Square Theatre, Chicago, June 4–15, 2008, as part of Night Caps 2. Directed by Phoebe Duncan. Cast: Beverly — Nicole Richwalsky; Frank — Jeremy Sorkin; Alice — Heather Irwin; Don — David Wilhelm; Sally — Kathleen Cawthon.

CHARACTERS
    DON: Twenties or thirties, saxophonist.
    BEVERLY: Twenties or thirties, drummer.
    FRANK: Twenties or thirties, trumpet player.
    SALLY: Twenties or thirties, keyboard player.
    ALICE: Twenties or thirties, bass player.

SETTING
    Minimal.

TIME
    The present.

• • •

A bluesy, winsome saxophone winds a heartbreaking melody through the dark theater. Soft blue light up on Don, a sax to his lips, his fingers caressing the keys. The music tears our hearts out, it's so sad and so beautiful. Don takes the sax away from his lips, but the music continues. Light up, whiter. Don lays down the sax, lights a cigarette, listens to the music. He wears an old sweatshirt, trousers. Beverly enters. A drum solo begins on the music. She mimes the drumming. As the drum solo reaches a crescendo of complex virtuosity, Don turns off the CD player. Beverly continues the drum solo, then stops.

BEVERLY: You quit smoking.
    (He nods, takes a drag.)
BEVERLY: Where are the others?
    (He looks at his watch.)
BEVERLY: They're always late. *(She watches him a moment.)* Are you seeing
    Alice again?
    (He tries to ignore her.)
BEVERLY: That explains it.
DON: I'm smoking because I want to smoke!
BEVERLY: Your lungs are the color of prunes!
DON: Alice loves me.
BEVERLY: Your breath sounds like a chain saw.
DON: She came over last night.
BEVERLY: Don't tell me.
DON: She was as seductive as ever.

BEVERLY: I don't know what love is. What is it? Heartbreak?

DON: That's country western.

BEVERLY: A good orgasm?

DON: You went to the Beethoven concert, didn't you?

BEVERLY: Dying for each other?

DON: Opera. Gounod.

BEVERLY: Habit? A habit you can't break?

(He gives her a look, stubs out his cigarette.)

BEVERLY: Quitting again?

(He nods. She smiles knowingly.)

DON: Alice wants you to —

(Frank enters, interrupting them. He carries a trumpet case.)

FRANK: I'm here, I'm here, I'm here because I'm here — how you doin', you guys, huh?

(Frank takes a battered trumpet out of the case, puts on a CD. A trumpet wails as he puts the trumpet to his lips and pretends to play. Don turns off the CD player.)

FRANK: What the hell? Is this a rehearsal or not? Don? Beverly?

(Don lights a cigarette.)

BEVERLY: He started again.

FRANK: *(To Don.)* You can't play the sax and smoke.

DON: Dexter Gordon smoked.

FRANK: You ruin it for the group. You're not the only one, you know. The sound depends on all of us.

(Don stubs out the cigarette. Frank turns on the CD player. A trumpet wails. Frank puts his trumpet to his lips. Beverly "drums." A sax comes in. Frank and Beverly look at Don. A few beats. He puts the sax to his lips. A keyboard comes in. The three of them hesitate, look around. Sally enters, drops her coat, "plays" a keyboard. A few beats. Frank turns off the player.)

BEVERLY: You're late.

FRANK: You missed a few notes.

SALLY: My fingers are stiff. Damn computer all day. I'm getting that carpal tunnel thing. Mail order adult videos — you know how many people want *My Back Door's Open and I'm Lonely for You?*

DON: Sounds like a country western song.

SALLY: It's number one this week.

BEVERLY: You watch?

SALLY: Descriptions on the box covers.

DON: How can you work there?

SALLY: When I was a telemarketer I was always pissing people off. Now I make people happy.

DON: Perverts.

SALLY: We don't use that term. Except as a compliment.

DON: It's filth.

SALLY: You're a mechanic. Your hands are black.

BEVERLY: His lungs are black.

SALLY: Did you start again?

FRANK: Alice.

SALLY: Oh God.

DON: She loves me.

SALLY: You're pitiful. Is she coming?

BEVERLY: Why wouldn't she come? She loves him.

SALLY: You loved him. Once.

BEVERLY: I loved you, too.

SALLY: You weren't going to tell that.

BEVERLY: I enjoyed it. Didn't you?

SALLY: Yes.

> *(Beat.)*

FRANK: She should be here. She playing trombone tonight? Guitar? Clarinet? I wish she'd make up her mind.

DON: *(To Beverly.)* Alice — last night — said she wanted you to —

SALLY: I don't want to hear about Alice.

> *(Frank puts on a CD. Discordant jazz. To Beverly.)*

SALLY: Why didn't you ever call?

BEVERLY: I was afraid.

SALLY: Of me?

> *(Frank begins to "play.")*

BEVERLY: What you'd think of me.

SALLY: I thought you loved me.

> *(Don begins to "play.")*

BEVERLY: Why does it have to be me who calls?

> *(On the CD the piano takes a solo. Frank and Don look at Beverly. Finally she "plays." A few beats. Alice enters. She wears a stained waitress's uniform. She watches them a moment, listens, exits, returns dragging an acoustic bass. She "plays" as the bass on the CD takes a solo. The others watch. When the solo ends, they quietly applaud. Beverly turns off the player.)*

ALICE: Sorry I'm late.

FRANK: Nice finger work.

ALICE: I love Don.

BEVERLY: He started smoking.

SALLY: Again.

ALICE: Don't blame me.

FRANK: Sally and Beverly —

(Don lights a cigarette.)

ALICE: I don't care. I made a hundred and three in tips. Two dollars in pennies.

FRANK: I leave pennies. Just to get rid of them.

ALICE: Take them to the bank. My legs ache.

SALLY: What was the special?

ALICE: Maybe I'm getting that fibromyalgia. Meat loaf.

FRANK: Again?

DON: *(To Alice.)* I love you.

BEVERLY: I don't need this.

DON: I would've loved you if you'd've let me.

BEVERLY: We tried it.

DON: We could try it again.

FRANK: Beverly . . .

BEVERLY: *(To Sally)* Do we still have that Brubeck we used to play?

FRANK: *(To Beverly.)* I've always loved you. Since we were kids.

BEVERLY: *(To Sally.)* What's it called?

ALICE: *(To Don.)* You still love her.

DON: *(To Alice.)* I love you.

SALLY: *(To Beverly.)* I love you.

FRANK: *(To Beverly.)* I dream about you.

(Beverly looks at Frank, at Sally. Don coughs. Alice takes away his cigarette.)

BEVERLY: *(To Alice.)* He's used to me, that's all. I'm like a bad habit.

ALICE: Is that what love is? A habit?

SALLY: I've watched hundreds of those videos, looking for love.

FRANK: It's a hurt, here. *(In the heart.)*

DON: Here it is. *(He pulls out a CD.)*

FRANK: You know love when you see it.

SALLY: *(To Beverly.)* Do you?

ALICE: Don't you?

FRANK: *(To Beverly.)* Since we were seven. You were swinging in that old green porch swing. You were barefoot. The chain squeaked.

(He actually plays the trumpet, a series of squeaks.)

FRANK: Back and forth. Kicking your bare legs.

(He plays a few more squeaks.)
BEVERLY: Why didn't you tell me?
FRANK: I was just the trumpet player.
DON: I know love when I see it.
SALLY: You can't see love.

(Alice puts on the CD. One by one they begin to "play." Light eases to a smoky blue, as in a nightclub, then fades as the music fades.)

END OF PLAY

Cabman

WILLIAM OREM

Cabman was first presented at the Stanford Calderwood Pavillion, Boston Center for the Arts, May 11, 2008, as part of the 2008 Boston Theater Marathon. Directed by Brett Marks. Cast: Cabman — Bill Bruce; Kev — Chris Lyons; Brett — Tyler Reilly; Douglas — Christian Daniel Kiley; White Businessman — Terrence P. Haddad; Black Girl — Rydia Vielehr.

An adaptation of the short story "Misery" by Anton Chekhov.

CHARACTERS

CAMAN: A black man, just too old for us to comfortably seeing him still working. He has a beautiful, soft, roughly treated face.

KEV, BRETT, DOUGLAS: Georgetown students; white, privileged, somewhat drunk. Douglas is smaller than the other boys.

WHITE BUSINESSMAN

BLACK GIRL

SETTING

A taxicab driving around Washington, DC.

TIME

Winter, the present.

• • •

Cabman is driving. Snow is falling outside the taxi. In the back seat are Kev, Douglas, and Brett. They speak quickly and trivially.

KEV: She was like, you're pre-med? That's so hot. I like a guy who knows how the body works.
(Laughter.)
BRETT: You're shit.
KEV: I swear to God. And I'm like, hey . . . we're all pre-med. Cause they don't understand that it just means what, you're a bio major.
DOUGLAS: *(Petulant.)* We're going to be late.
KEV: Shut up. Are we? *(To Cabman.)* Hey, what's the deal here?
CABMAN: Construction.
KEV: Find a way around it, whatever. *(To Brett.)* So I decided, I'm not going with my family. I mean, Caymans?
BRETT: Your mom will freak.
KEV: Have you got my cell?
CABMAN: Always somethin' being put up in the city. Or somethin' bein' torn down. They don't take care of the streets.
KEV: Fuck, this is an ipod. I need one of those breath things.
CABMAN: We used to . . . you boys are too young to remember this . . . back when Marion Barry was mayor, we used to call the potholes Barrys.

There's another Barry, we'd say. Look out for the Barry. 'Cause they was so big you could get buried in 'em.

DOUGLAS: Call them and say we're going to be late.

KEV: We're not going to be late. Hey, what the hell, man? Can't you speed it up?

(Brett dials number.)

CABMAN: You got to watch for the snow.

KEV: Let me talk to her. Is this that blonde with the Britney face?

BRETT: *(He has Kev's cell phone.)* Back off, jack-off. You sniffing around her panties I don't need. Not when I'm trying to sniff around her panties.

KEV: *(Sings.)* Beat me baby, one more time.

BRETT: *(On cell.)* Hey, Carolyn? Who is this, Claudia? Hey, it's Brett. Brett, from Georgetown, you met . . . and Kev and Douglas. Oh, you remember Kev.

KEV: I bet she remembers me. *(Sings.)* One more time . . .

BRETT: We're . . . I know, we're in a cab. We're coming. No, we're still on Capitol Hill. I can see the Washington Monument.

DOUGLAS: He' not speeding up. I don't think he's even trying.

CABMAN: If you boys look at the monument, you can see the line where the workmen stopped. Look at the bottom there, just above the flags. The marble is a different color. That's where they had to stop, because of the war. That happened during the Civil War.

KEV: Tell them to wait at the bar. Don't go without us. Let me talk to her.

BRETT: No, put Carolyn on. I'm serious, put her on! Calli? It's Brett. Yeah, and Kev . . . yeah, he's here too. *(To Douglas.)* She calls you little Douggie.

DOUGLAS: Bitch!

KEV: Little Douggie! *(To Brett.)* Are you going to let me talk to her?

BRETT: Just stay at the bar, we're going to be there in a minute and we'll all go over together. Why? Who's that in the background? Tell her because it's more fun to go together. We haven't been drinking hardly at all, we need to catch up.

CABMAN: You boys from Georgetown? That's what I heard your friend say.

KEV: What? Freshmen. *(Takes breath mint.)*

DOUGLAS: You don't have to answer him.

BRETT: *(About the mints.)* Gimme.

CABMAN: I have a son just about your age. And he's smart, like you boys are smart. He could go to Georgetown University. He could do anything. If they would take a look at what he can do, you see. He's smart, just like you boys are smart.

KEV: *(Smart-ass.)* Oh yeah? What's his name? Maybe I know him.

DOUGLAS: He's supposed to be doing a job.

BRETT: I'm gonna call Howie. See if he can make it.

KEV: Howie? Fuck that guy.

CABMAN: Carter's my name. Julius Carter. My son's name is Anton Carter. Private Anton Carter.

KEV: Private, huh? *(Tries to take phone from Brett.)*

BRETT: Fuck off. I mean it.

CABMAN: He signed up when the recruits set up those tents in front of the Jefferson Memorial. It was fourth of July, they were handing out these papers to read. Two recruits start talkin' to him when he was readin' the papers. Then he says to me, Daddy, it's so I can go to school afterward. The recruiters are gonna give him money so he can go to college.

BRETT: Are you still there? Oh fuck, I dialed you again by mistake. *(Laughs.)* Just tell her I'm looking forward to seeing her. Yeah. No, tell her Brett is. *(Gives finger to Kev, who returns gesture.)*

CABMAN: Anton Tyrone Carter is his name. He's the supply person. He carries supplies, for those jeeps they have. But he's going to go to college. He can do things with his hands. One day I took him down the garage with me, and he looked at the engines. He could see what was wrong, just lookin'.

DOUGLAS: Jesus. Is this a game you play? Instead of driving? This is some kind of a game you play to make everything take longer and get more money out of the white kids.

(Brett bangs on window and points, indicating Cabman is to pull over.)

BRETT: *(Into cell.)* I can see you! Yes, that's me in the fucking cab! I know we're fucking late, this stupid-ass cabbie is trying to pull some shit.

CABMAN: *(Stopping cab.)* Here we go.

(The boys climb out.)

BRETT: *(Outside.)* Christ, it's snowing like shit! Is everybody inside still?

KEV: *(Tossing money in front seat.)* Here's twenty. *(Outside.)* Car-o-line!

DOUGLAS: *(Quietly, as he exits.)* Nigger.

(Cabman takes the money and places it inside an old cardboard shoebox without looking at it. Drives; picks up another fare. This is a White Businessman.)

WHITE BUSINESSMAN: Good evening. The Embassy Suites at Dupont Circle, please.

CABMAN: All right. That's a nice hotel. *(Drives.)* It's winter, m-m. Starting for real now. You can always tell. *(Drives.)* I remember when it snowed back in nineteen ninety-seven. You was in the city in nineteen ninety-seven? We had snow that year. Broke down the 'lectricity lines . . . it made this sound, everywhere you could hear it.

One night, I stopped my taxi at Farragut Square, just around nine o'clock and rolled down the window and I heard it. First everything was quiet, there was no cars on the streets. Nobody out walkin'. And then this sound. This sound. The snow had got so heavy it was breaking the trees. It was breaking the . . . the . . .

WHITE BUSINESSMAN: *(He is looking through a newspaper.)* Limbs.

CABMAN: That snow just about covered everything up. Next morning, it was like the city was gone. *(Drives.)*

You know? I have a son in the army. You just reminded me of him, just there that moment. In that nice suit. When he wears his uniform, he looks like that, you see I'm sayin'. He has dignity. You understan'? Dignity.

WHITE BUSINESSMAN: *(Uninterested.)* You must be proud.

CABMAN: Anton Carter is his name. He sent me a picture, a photo, of him wearing his uniform. Dignity, see I'm sayin' . . . I have it here . . .

WHITE BUSINESSMAN: Here, please.

CABMAN: A'ight. *(Pulls over. Pause.)*

WHITE BUSINESSMAN: What's the fare?

CABMAN: All right. Scuze me?

WHITE BUSINESSMAN: The fare. You don't have the meter on.

CABMAN: Oh, that's right.

WHITE BUSINESSMAN: Shall we say five dollars.

CABMAN: *(Beginning to fumble with shoebox.)* He's in the desert now . . . this . . . Salam. That's the name of a place there. Salam, somethin' . . . a hundred, a hundred an' fifteen degrees. Any day, hundred and fifteen degrees. An here it's snowin'. It doesn't seem right, a hundred degrees there, and here it's snowin'. Somethin' ain't right . . . about that. You see what I'm sayin'?

He sent me a picture. I don't think they took the picture there. It looks like one of them pictures with the sky behind, only it's a wall, with clouds on it . . .

WHITE BUSINESSMAN: Excuse me.

(White Businessman climbs out. Cabman fumbles with the money for a moment, as if unsure what to do with it. Then he puts it in the box and drives. He picks up another passenger. This is a Black Girl, a teenager, tough.)

BLACK GIRL: Hey. Just go to the playground at the other side of the park.

CABMAN: Oh. A'ight. *(Drives.)* Cold in the winter. Then in the summer we get the mist. It's why they call it Foggy Bottom.

BLACK GIRL: *(On cell.)* You still there, bitch? I'm gonna be there in five minutes. You know who. Don't give me who.

CABMAN: Foggy Bottom is what they used to call it. Because when those people came here in the revolutionary war days, the city was a swamp. An' it was just fog . . . clouds and fog, everywhere they went.

BLACK GIRL: The fuck you sayin'? Drive the cab, man.

CABMAN: Oh. Uh-huh. *(Drives.)*

You know, I don't generally say nothin'. To people in my taxi, you understand. People want a quiet ride. But you remind me of someone. Your eyes.

I got a letter . . . I have it here . . . an official letter. From . . . "Commanding Officer," is how they say it . . . it has a gold seal.

BLACK GIRL: Can't you speed it up?

CABMAN: All right. *(Drives.)* You have to be careful. Night like tonight. They don't take care of the streets. The letter came just this week . . . it has a picture.

BLACK GIRL: This is good enough. Stop here. The red apartments. By the liquor.

CABMAN: Red house.

(Stops. Black Girl gets out of cab.)

BLACK GIRL: *(Checking her pockets.)* Oh shit. Look, man. I got to go inside and get some money from my sister. I be right back out.

CABMAN: A'ight. Go ahead.

(Black Girl pauses, about to leave. Looks at Cabman.)

BLACK GIRL: Nigger, what's wrong with you?

CABMAN: Wrong, nothing. You take your time.

BLACK GIRL: Bullshit. You know I'm shittin' you right now. You know I ain't comin' out with no money. You let me go, I'm just gonna walk in the front door of this apartment house an' straight out the backdoor and keep walkin' where I'm really goin'. How come you don't know that?

CABMAN: Oh. I suppose I know that.

BLACK GIRL: You old enough to be a grandfather. What you doin' driving a cab?

CABMAN: This cab? *(As if seeing it for the first time.)* I can go anywhere. I can go into Southeast. The red light. Anacostia. I can go anywhere. I don't mind. An' I get to talk. To people. You understan'? To people.

BLACK GIRL: Ain't you got no woman?

CABMAN: A woman? No . . . no. I have a son . . . they sent me his picture. *(Suddenly animated; his last chance.)* Can I tell you . . . if I could just . . . talk to you . . . just for a minute . . . about my son . . .

BLACK GIRL: What?

CABMAN: I want to tell you . . . about my son . . .

(Desperate, Cabman opens the door and begins to step out. It is a painful process.)

BLACK GIRL: The hell are you doin', man?

CABMAN: I won't touch you . . . I just want . . . I want you to listen. I just want you to listen to me. Just for a minute . . . please . . . please . . .

BLACK GIRL: Go home, old man. Get yourself a woman.

(Black Girl exits. Pause. Cabman standing in the street, facing in the direction where she left. He looks up at the falling snow. He looks at the empty street, begins walking around as if to find something. Finally he returns to the cab, wiping the snow away from the windshield and then running his hand across it almost lovingly. He sees his own face in the windshield.)

CABMAN: He looks a lot like you. Smart, like you. With dignity. And he has your eyes. I knew that soon as you got in. I saw your eyes and I thought, I have a son. I have a son. A good boy, so smart. Good with his hands. And I can see him. In you. In your eyes.

END OF PLAY

An Epic Story of Love and Sex in Ten Minutes: Chapter One

RICHARD VETERE

An Epic Story of Love and Sex was first presented by the New York Playwright's Lab at Cherry Lane Theater, New York City, January 8, 2008. Directed by Richard Vetere. Cast: Man, Man as Boy, Man as Teenager, Man as Young Man — Lou Martini; Ralphie, Tough Teenager, Young Man with Guitar, Gino — Michael Bakkensen; June Arroyo, Sara Viola, Teen Girl 2, Lucia — Margo Passalaqua; Carol Pappappetro, Young Wife, Teen Girl 1, Perfect Female, Luneta — Antoinette LaVecchia; Dolores, Sister, Teen Girl 3 — Christine Broccolini.

Two men, twenties to fifties, play all the male parts. Male lead plays:
    MAN
    MAN AS BOY
    MAN AS TEENAGER
    MAN AS YOUNG MAN

Second male actor plays:
    RALPHIE
    TOUGH TEENAGER
    YOUNG MAN WITH GUITAR
    GINO

Three women play all the female parts:
    JUNE ARROYO
    CAROL PAPPAPPETRO
    YOUNG WIFE
    DOLORIES
    SARA VIOLA
    TEEN GIRL 1
    TEEN GIRL 2
    TEEN GIRL 3
    PERFECT FEMALE
    SISTER
    LUCIA AND LUNETTA

SETTING
    Bare stage, lights.

TIME
    The present.

• • •

MAN: So, you want to hear about my ex-lovers? OK, I'll tell you about my ex-lovers. Here is An Epic Story of Love and Sex in Ten Minutes. *(Then.)* Chapter One. I'm in the fifth grade. I am a complete nebbish. An amoeba has more charisma.
    (He hunches over and transforms into a completely nondescript boy.)

MAN AS BOY: Neither sex or love have ever entered my mind until . . .

(Lights up on June. Though thirteen, she radiates sexuality.)

MAN: June Arroyo sits next to me.

(Man and June sit side by side. He is so overwhelmed, he has to catch his breath. He can hardly look at her. He steals glances then stares down at his desk, in the other direction, anywhere but at her.)

MAN AS BOY: I have no idea what "having sex" means but I do know one thing — *(He turns to June.)* I love you.

(She smiles sweetly but doesn't look at him.)

MAN AS BOY: I can't even imagine what specific female body parts having sex actually involves, however, I do know one thing — *(To June.)* I love you. *(Then.)* I write her two love letters and nine poems. *(To June.)* I love you.

(She turns to him, demurely, and says:)

JUNE: I have a boyfriend in the army. He's in Vietnam.

(She looks at him, unattainable. He steps away from her.)

MAN AS BOY: *(To audience.)* Strike me dead now! There is no love in this world for me! I swear that I will never love another woman! I am cursed to be unloved! So, I officially proclaim with Hop Along Cassidy lunch box in hand under a gloomy November sky.

(Man looks to June who smiles sweetly. Lights out on June.)

MAN AS BOY: With heavy heart, I barely exist. I move through the following years like a slug. Until one bright sunny day, after a blizzard, I meet the older Carol Pappappetro sleigh riding down Snake Hill.

(Lights up on Carol.)

CAROL: Where's your sleigh?

MAN AS BOY: Some big guys took it.

CAROL: You want to ride down on mine?

MAN AS BOY: Yeah, all right.

CAROL: I'll get on my stomach and you lie down on top of me. *(Off his stunned look.)* So you can steer better.

(Man turns to the audience.)

MAN AS BOY: Snake Hill is a tenth of a mile long but not once, not once, do I think about running into a single parked car, concrete sidewalk curb, or cast-iron lamppost! All I care about is what is happening on the sleigh beneath me.

(He and Carol now walk hand in hand. He can't take his eyes off her bottom.)

MAN AS BOY: And for the rest of that year I don't let Carol out of my sight nor out of my grasp since, everywhere we walk — the grocery store, school, church — I have my hand planted firmly on her ass.

(Man slowly and with trepidation, places his hand on Carol's bottom. Her reaction is swift and clear.)

CAROL: *(Smiling.)* I like it there.

(They walk with his hand on her ass.)

MAN AS BOY: And everything is perfect in my small universe until one Saturday afternoon, Ralphie Maccia, pulls me aside.

(Lights up on Ralphie who pulls Man as Boy aside as Carol stands away from them smilingly but not paying attention.)

RALPHIE: But what's wrong with you?

MAN AS BOY: What's wrong with me?

RALPHIE: *(Hysterical.)* It's a sin!

MAN AS BOY: What's a sin?

RALPHIE: You got your hand on Carol's ass! Everywhere you walk! The entire block sees it. What's wrong with you? You better go to confession right now or you are going straight to hell! I knew you were a pervert. God ain't gonna like it, man.

(Lights down on Ralphie. Man to audience.)

MAN AS BOY: So God is watching me put my hand on Carol's ass? That's embarrassing. And now God wants me to take my hand away?

(He ponders his predicament.)

MAN AS BOY: I deliberate. God . . . Carol's ass . . . So, I make a forthright decision. I decide that I have no intention of confessing my newfound and, I thought, secret pleasure to anyone, other than the older and wiser Carol. True, it's my soul in jeopardy, but it is her ass we're talking about.

(Man turns to Carol. She thinks it over.)

CAROL: It's only a venial sin.

(Man sighs in relief and places his hand on her bottom again. Man looks up.)

MAN AS BOY: God can watch all He wants.

(Lights out on Carol.)

MAN AS BOY: Somewhere before high school, in that fog of long ago, a young wife, who lives a few houses away, talks to me.

(Lights up on Young Wife. She gives him big, soulful looks while he nervously twitches.)

MAN AS BOY: *(To audience.)* She tells me some fascinating stuff that's she's noticed.

YOUNG WIFE: I watch you . . . watching me.

MAN AS BOY: She considers me a man's man and has some chores for me to do.

YOUNG WIFE: I need help pulling weeds out of my backyard.

(She takes his hand and they take a step to the backyard. They pull weeds together.)

MAN AS BOY: *(To audience.)* She has a husband. But doesn't say much about him.

(Lights up on man in chair, looking out. Man looks at husband.)

MAN AS BOY: He's older than her. He was paralyzed by a mortar on Normandy Beach. So, he spends all day sitting on the porch with a six pack.

YOUNG WIFE: You're the quiet type, aren't you?

(She turns her back to him, and he watches her closely as she bends down pulling out weeds. She sees him watching her, and she becomes even more seductive.)

MAN AS BOY: When I was done pulling weeds, she tells me I did a good job.

YOUNG WIFE: You have strong hands.

MAN AS BOY: She tells me I'm probably a bright kid.

YOUNG WIFE: I like how serious you are.

MAN AS BOY: She tells me that I'm probably the most fascinating kid on the block.

YOUNG WIFE: I have to pay you for your work. Come inside the house.

(The Young Wife turns to him and smiles. He looks back at the husband then follows her into the house. They look at one another for a beat, then she hands him money. He takes it. Then she says:)

YOUNG WIFE: I can't send you home dirty. I'll make you a . . . bath.

(She takes a few steps, stops and turns to him, waving him along. Man looks to audience.)

MAN AS BOY: She made a bath, all right. With bubbles. When I leave, she tells me that I've changed her life forever.

YOUNG WIFE: This never happened. You were never here. Don't come back.

(Lights down on Young Wife.)

MAN AS TEENAGER: Sometime during high school, some gland kicks in.

(Music plays and bright sunshine is everywhere.)

MAN AS TEENAGER: I'm suddenly a juvenile delinquent. My folks send me away for the summer to a place called Fiscarelli Farm where I'm supposed to rehabilitate myself. It was a converted motel in the Poconos for Italian families to place their deranged teenagers. When I get there, I find out a few important things. First, if your family doesn't have a criminal record, make one up.

(Tough Teenager to Man as Teenager.)

TOUGH TEENAGER: Yeah, my father's away . . . upstate. He's doin' ten to fif-teen. He robbed a bank, beat up the teller, and shot a cop.

MAN AS TEENAGER: *(Truly stunned.)* Unbelievable.

TOUGH TEENAGER: Hey, you gotta feed your family, right? So, what did your old man do?

MAN AS TEENAGER: My father? Wow. He's f'in mean. Scares the shit out of me. And everybody else too, obviously.

TOUGH TEENAGER: Hey, but what did he do?

MAN AS TEENAGER: Do? Oh, yeah, right, well, he shot a cop, beat up a teller, and then robbed a bank.

TOUGH TEENAGER: No shit?

MAN AS TEENAGER: Not the same cop your father shot, I don't think. But it coulda been the same bank. Not sure about the teller though.

(Lights down on Man as Teenager as Tough Teenager looks around.)

MAN AS TEENAGER: Besides the fascinating conversations with the guys my own age, I notice things about the girls at Fiscarelli Farm.

(Man smiles as lights up on hot girls.)

MAN AS TEENAGER: These young girls from Brooklyn were friggin' hot. They had big hair, big tits, long fingernails, wore no panties, and bragged about things they could do to your penis with their well-manicured toes.

DOLORES: You're cute. You want to make out?

MAN AS TEENAGER: That was Dolores. She was gorgeous and fifteen.

(Man as Teenager makes out with Dolores.)

MAN AS TEENAGER: I learned a lot about Dolores, her family, women in gen-eral and finances in particular. Every time I kissed her lips, it cost me a dollar. Anywhere I else I kissed her, it cost me five bucks. By the time Labor Day rolled around I owed this guy everybody called "Uncle Funzi" half a C note not counting the vig.

(Lights out on Dolores. Lights up on Young Man with Guitar with his arm around two young women.)

MAN AS TEENAGER: Hanging out one afternoon, I met this cool guy with long hair and a guitar in one of the rooms lying on the bed with his arm around two girls. It wasn't what he was doing . . . it was how he was doing it. It was like he was saying . . . "This is natural, man. Like, this the way it's supposed to be." *(To audience.)* He knew something.

(Man as Teenager faces Young Man with Guitar.)

YOUNG MAN WITH GUITAR: It's the shirts.

MAN AS TEENAGER: Shirts?

YOUNG MAN WITH GUITAR: Yeah, man, you gotta wear the right shirts. And jeans. Bell-bottoms. And don't forget the boots. Cowboy boots. Chicks dig it.

(Young Man with Guitar walks away. He is clearly cool. Lights out on him.)

MAN AS TEENAGER: He forgot to mention that the guitar had something to do with it. But I realize then and there — I want to be him. And that summer, guitar or not, I was.

(Man as Teenager smiles and looks at a series of women who smile and flirt at him.)

MAN AS TEENAGER: And there were girls who noticed that I was. Nancy, Diane, Patty, Laura. Odd thing, though, they all wanted to keep their virginity for their future husbands. So, despite all the sex we had. They never actually considered any of it sex.

TEENAGE GIRL 1: You want a hand job? Sure, that's not sex.

TEENAGE GIRL 2: You want a blow job? No problem. That's not sex.

TEENAGE GIRL 3: I don't care what anybody says. Anal is not sex.

MAN AS TEENAGER: I felt like I was in a Felini movie when all of a sudden, I meet Sara Viola.

(Sara steps out into a bright light.)

MAN AS TEENAGER: I carve her initials in the wooden bridge. She wears my jacket and I wear her sweater. We are like a team, a twosome . . . it's the first time in my life I feel really, really, really close to one particular woman until she says to me —

SARA VIOLA: My boyfriend, Gino, runs this gang, you know, back in Bay Ridge. The Golden Guineas. And he's coming up to see me. So, unless you want to be dead. We have to break up.

(Lights up on Gino as Sara watches.)

GINO: Who are you?

MAN AS TEENAGER: *(Petrified.)* Nobody.

GINO: You want to die?

MAN AS TEENAGER: Not really.

GINO: Then . . . disappear.

(Lights out on Gino and Sara. Man as Teenager is now alone onstage and slowly grows up.)

MAN AS YOUNG MAN: So, I grow up a little more. And one night, down the park, I meet a girl.

(Lights up on Perfect Female. Man looks.)

MAN AS YOUNG MAN: I see an aura over her head.

(Man steps over to Perfect Female.)

MAN AS YOUNG MAN: There's a aura over your head. You're the perfect female.

PERFECT FEMALE: My boyfriend doesn't think so.

MAN AS YOUNG MAN: Get rid of him. I'm here now.

> *(Man smiles and takes her hand.)*

MAN AS YOUNG MAN: She gets rid of the boyfriend. We make love day and night . . . we even do the alphabet together.

> *(To her.)* A . . . is for how adorable you are.

PERFECT FEMALE: B is for how brilliant you are.

MAN AS YOUNG MAN: C is for how cuddly you are.

> *(To audience.)* Months pass . . . we do everything together and then out of nowhere, her little sister grows up. One day, we find ourselves completely alone.
>
> *(Lights up on sister. Perfect Female steps away and Man as Young Man walks over to sister.)*

MAN AS YOUNG MAN: You grew up.

SISTER: Glad you noticed.

MAN AS YOUNG MAN: Then . . . as if it had a life of its own . . . I watch as my hand goes directly to her . . .

> *(Man as Young Man places his hand on sister's bottom. She smiles.)*

SISTER: I like it there.

> *(Perfect Female glares at him.)*

PERFECT FEMALE: Get out of my life! Never call me again!

MAN AS YOUNG MAN: Strike me dead now! There is no love in this world for me! I swear, I will never love another woman! I am cursed to be unloved!

> *(Lights out on Perfect Female and her sister. Man as Young Man stops. He then turns to the audience.)*

MAN AS YOUNG MAN: Or so I thought, until I went to my uncle Carmine's wedding in Jersey and meet the Narducci sisters . . .

> *(Lights up on Lucia and Lunetta.)*

MAN AS YOUNG MAN: . . . Lucia and Lunetta. They were the maids of honor and they called me their . . .

> *(He turns to them.)*

LUCIA AND LUNETTA: *(Big smiles.)* Flower boy . . .

> *(They wink at him; he winks at the audience.)*

MAN AS YOUNG MAN: Well, that was my life so far.

> *(Lights out.)*

END OF PLAY

First Time for Everything

JOHN SHANAHAN

First Time for Everything was first performed at Curtain Call Theatre, Braintree, Mass., March 2008. Directed by Stacey Shanahan. Cast: Dorie Schulmann — Shannon Lillian Hogan; Ben Kaufman — Steve Abouzeid; Tracey — Martha Sawyer; Luanne — Marianne Withington.

CHARACTERS
    DORIE SCHULMAN: Twenties.
    BEN KAUFMAN: Twenties.
    TRACEY: Preferably fifties or up, a waitress.
    LUANNE: Same, a waitress.

SETTING
    A small restaurant.

TIME
    Early morning, the present.

• • •

Ben and Dorie are seated at a table, looking over menus. They're very happy and a bit flirty.

DORIE: Know what you're going to have?
BEN: Everything looks good.
DORIE: Does it really?
BEN: The French toast, the waffles . . . I can't decide! How about you?
DORIE: Maybe I'll have what you're having, once you figure it out.
BEN: Copycat.
    (Tracey enters, carrying a pot of coffee.)
TRACEY: Good morning! Coffee?
BEN: Please.
DORIE: Yes.
TRACEY: About ready to order?
BEN: I think so. You?
DORIE: Yes! Good.
BEN: You first.
DORIE: You're still thinking, aren't you?
BEN: Maybe . . .
DORIE: I knew it. OK. I'll have —
TRACEY: Oh my goodness!
DORIE: Yes?
TRACEY: You two just made love for the first time, didn't you?
BEN: Excuse me?
TRACEY: Oh, I can see it! You're positively glowing!

DORIE: *(Stunned.)* I, uh . . .

TRACEY: I love it! I love that look!

DORIE: Can I —

TRACEY: *(To Ben.)* Oh, and she's so beautiful!

DORIE: Waffles? Get waffles? Can I?

TRACEY: It's so wonderful! Make a little love, have a little breakfast, talk about the future. Oh!

DORIE: I like waffles.

TRACEY: *(To Ben.)* So how was it? Good? Did you do well?

BEN: Uh . . . so, I . . . heh.

TRACEY: Oh, don't mind me! I think it's lovely! Just lovely! *(To Dorie.)* Oh, it was good, wasn't it? Look at the color in your cheeks! *(Calling off.)* Lu-anne! Luanne, come here a minute!

BEN: Could we just order?

DORIE: Waffles?

(Luanne enters and stands by Tracey.)

TRACEY: Look! Look at this!

LUANNE: Oh my stars, you two just got done doin' it for the first time, didn't ya?

TRACEY: Look at her cheeks!

LUANNE: *(Leaning in.)* Oh, mercy! You're still feelin' it, ain't you?

DORIE: *(To Ben, because it's all she can spit out.)* Ben? Waffles?

BEN: Can we —

LUANNE: So how was it?

TRACEY: I asked, but they haven't said.

BEN: It was good, OK?

LUANNE: Well of course it was, for you!

BEN: Sorry?

LUANNE: It's always good for the man.

TRACEY: Oh, Luanne, give the boy a little credit. Look at her cheeks. I'd say he did the job right.

LLUANNE: *(To Dorie.)* Did he do the job right, honey? Did he give you an orgasm?

DORIE: Yes. No! I mean . . . He did. But I . . . I need to eat. Now. Pancakes?

LUANNE: Well of course you need to eat, gettin' all loved up like that first thing in the morning. That'll work up a hunger. Look at those cheeks!

TRACEY: We have a special for first-timers, don't we, Luanne?

LUANNE: We sure do. Because you know as sure as all get out that when you're done here you're going right back for round two!

TRACEY: Oh, I used to love that second one!

LUANNE: Seems to go on forever, don't it?

TRACEY: You are going to go do it again, right?

(Ben and Dorie just stare at each other.)

TRACEY: I knew it!

LUANNE: Our first-timer special has lots of protein and carbohydrates to give you a li'l energy boost. Not too heavy though.

TRACEY: Can't make love on a full stomach!

LUANNE: Right. This'll take you right through the afternoon.

TRACEY: Right through! So can I get you two of those?

DORIE: I like waffles.

TRACEY: OK, then! One first-timer's special with waffles. How about you, stud?

BEN: This really isn't appropriate.

LUANNE: Well of course it is, the way you two are looking at each other! You had a darn fine time of it, any fool can see that. Probably a long time coming, wouldn't you say, Tracey?

TRACEY: Oh, I see it. I see it!

LUANNE: You two known each other long?

DORIE: Yes.

BEN: Years.

TRACEY: There you go!

LUANNE: Lots of things going unsaid all that time, and all that grrrrr has been building up like you want to go touching each other but somehow you thought maybe it wasn't right?

TRACEY: Sometimes it's a bad idea.

LUANNE: I'm guessing maybe a bottle of wine or two was involved?

BEN AND DORIE: Yes.

DORIE: Two.

LUANNE: And that's OK, too! What's that saying, Tracey? About wine and truth?

TRACEY: "In vino, varied gas."

LUANNE: Exactly. And it brought you together.

TRACEY: Meant to be.

LUANNE: Now if you two were sitting here and you weren't talking to each other, that would mean it was a bad idea. We have a special for that, too.

TRACEY: Walk of Shame breakfast.

LUANNE: One egg and a single piece of toast. Get you in, out and away from the other person in under half an hour. Guaranteed.

TRACEY: Because sometimes it's just a bad idea in the first place.

LUANNE: But not you two!

TRACEY: No.

LUANNE: We can see that.

TRACEY: Look at the cheeks!

LUANNE: So . . . two first-timer specials?

BEN AND DORIE: Please.

TRACEY: Coming right up!

(Tracey and Luanne exit. Ben and Dorie sit through an awkward pause.)

BEN: So.

DORIE: Yeah.

BEN: That was . . .

DORIE: Embarrassing.

BEN: To say the least.

DORIE: But accurate.

BEN: True. I give them that.

DORIE: Is there really something going on with my cheeks?

BEN: You're a little flushed.

DORIE: Oh, God.

BEN: So . . . it was OK, huh?

DORIE: It really was.

BEN: Honest?

DORIE: You did good, rookie.

(They laugh.)

DORIE: And nothing's changed, right?

BEN: You mean between you and me?

DORIE: I mean in general.

BEN: Oh. No.

DORIE: Not at all?

BEN: No. Same as it ever was.

(Pause.)

DORIE: I can't believe they knew!

BEN: I know! It was like waitress ESP.

DORIE: Scary.

(Pause.)

BEN: I wonder if they know I'm gay.

(Black out.)

END OF PLAY

Good Girl

JULIA BROWNELL

Good Girl was first produced by the Actors Theatre of
Louisville Apprentice Company, January 19, 2009, as part of
The Tens, a ten-minute play festival. Directed by Mike Brooks.
Cast: James — Aaron Matteson; Jenna — Julia Bentz;
Rosalind — Alison Clayton; Celia — Ami Jhaveri.

CHARACTERS
 JENNA: Twenty-four.
 JAMES: Twenty-five, her boyfriend.
 ROSALIND: A cockatiel.
 CELIA: A parakeet.

SETTING
 A small, nicely furnished apartment in Brooklyn.

TIME
 Morning, the present.

NOTE: Rosalind and Celia are pet birds, represented by female actors in their twenties, preferably on stools.

• • •

At rise: The living room of a very small but nicely decorated apartment in Brooklyn. Morning. Two birds, a parakeet and a cockatiel, sit in two bird-cages. Jenna enters.

JENNA: Morning birdies! Morning, Rosalind! Morning, Celia!
 (Jenna puts a sheet over the cages. The birds squawk.)
JENNA: Time for a little morning nap. Don't tell James.
ROSALIND: Good girl!
 (James enters from a run. Sweaty.)
JENNA: Hi sweetie! How was your run?
 (James takes the sheet off the cages.)
JAMES: Great! Hi girls! Did you miss me?
ROSALIND: Good girl! Good girl! I love you!
JAMES: Oh my God! She said it. Did you hear that? Why is her cover on?
JENNA: Sorry, I wanted some quiet.
JAMES: Can you believe she said, "I love you!"? She's so smart! You're so smart, Rosalind!
ROSALIND: Good girl! Good girl!
 (Celia, the parakeet, squawks.)
JAMES: Celia's happy for her! She's happy for Rosalind! She's squawking! She's cheering!
JENNA: Good girl, Celia!

(Celia squawks happily.)

ROSALIND: Good girl!

JENNA: God, Rosalind's such a bitch.

JAMES: Shhh . . . what are you talking about? She's the sweetest bird that ever lived.

JENNA: She's always stealing Celia's thunder.

JAMES: No, she was happy for her. Rosalind was calling Celia good girl, not herself!

JENNA: How do you know?

JAMES: I can tell by the way she said it. She was looking RIGHT AT Celia. Besides, she would never hurt Celia's feelings. She's too much of a sweetheart.

JENNA: I guess.

JAMES: You were just kidding. But don't say those words in front of the girls again, OK? I don't want them to pick anything up.

JENNA: All Rosalind can say is "Good girl," "Go Mets," and now, "I love you." And Celia still can't say anything. *(Jenna imitates Rosalind as she speaks.)*

JAMES: Still, I don't want Celia's first word to be a curse.

JENNA: I thought you said parakeets never speak.

JAMES: Most parakeets never speak. I think Celia is an exception.

(Celia squawks proudly.)

ROSALIND: Good girl! I love you!

JENNA: You should probably get in the shower. It's going to take an hour at least to get to my parent's house.

JAMES: I love you too, Rosalind. OK, I am, I just need something to drink first.

(James exits into the kitchen. Jenna turns to straighten the apartment.)

ROSALIND: Bitch!

JENNA: What?

ROSALIND: Bitch!

JENNA: Oh my God.

(James enters with an empty glass.)

JAMES: Did you say something, sweetie?

JENNA: No, but Rosalind just said –

ROSALIND: Good girl!

JAMES: Aww, she's such a good girl. She loves you, Jenna. We're so glad you moved in. I'm hurrying!

(James goes back into the kitchen.)

JENNA: *(To the bird.)* You little —

ROSALIND: Bitch!

(Jenna gasps. Celia squawks. It sounds suspiciously like laughter.)

JENNA: You are such a little —

ROSALIND: Slutty Mc-Ho-bag!

JENNA: What did you just say?

(James enters, shirt off.)

JAMES: Did Rosalind say something new?

JENNA: Yeah.

JAMES: Did she say what I think she said? I've been teaching her something special for you, ever since before you moved in.

(Rosalind and Celia squawk uproariously.)

JENNA: What did you teach her?

JAMES: I want it to be a surprise when she says it.

JENNA: I'm not sure the birds like me living here.

JAMES: What are you talking about? They love it! They're almost as glad as I am that you got evicted and had to move in. Aren't you happy, girls?

(Celia squawks loudly. Rosalind says something that sounds suspiciously like "discharge omelet.")

JAMES: They're such good girls. I'm popping in the shower. I'll be quick.

JENNA: *(A come-on.)* Want me to join you?

JAMES: Aww, I would, but I gotta be quick. I don't want to be late for your parents.

JENNA: We can be a little late.

JAMES: Besides, I can't look your dad in the eye if I've just nailed his daughter. Bye girlies! I'll be right back. Sweetie, will you talk to them? I'm worried they're going to be lonely all day.

JENNA: They've got each other.

JAMES: *(As he exits to the bathroom.)* You're the best.

JENNA: Hi, Rosalind. Hi, Celia.

ROSALIND: Good girl!

JENNA: Good girl, Rosalind. You're a —

ROSALIND: Cum dumpster!

JENNA: All right, that's not even fair. Do you see us having sex? We're NOT having sex right now. We haven't had sex since I moved in because you're too damn loud and he "doesn't want to upset you."

ROSALIND: Good girl!

(Celia squawks in approval.)

JENNA: If you insult me again I'm going to put the sheet over you.

Silence. The birds stop squawking.

JENNA: Thank you. God, silence. It's the first time it's been quiet since you got here.

Silence continues. Jenna starts to get uncomfortable.

JENNA: Stop — stop blinking at me, OK? That's weird.

(Rosalind emits a small cough. James rushes in, a towel around his waist.)

JAMES: Is everything OK? I heard Rosalind cough!

JENNA: You heard that?

JAMES: Are you OK, honey? Is everything all right?

JENNA: Everything's –

JAMES: Oh, sweetie! I was talking to Rosalind! Did you think I was talking to you? That's so cute.

JENNA: Yeah.

JAMES: I'm going to hop back in the shower. Tell me if she coughs again, OK? Just come get me out of the shower.

JENNA: OK.

JAMES: If Rosalind's sick, maybe I shouldn't go to your parent's house.

JENNA: It's my mom's birthday.

JAMES: And I wouldn't miss it for the world, honey, not for anything. But obviously I can't go if Rosalind is coughing.

JENNA: Why not?

JAMES: It would kind of ruin your mom's special day if we came home and Rosalind was dead, wouldn't it?

JENNA: I doubt it.

JAMES: You are such a goof today. Are you getting sick? I hope you didn't give it to the birds.

(James exits. Rosalind and Celia squawk happily.)

JENNA: Jesus Christ.

ROSALIND: I win.

JENNA: What?

ROSALIND: I win.

JENNA: You're just a bird. You're never going to win. I'm his girlfriend, for God's sake, I take —

(Rosalind coughs quietly.)

JENNA: Oh, don't you dare.

(Rosalind coughs a little louder.)

JENNA: You bitch.

(Rosalind coughs, loudly this time.)

JAMES: *(Offstage, in the shower.)* Honey? Is that Rosalind?

JENNA: She's fine. *(To Rosalind.)* Cough all you want. Do you give blow jobs?

ROSALIND: Bitch!

JENNA: Because until you give blow jobs, I think James is going to stick with me.

ROSALIND: *(As orgasmically as possible.)* Oh, Melanie!

(Jenna gasps.)

ROSALIND: Melanie! Melanie!

JENNA: How dare you. How dare you bring up Melanie?

ROSALIND: Melanie!

JENNA: Bitch!

(Jenna opens the cage door as if to hurt Rosalind. James runs out of the shower, a towel around his waist. Jenna closes the cage.)

JAMES: Is Rosalind coughing again?

JENNA: No, she's saying Melanie over and over.

JAMES: Oh . . . that's awkward. But you know that the girls and I lived with Melanie for over a year — we got the birds together —

JENNA: She's not just saying it. She's saying it . . . orgasmically. Like she's getting off.

JAMES: Sweetie, what are you talking about? Melanie never got the birds off.

JENNA: Like she's you — getting off.

JAMES: Now you're just being paranoid. Birds don't do that kind of thing. And please don't say "orgasm" in front of the birds again. I don't want to upset Celia.

(James exits to get dressed.)

ROSALIND: Melanie! Melanie! Melanie!

(Celia laughs. Jenna's phone rings.)

JENNA: Shut the fuck up! *(Into her phone.)* Hi Mom. Yeah, no we're coming. Before noon.

ROSALIND: Cum dumpster!

JENNA: What? No, that wasn't anyone. It was — nobody. Yes, James lives in a safe neighborhood. No, I don't need to move back home. Yes, I understand it's a big step to move in with my boyfriend. We'll be there in an hour.

(Jenna hangs up her cell.)

JENNA: Rosalind, would you like to come out of your cage? Fly around a little?

(Rosalind squawks happily. Jenna opens the cage and takes Rosalind out on her finger.)

ROSALIND: Good girl! I love you!

JENNA: Oh no, Rosalind. Today we're going out on the fire escape. We're going to fly outside!

ROSALIND: Good girl!

(Jenna takes Rosalind out the fire escape door, offstage.)

JENNA: *(Offstage.)* OK, sweetie. Time to fly.

CELIA: *(Loudly.)* Do it, bitch!

ROSALIND: *(Offstage.)* Good girl! Good girl!

(Pause. A loud crash offstage. James comes rushing in, towel around his waist.)

JAMES: *(To Celia.)* Celia, where's Rosalind? Where's Rosalind?

CELIA: *(Frantic.)* Do it! Good girl! Do it! Good girl! Good girl!

JAMES: Celia! You're talking! I'm so proud of you!

(Rosalind flies back in the apartment, directly to her cage.)

JAMES: Rosalind, Celia talked! Can you believe it? Aren't you proud of her?

CELIA: Good girl! Good girl!

ROSALIND: Good girl! Good girl!

JAMES: Where did Jenna go? We're going to be late.

CELIA: Good girl!

(Police sirens in the background as lights fade.)

END OF PLAY

Open House

Michael J. Grady

Open House was first produced at the Stanford Calderwood
Pavillion, Boston Center for the Arts, May 11, 2008, as a part
of the Boston Theater Marathon. Directed by Dawn Simmons.
Cast: Rankle — Jason Cross; Woody — Mark Sickler;
Lesser — Nathanael Shea; Blot — Adelmar Pereira;
Puppeteer — Shauday Johnson.

CHARACTERS

>JAYK LESSER: Late twenties to early thirties, a senior real estate agent at Rankle Realty.
>
>WOODY BENCH: Early thirties, a potential buyer.
>
>KENNY BLOT: Midtwenties, an agent-in-training.
>
>MR. RANKLE: Early to midfifties, the owner and founder of Rankle Realty.
>
>LARGE FLESH-EATING MONSTER: Unknown age or origin.

SETTING

>A well-appointed living room.

TIME

>The present.

• • •

>*At rise: A dream living room, furnished to perfection by Rankle Realty to create a good impression. The most remarkable thing about the room, however is the presence of a large, menacing thing, writhing, growling, and groaning under a large tarp. Jayk Lesser stands on a couch looking down at the creature. His palms are flat against the wall. It is as if he is trying to back away from the monster but the wall prevents him. Lesser stands for a moment fixated on the monster, mumbling to himself. The doorbell rings. Lesser moves carefully to the door, keeping his eyes fixed on whatever it is he is watching. The doorbell rings again.*

LESSER: *(Calling out.)* Just a minute. *(Lesser walks downstage, presumably to a mirror.)* See the positive. *(Lesser opens the door.)*

WOODY: Is this the open house?

LESSER: Of course. Of course. Mister?

WOODY: *(Pause.)* Bench . . . but you can call me . . . Woody.

LESSER: *(Pumping his hand.)* Well Woody; Jayk Lesser; nice to meet you.

WOODY: I couldn't wait to see the place. I brought along a bunch of questions; I hope you don't mind.

LESSER: Not at all, not at all.

WOODY: I've been doing a lot of research online.

LESSER: Good to hear. We at Rankle Realty like it when our customers are well informed. It saves a lot of time. Please, please come in. Can I take your coat?

(*Woody enters and stares at the middle of the room, with horror. Lesser looks at the center and back to Woody.*)

LESSER: May I take your coat?

WOODY: (*Still fixated.*) Sure, sure. Absolutely.

LESSER: Something wrong?

WOODY: Wrong? Wha-uh . . . no, no, of course not. It's a great place. Very nice.

LESSER: Would you like a Coke? I can get you a Coke. Do you want a Coke?

WOODY: What?

LESSER: Would you like something to drink?

WOODY: A Coke?

LESSER: Just one minute.

(*Lesser walks toward the center of the room. At the last second, he turns and walks across the couch to the refrigerator. He gets a can and cautiously walks back.*)

WOODY: Thanks.

LESSER: My pleasure. (*Pause.*) I just cleaned the place.

WOODY: It's very nice.

LESSER: Thank you. (*Pause.*) So ah, let me show you around. Over here, we have the bedroom.

WOODY: Very nice.

LESSER: Nice closet space, uh? It's like having a second bedroom. You won't have much trouble with storage with a monster closet like that.

WOODY: Wow.

LESSER: Now, let me show you the bathroom.

WOODY: OK.

LESSER: I promise you, Woody, you will be amazed.

WOODY: I am.

(*They walk back into the living room and Woody faces the middle, walking backwards to the door to the bathroom. Lesser enters the bathroom, offstage. Woody stares at the creature with distracted horror.*)

LESSER: (*Offstage.*) See that?

WOODY: How could I miss it?

LESSER: (*Offstage.*) An griffen-clawed bathtub. You don't see so many of these, nowadays. Pretty big huh? How many gallons of water do you think that will hold? Think you can you guess?

WOODY: A lot.

LESSER: *(Offstage.)* Right.

WOODY: It's a beast.

LESSER: *(Offstage.)* Sure is.

WOODY: A big beast.

LESSER: *(Offstage.)* A real monster. They don't make tubs like that anymore. No sir.

WOODY: Very nice.

LESSER: *(Offstage.)* And this toilet, look at this, huh. She's a beauty. *(The sound of a flush. Lesser reenters.)* Listen to that, huh! Music.

WOODY: You don't hear many flushes like that.

LESSER: Not these days.

WOODY: Nope.

LESSER: Of course there is also . . . the kitchen.

WOODY: Yeah.

LESSER: Over there.

> *(Lesser points to the other side of the room [past the floor thing]. They do not move.)*

WOODY: It looks nice.

LESSER: You like it?

WOODY: Sure *(Pause.)* very, impressive.

LESSER: Would, ah, would you like to see it . . . a little closer? *(Pause.)* Hmm?

WOODY: *(Pause.)* Now?

LESSER: Sure. Right this way.

> *(Lesser walks up on the couch, looking center. Woody stands back, looking at him suspiciously.)*

LESSER: I just cleaned the floor. It could be wet. I wouldn't want you to slip. *(The floor thing twitches and makes digestive noises.)*

WOODY: We wouldn't want that. I can see it all right from here.

LESSER: Come on.

WOODY: Maybe I can come back when the floor is dry.

LESSER: Very smart, Mr. Bench.

WOODY: Thank you.

LESSER: You really did your homework.

WOODY: I told you.

LESSER: You're a hard man, Mr. Bench, and you have me against the ropes.

WOODY: Well, I'll go easy on you.

LESSER: No, no, please, please, I love to see a master at work and I believe in rewarding great negotiations. Your courage is what really gets me. It's astonishing.

WOODY: Thank you.

(Lesser and Woody walk to the other side, moving very slowly and carefully. Blot enters on his cell phone.)

LESSER: I think you'll be very impressed with the kitchen. Whereas the bathroom has those wonderful antique bathroom fixtures, the kitchen is fitted with brand-new plumbing and a refrigerator with an ice cube machine.

WOODY: Really? I love ice cubes.

BLOT: And I was walking around with my fly open all day. Can you believe that? I must be getting senile or something . . . Yeah, it's so weird. Nobody told me. . . What? . . . You saw it, too? Oh my God! Why didn't you tell me, you goof? . . . That is so funny *(He laughs.)* You little goof. Yeah, well I have to get back to work . . . I dunno, until — *(Blot sees it in the center of the room. Blot is horrified. Long fixation.)* What? Oh yeah, sorry. Six o'clock. OK. Bye.

(Long fixation.)

BLOT: Holy Shit!

LESSER: Hello?

BLOT: Oh, hi. *(Beat.)* Sorry I didn't see you there.

(Walks around the room via the couch, keeping his eyes on the thing in the center of the room.)

BLOT: Hiiiiiiiii. Lesser.

LESSER: *(Taking him aside.)* You're late.

BLOT: Sorry.

LESSER: Mr. Bench. This is Kenny Blot. He is an associate in training.

BLOT: Nice to meet you, Mr. Bench.

WOODY: Woody.

BLOT: What do you think, Woody?

LESSER: So?

(Woody looks to the middle and back at them. Lesser and Blot smile expectantly.)

WOODY: Ah, well. I'm really not sure.

LESSER AND BLOT: Why?

WOODY: Well, ah. I'm not sure.

(The doorbell rings. They look at each other. The doorbell rings again.)

LESSER: I bet that's another buyer.

(The doorbell rings.)

BLOT: I bet it is.

LESSER: If you don't scoop this up he probably will.

BLOT: Yep. *(The doorbell rings.)* Yes. Well . . . I guess I will get it. *(The door-bell rings twice.)* Coming! *(Facing the center of the room, Blot gets up on the couch.)* Be right there!

(The doorbell rings with increasing impatience.)

LESSER: Can you get that, Kenny?

BLOT: I'm on my way.

(Blot crosses to the other side and answers the door. Mr. Rankle enters, un-fazed.)

RANKLE: Took you long enough.

BLOT: Mr. Rankle.

RANKLE: Time is money, Blot. The "For Sale" sign is still up. What am I pay-ing you for?

BLOT: We have a potential buyer.

RANKLE: Good. Maybe I have underestimated you, Blot.

BLOT: Thank you, sir.

RANKLE: Your fly is open.

BLOT: Sorry, sir.

RANKLE: Hello?

LESSER: Mr. Rankle! *(To Woody.)* It's Mr. Rankle. *(Whispers.)* Big cheese. *(To Rankle.)* We were just about to close with Mr. Bench, here.

RANKLE: Really? Well, Mr. Bench. You are making quite a deal; you won't re-gret it. This place is a rarity; it will probably outlive you. When they built this house they really knew how to make them; you won't regret it. Congratulations!

(Rankle holds his hand out.)

WOODY: Oh, ah, ok. Very nice to meet you sir.

(Woody walks along the wall and trips, falling to the center of the room. The creature sucks Woody in and begins to devour him up to the waist as he screams.)

BLOT: Hold on, hold on!

(Blot pulls the vacuum out of the wall and throws Woody the chord. Woody takes hold of and is swallowed by the monster. Blot continues to pull against the chord and goes back and forth with the monster. Blot hits the monster with the vacuum, and the monster spits out a big lumpy mass, covering Blot with blood and lumpy bits of viscera. Fixation. Everyone but Rankle is horrified.)

RANKLE: Damn it, Lesser, you lost another sale!

(The thing burps)

BLOT: What the hell is that?

(Pause. The thing makes a loud digestive noise.)

RANKLE: What?

BLOT: What? That thing that thing!

RANKLE: What thing?

LESSER: Yeah, what thing?

BLOT: The the the thing — the thing that ate Woody.

RANKLE: You're crazy. Woody . . .

BLOT: Yeah?

LESSER: Woody. . . left.

RANKLE: Yes. You scared him off.

BLOT: I'm going.

RANKLE: Really? I thought better of you, Blot.

LESSER: Come on. Don't be a party pooper.

(There is a farting sound.)

BLOT: Oh my God.

RANKLE: What?

LESSER: *(With a handkerchief over his nose.)* What?

BLOT: That smells horrible!

LESSER: Who smelt it dealt it.

BLOT: I didn't do it. The floor did it.

RANKLE: That's right. Blame it on the floor.

LESSER: Always the floor.

BLOT: Dear God!

RANKLE: That's nothing more than the stink of desperation. You reek of it. It's your excuses that stink up this place. "See the positive" not excuses. I hate excuse makers. "The floor farted." "The floor ate Woody." I'm tired of your shirking responsibility. I am this close to asking you to leave.

LESSER: Maybe you ate Woody.

BLOT: I ate Woody?

LESSER: At least he admits it.

RANKLE: You both make me sick with your ridiculous excuses.

BLOT: This is crazy. You mean to tell me that you actually don't see it?

LESSER: What?

BLOT: That thing.

RANKLE: Blot, you're absolutely hopeless.

LESSER: Why do you keep harping on about the thing?

BLOT: Lesser, if you don't see anything over there than why don't you come over here?

LESSER: Why? Why don't you come over here?

BLOT: You see! You're afraid to come over here.

LESSER: No I'm not.

RANKLE: I've given you the book, the tape series, the little card to keep in your wallet. "See the positive." Losers look at a house and see monsters. I've had quite enough of this stalling. I am paying you to sell. Lesser, just come over here and put an end to this nonsense.

LESSER: What?

RANKLE: Show this fool how wrong he is.

LESSER: But

RANKLE: But what, Lesser?

(Lesser moves up the couch and walks toward them.)

LESSER: What?

BLOT: Why didn't you walk on the floor?

LESSER: What are you fucking crazy?

BLOT: Aha! You see! Why am I crazy?

LESSER: The floors wet. I'd slip and — and break my head open.

BLOT: The floor isn't wet.

LESSER: Then why don't you walk on it?

BLOT: Because there is a *(Gestures, trying to describe it in many different ways.)* thing over there.

RANKLE: There you are focusing on the negatives again. That is why you will never be a winner. A good salesman will look at a place like this and see money, all you see are wet floors and man-eating predators with digestive problems. You want to work on commission or do you want to scrape by on an hourly wage. It's up to you.

BLOT: I'm going.

RANKLE: Go ahead.

BLOT: *(Exiting.)* Good luck.

RANKLE: Winners don't need luck; they see the potentiality all around them. The winner draws the forces of wealth and potentiality from the four corners of the world and it cleaves to him. People see it and they seek him out. They throw their money at his feet in adulation.

LESSER: Wow. So ah, do you have any advice about the uh?

RANKLE: You know, Lesser . . . you remind me of myself when I was your age.

LESSER: Really?

RANKLE: Yes. You're not as smart, good-looking, skilled, or charismatic but in some ways you remind me of myself. You know why?

LESSER: Why?

RANKLE: Because I see the positive. I imbue you with my positivity.

LESSER: Thanks Mr. Rankle.

RANKLE: No need to thank me, Lesser. It's what I do.

LESSER: So what should we do?

RANKLE: It is clear, what we have to do, Lesser: Sell.

LESSER: But shouldn't we deal with the, uh?

RANKLE: Enough excuses, Lesser. You must direct your energies to more productive enterprises. Find me a buyer or find a nice hourly wage.

LESSER: Yes, sir.

RANKLE: Good-bye.

LESSER: Bye, sir.

(Rankle exits.)

LESSER: Focus on the positive and they will see the positive. Focus . . . focus . . . it's a nice kitchen. The refrigerator makes ice cubes. Big closet . . . above ground . . . bathtub . . .

(Lesser faces the monster, walks up on the couch, grasping the wall. He stares into the monster. Lights fade to black.)

END OF PLAY

The Real Story

NEIL OLSON

The Real Story was first produced by The Drilling CompaNY at the 78th Street Theater Lab, New York City, April 11–27, 2008. Directed by Bradford Olson. Cast: Jack — Dan Teachout; Miranda — Jane Guyer; Danny — David Adams; Carlos — Adam Fujita

CHARACTERS

JACK: Fifties or older (though played by a forty-something), burned-out international journalist.

MIRANDA: Twenties or early thirties, American magazine journalist, quick-witted but naïve.

DANNY: Twenties, a native of the country (never specified, but played as African in this production), translator.

CARLOS: Thirties or forties, successful, thrill-seeking international news photographer, probably Spanish.

SETTING

Bare stage with a few chairs.

TIME

The present.

• • •

The sound of faraway gunfire, and lights come up on a small room, bare but for a few chairs. Jack, older than the others, divides his attention between a satellite phone and a whiskey flask. Danny, a local, sits quietly and stares. Miranda, somewhat younger, paces the room, continually playing with her cell phone. All are dressed for hot, rugged outdoor conditions.

JACK: Give it up, kid, you won't get a signal out here.

MIRANDA: What are they doing with Carlos?

JACK: There isn't a cell tower for a hundred miles.

MIRANDA: Danny, what are they doing with Carlos?

DANNY: I cannot say, miss.

MIRANDA: Do you think they're hurting him?

JACK: Nothing. A few questions.

MIRANDA: Danny? Do you?

DANNY: I am sure he is well.

MIRANDA: He photographed them shooting that boy.

JACK: So they'll take his film. Maybe slap him around a bit.

MIRANDA: Christ.

JACK: You think boys aren't shot in these parts every day? Put the phone away and have a drink.

MIRANDA: I thought maybe up in the hills I'd get something.

JACK: The hills would only block it. Don't they teach you girls anything?

MIRANDA: What's up with your sat?

JACK: Dead. Batteries.

MIRANDA: You left K-town without a working satellite phone. That's great, Jack.

JACK: It was working when we left, and you can't find D batteries in this joke of a country for love or money.

MIRANDA: But somehow you can find whiskey.

JACK: I can always find whiskey.

MIRANDA: You should have brought more batteries.

JACK: Maybe that slick magazine of yours should have bought you a satellite phone.

MIRANDA: I didn't think I was going any place I would need it.

JACK: Ah, but you wanted adventure.

MIRANDA: Do not put this on me. Danny told you to turn around at the last checkpoint.

JACK: Danny would never say such a thing. What did you say, Danny?

DANNY: That it would be dangerous to continue.

JACK: Dangerous to continue. You know what that's code for? I am a translator, not a soldier or hack journalist, and you owe me a fat bonus when we get back to K-town, Mister Jack. That's all Danny was communicating.

MIRANDA: You're an asshole.

JACK: Sweetheart. Listen. The real story is always in the places they don't want you to go.

MIRANDA: Is that why you spent your Baghdad posting getting drunk in the Green Zone?

JACK: Perpetuating evil rumors is no way for a professional reporter to behave.

MIRANDA: Rumors.

JACK: You weren't there. There was no story in Iraq. Or it was the same story over and over. That's why we've come to the ass end of the world, to find fresh atrocities for the breakfast table reading of America. Not that they give a shit, mind you. They'll take a look at the photo — one of Carlos's heartbreaking masterpieces — they'll tsk tsk, and flip the fucking page.

MIRANDA: So why are you still doing this?

JACK: Because I'm no longer fit for civilization. Not too late for you though, kid.

MIRANDA: I hope you're right. You think they're going to let us leave?

JACK: Eventually.

MIRANDA: What, in six months, a year?

JACK: You got someplace to be?

MIRANDA: They didn't take our stuff. Our phones or notebooks or anything. What does that mean?

JACK: Nothing.

DANNY: Mister Jack is correct. We can draw no conclusion by their failure to confiscate your possessions. It could be simple carelessness.

MIRANDA: Are they going to kill us? Because of what we saw?

DANNY: What is it you believe you saw?

MIRANDA: A massacre. Or the end of one. Those bodies out in the fields. The boy. We haven't seen anyone in the village but men with guns.

JACK: Men with guns, listen to you. They're rebels, dear. You can tell from the headbands and lack of uniforms.

MIRANDA: Are they? Do we know? Danny, are we getting all of this wrong?

DANNY: They are the forces in opposition to the government, certainly. What has happened . . . It is unwise to draw swift conclusions. There may have been a battle. The villagers may have fled, or . . .

JACK: Or, there might have been a government informer here, so they slaughtered everybody in the place.

DANNY: That is of course possible.

JACK: Oh, look at her face, Danny. She wants the rebels to be the heroes. Poor Miranda.

MIRANDA: I'm going to find Carlos.

DANNY: Miss, you cannot go out there.

MIRANDA: Why, are they going to shoot me?

DANNY: That is quite likely, if you attempt to leave. You do not seem to have completely registered the gravity of the situation.

JACK: She's getting there.

MIRANDA: Shut up, Jack, this is your fault.

JACK: If you'll remember, I tried to talk you out of coming. So did your boyfriend Carlos.

MIRANDA: He's not my boyfriend.

JACK: I'm sorry, what's the current phrase? Fuck-buddy? You insisted.

MIRANDA: I thought you knew what you were doing. Everybody said that if I wanted the inside story on what was happening here, I should follow Jack Mercer around.

JACK: And now — tada — you are the story. Clearly these weren't the same people who painted me the Green Zone drunk. I'm glad to know you consulted multiple sources.

(Carlos is shoved into the room, limping and with fresh bruising — or possibly a cut — on his face. Miranda helps him to a chair.)

MIRANDA: Oh God, are you all right? I was afraid they killed you.

CARLOS: I believe they considered it seriously.

JACK: Decided you weren't worth the bullet.

CARLOS: Lucky for me.

MIRANDA: I'm glad you guys think this is funny.

CARLOS: Oh, there was nothing funny about it.

MIRANDA: Did they hurt you badly.

CARLOS: Not so bad. The worst was watching them smash my cameras. I had that Leica ten years.

DANNY: Did they ask you any questions?

CARLOS: Not really. None I understood. It was mostly just kicking and laughing. They were only boys. Boys with big boots.

MIRANDA: So what does that mean, the no questions? Danny?

DANNY: It is not such a good sign if they did not ask questions.

MIRANDA: That's it. *(Going to the door.)* I'm getting some answers.

DANNY: I have said you cannot.

MIRANDA: They could have shot us already if they were going to.

DANNY: They are awaiting their commander. Not the young one out there, but the true leader. He will be wearing a white cap and have a scar on his neck. It is he who will decide our fate.

MIRANDA: I'll find him.

CARLOS: Miranda, don't be ridiculous.

MIRANDA: I'm not waiting here to be shot. I don't see the guards.

CARLOS: I think they went behind the stone wall to get high.

DANNY: Miss Miranda, do not. *(She rushes out, he pursues to the door.)* Miss Miranda!

JACK: Don't do it, Danny. They're more likely to shoot you than her.

DANNY: She cannot even speak the language. You are letting her go?

JACK: Don't look at me, she's his girlfriend.

CARLOS: I can barely stand. Besides, you can't tell American women anything.

JACK: You pretty much informed her we were going to be executed. What did you expect her to do? Sit here and get drunk, like me?

DANNY: I did not intend . . . but of course you are correct. May I see your phone, please?

JACK: Sure. But trust me, it's dead. Have a drink, Carlos?

CARLOS: Your terrible whiskey. You know, I think I will.

JACK: Sorry about the cameras.

CARLOS: Yes, well, it's not the first time. Maybe the last.

JACK: Sorry I dragged you out here.

CARLOS: No one dragged anyone. We all came for our own reasons. Should I go get her?

JACK: They'll have her back here in a minute.

CARLOS: She is brave.

JACK: Yes. Like you.

CARLOS: No, I just enjoy the lifestyle. If I did not do this I would have to sky dive, or, what do you call it? Bungee jump. She seeks the truth. *Una chica loca.*

DANNY: I will attempt to find batteries.

JACK: Among this crew?

DANNY: They use many electronics. They may have what we need, for the right price.

JACK: And what's the goal?

DANNY: So that you may contact your newspaper. Or your embassy. To arrange a ransom.

JACK: Fat fucking chance.

DANNY: Are you so invested in this sense of failure, in your self-indulgent cynicism? Will you not even try to save yourself? To save your colleagues?

JACK: Don't pretend it's me you're worried about.

CARLOS: Why not let him try, Jack?

JACK: What will you buy the batteries with?

DANNY: I will require money.

CARLOS: They took everything I had.

DANNY: Mister Jack is carrying more than enough. Euros and dollars, not the local currency. All of it, please.

JACK: OK. OK, Danny boy, why not? Not like I need it. But I know your game.

DANNY: I will return as soon as I can. If they kill me, I suggest you run. Better to go that way . . .

(He exits. Carlos hobbles to the doorway to watch.)

JACK: They shoot him yet? Maybe club him to death?

CARLOS: No.

JACK: Good, I can do it when he comes back.

CARLOS: He is speaking to one of them, the rebels. Older. No visible weapon.

JACK: White cap?

CARLOS: No. And there is Miranda, thank God. She is coming this way now.

JACK: Oh, joy. (*She enters.*) Hello dear, learn any new words?

CARLOS: Sit down, you look terrible.

MIRANDA: I'm fine. It wasn't a massacre. The whole village cleared out before they arrived. Except four or five young men, who stayed behind to steal food and guns. That's who they killed.

CARLOS: Who told you?

MIRANDA: The only one of them who speaks English. I think he's a doctor. They took him from a captured town to care for their wounded. I guess the wounded are all the same to a doctor, the sides don't matter. He also said we were going to be shot. He seemed sorry about it.

JACK: Damned decent of him. And there's you, little Brenda Starr, still ferreting out the facts while they're tying on your blindfold. A reporter to the end. I'm proud of you, kid.

MIRANDA: What's Danny up to? He took my phone and my watch.

CARLOS: Trying to buy batteries.

JACK: Is that what you think? Three hundred dollars for batteries? You surprise me, Carlos. He's trying to buy his way out.

MIRANDA: Why are you so hard on Danny? He's taken good care of you, and you don't even know his real name.

JACK: I didn't say I had a problem with it. He's coastal, these guys are a mountain tribe. No love there. You know what they'll do to him before they get around to killing him? Hell, I hope his little ploy works. Everybody looks out for themselves.

CARLOS: So. Anyone seen any good movies lately?

MIRANDA: Where are the keys, Jack?

JACK: Still in the Jeep, unless they took them.

MIRANDA: The Jeep is thirty yards from that door. No guards around. We make a run for it. I'm serious, what have we go to lose?

JACK: A blaze of glory, like Butch and Sundance.

CARLOS: Except we have no guns.

JACK: Right. And you can't even walk.

CARLOS: I'll hide behind you. She's right, let us try.

JACK: You two go ahead, I'll finish my whiskey.

MIRANDA: Fine, leave him. He quit on everything years ago. Come here now, put your arm over my shoulder.

(*Danny enters.*)

DANNY: You are free to leave. Do not delay, go to the vehicle at once.

MIRANDA: What about you?

JACK: You heard the man, get going. Danny and I will be right behind you.

Carlos, get her out here. *(Carlos leads Miranda out.)* Danilo Musab, how did you manage it?

DANNY: I convinced the commander that you are an alcoholic who had been exiled here by your newspaper, which never publishes your stories anyway.

JACK: The truth, a bold strategy.

DANNY: And that Carlos and Miranda are stupid American tourists. He decided that the money, the watch, and the two phones were sufficient ransom.

JACK: And you?

DANNY: I am to be kept for further questioning. You must go now, he could change his mind at any moment.

JACK: Well, that just won't do.

(Carlos enters.)

CARLOS: Jack?

JACK: You'll never believe it. Danny's gotten me an exclusive with their commander. Don't tell your girl, she'll want in.

CARLOS: You're right, she will. Jack, are you . . .

JACK: Go, Carlos. Drive out of here quick.

(Carlos exits.)

DANNY: You cannot protect me.

JACK: We'll see about that. Maybe I just want my phone back. Have a drink, Danny?

DANNY: You know I do not drink.

JACK: Make an exception today.

END OF PLAY

Rights and Permissions

Plays for Two Actors

ALL GOOD CRETINS GO TO HEAVEN. © 2008 by Kathleen Warnock. Reprinted by permission of the author. For performance rights, contact Smith and Kraus (www.smithandkraus.com).

THE CAN CAN. © 2008 by Kelly Younger. Reprinted by permission of Bruce Miller, Washington Square Arts. For performance rights, contact Bruce Miller (bmiller@washingtonsquarearts.com).

COUNTING RITA. © 2000 by Patrick Gabridge. Reprinted by permission of the author. Anyone interested interested in producing *Counting Rita* or using it in competition must contact Brooklyn Publishers, 1-888-473-8521, 1841 Cord Street, Odessa, TX 79762 (info@brook pub.com) (www.brookpub.com). All others should contact the author (pat@gabridge.com).

CRITICAL CARE. © 2008 by Bara Swain. Reprinted by permission of the author. For performance rights, contact Smith and Kraus (www.smith andkraus.com).

CROSSING THE BORDER. © 2008 by Eduardo Machado. Reprinted by permission of Pat McLaughlin, Beacon Artists Agency. For performance rights, contact Pat McLaughlin (beaconagency@hotmail.com).

CROWS OVER WHEATFIELD (or, The Nuance of the Leap). © 2006 by Gregory Hischak. Reprinted by permission of the author. For performance rights, contact Smith and Kraus (www.smithandkraus.com).

DÉJÀ VU ALL OVER AGAIN. © 2008 by Robin Rice Lichtig. Reprinted by permission of the author. For performance rights, contact Smith and Kraus (www.smithandkraus.com).

FEEDING TIME AT THE HUMAN HOUSE. © 2008 by David Wiener. Reprinted by permission of the author. For performance rights, contact Smith and Kraus (www.smithandkraus.com).

A FIGMENT. © 2008 by Ron Weaver. Reprinted by permission of the author. For performance rights, contact Smith and Kraus (www.smithand kraus.com).

426

Plays for Three or Four Actors

Plays for Five or Six Actors